.

The double game of music

Manchester University Press

MUSIC AND SOCIETY

Music and Society aims to bridge the gap between music scholarship and the human sciences. A deliberately eclectic series, its authors are nevertheless united by the contention that music is a social product, social resource, and social practice. As such it is not autonomous but is created and performed by real people in particular times and places; in doing so they reveal much about themselves and their societies.

In contrast to the established academic discourse, *Music and Society* is concerned with all forms of music, and seeks to encourage the scholarly analysis of both 'popular' styles and those which have for too long been marginalised by that discourse – folk and ethnic traditions, music by and for women, jazz, rock, rap, reggae, muzak and so on. These sounds are vital ingredients in the contemporary cultural mix, and their neglect by serious scholars itself tells us much about the social and cultural stratification of our society.

The time is right to take a fresh look at music and its effects, as today's music resonates with the consequences of cultural globalisation and the transformations wrought by new electronic media, and as past styles are reinvented in the light of present concerns. There is, too, a tremendous upsurge of interest in cultural analysis. *Music and Society* does not promote a particular school of thought, but aims to provide a forum for debate; in doing so, the titles in the series bring music back into the heart of socio-cultural analysis.

To buy or to find out more about the books currently available in this series, please go to: https://manchesteruniversitypress.co.uk/series/music-and-society/

The double game of music

Paradoxes of power, status and class in music education

Edited by
Live Weider Ellefsen,
Petter Dyndahl, Anne Jordhus-Lier
and Siw Graabræk Nielsen

MANCHESTER UNIVERSITY PRESS

Published by Manchester University Press
Oxford Road, Manchester, M13 9PL
www.manchesteruniversitypress.co.uk

British Library Cataloguing-in-Publication Data
A catalogue record for this book is available from the British Library

ISBN 978 1 52618724 6 hardback

First published 2025

The publisher has no responsibility for the persistence or accuracy of URLs for any external or third-party internet websites referred to in this book, and does not guarantee that any content on such websites is, or will remain, accurate or appropriate.

EU authorised representative for GPSR:
Easy Access System Europe, Mustamäe tee 50, 10621 Tallinn, Estonia
gpsr.requests@easproject.com

Typeset
by Deanta Global Publishing Services, Chennai, India

Contents

Contributors

Live Weider Ellefsen, Professor of Music Education, University of Inland Norway

Petter Dyndahl, Professor of Musicology, Music Education and General Education, University of Inland Norway

Anne Jordhus-Lier, Associate Professor of Music Education, University of Inland Norway

Siw Graabræk Nielsen, Professor of Music Education, Norwegian Academy of Music

Sidsel Karlsen, Professor of Music Education, Norwegian Academy of Music

Ingeborg Lunde, Professor of Music Education, University of Inland Norway

Kari Marie Manum, PhD Candidate, University of Inland Norway/ Assistant Professor of Music and Arts Education, University of Stavanger

Friederike Merkelbach, Associate Professor of Education and Music Education, University of Inland Norway

Odd Skårberg, Emeritus Professor of Musicology, University of Inland Norway

Preface

The field of music education is traditionally concerned with the teaching and learning of music. The overwhelming majority of those engaged in music education do so on the basis of a deep belief or conviction that music offers significant opportunities for aesthetic experience, insight, knowledge and mastery, both at the individual and collective levels. This assertion also applies to us, the authors and editors of this book. Our collective experience as music educators spans a diverse range of educational contexts, including primary and secondary schools, schools of music and arts, as well as higher music education, particularly in the field of teaching and teacher education. A number of us are also graduate musicians or musicologists.

However, drawing upon our own experiences and those of our students, we recognise the aesthetic learning experiences and social interactions that occur outside the formal music education environment. These influences have shaped our perspectives and understanding of music. It is our intention to establish connections with music education initiatives that have been implemented with the objective of integrating informal and non-formal methods of musical learning, in addition to the conventional formal education within an institutional framework. Moreover, we seek to include contexts and arenas for musical upbringing and socialisation that have hitherto received relatively little attention in music education research.

Furthermore, as researchers with a specific interest in examining music and music education in a comprehensive manner, with a particular emphasis on sociological, philosophical and historical perspectives, which are frequently complemented by critical and political insights, we seek to shift the relatively one-sided focus on the acclaimed attributes and potential of aesthetic practice and experience towards a more analytical approach that elucidates the less overt aspects associated with music and music education.

Nevertheless, it is not our intention to advance an alternative, negative representation of music education in contemporary society. Neither do we subscribe to the view that music is of lesser importance than that attributed to it by musicians, music teachers and music enthusiasts. Conversely, our objective is to underscore the notion that music is likely to be of greater consequence than is commonly acknowledged, and that its import may extend well beyond the realms to which we typically ascribe it. Similarly, we aim to present a more expansive view of the typical scope of music education. In doing so, our intention is twofold: firstly, to expand the field of research; and secondly, to transcend the boundaries between music education and other related disciplines, including the sociology of music, the sociology of culture, the sociology of education and perhaps also general sociology.

It should be noted that both the research that forms the basis of the book and the educational and social context in which it is situated are focused on the Scandinavian welfare state (particularly within Norway) in the post-World War II era, with an emphasis on the current situation. However, it is our intention to demonstrate that the transferability of the book's insights to other contexts is both possible and profitable, given that we also draw extensively on international research contributions and theoretical frameworks.

It is now recommended that the reader consult the subsequent chapters in order to gain further insight into the concept of 'the double game of music', as it is referred to throughout this book. The chapters can be read in any order, but we recommend starting with the Introduction and Chapter 1.

Acknowledgements

The accomplishment of the research outcomes detailed in this publication is inextricably linked to the provision of public funding, in this instance, facilitated by the Norwegian welfare state. The Research Council of Norway has provided financial support for the projects in question for almost a decade through its scheme for independent research (FRIPRO). The project *Musical Gentrification and Socio-Cultural Diversities*, which was completed between 2013 and 2017, was led and conducted by Petter Dyndahl, Sidsel Karlsen, Siw Graabræk Nielsen and Odd Skårberg. Moreover, post-doctoral researcher Mariko Hara, doctoral student Stian Vestby and the international visiting researchers Ylva Hofvander Trulsson and Ruth Wright must be acknowledged for their invaluable contributions to the project.

This work was continued in the 2018–2022 project, entitled *The Social Dynamics of Musical Upbringing and Schooling in the Norwegian Welfare State* (DYNAMUS). The project involved the management and participation of Petter Dyndahl, Live Weider Ellefsen, Anne Jordhus-Lier, Sidsel Karlsen, Ingeborg Lunde, Kari Marie Manum, Friederike Merkelbach, Siw Graabræk Nielsen and Odd Skårberg. We would like to express our gratitude to the international reference group that has followed the project, comprising Evert Bisschop Boele, Lucy Green, Andreas Lehmann-Wermser, Karin Lesnik-Oberstein, Anna Sparrman, Lauri Väkevä and Ruth Wright. We are grateful for the support they provided, despite the challenges and limitations imposed by the global pandemic.

Furthermore, we would like to acknowledge our institutions, the University of Inland Norway and the Norwegian Academy of Music, for providing us with favourable conditions to conduct research, both within and independently of the aforementioned larger projects. The University of Inland Norway has ensured the availability of open access to the book. The contributions of several in-house research groups have been conducive to the establishment of optimal research environments and the provision of invaluable forms of research support. In particular, we would like to acknowledge the *Centre for Educational Research in Music* (CERM) at the Norwegian Academy of Music and the research group *Music Education and Cultural Studies* at the University of Inland Norway, including visiting professors Hilde Synnøve Blix, Alexandra Kertz-Welzel and Anna Sparrman, for their significant contributions to the realisation of our endeavours.

On a national level, we would like to express our gratitude to the representatives from other Norwegian research project groups, as well as from public councils, non-governmental organisations, special interest groups and trade unions in the field of music and cultural policy, who have participated in seminars held under our auspices. Their contributions have been of immense value in enabling us to fulfil our societal mandate regarding the communication and dissemination of research.

In addition, we are grateful to have had the opportunity to participate in a number of international research networks. In this context, our research environment has also served as the venue for significant research conferences, including the International Society for the Sociology of Music Education (ISSME) and the Nordic Network for Research in Music Education (NNRME).

Moreover, we would like to express our gratitude to all those who have provided us with invaluable feedback, which has been instrumental in developing the arguments presented in this book. This encompasses all reviews and comments received on papers and other versions of chapters that ultimately formed part of the book, as well as oppositions and discussions at conference presentations. In the context of the aforementioned research groups and projects, we have been privileged to extend invitations to a number of distinguished researchers who have contributed their insights on a range of significant issues pertaining to the book's subject matter. These include sociological and cultural perspectives on music (education) and childhood, genre, media, intersectionality, diversity, equity, social justice, activism, democracy, politics and other matters of importance. Seminars and conversations with individuals such as Margaret Barrett, Tyler Bickford, Kim Boeskov, David Brackett, Anna Bull, Patricia Shehan Campbell, David Hesmondhalgh, Juliet Hess, Liam Maloy, Nasim Niknafs, Silje Valde Onsrud, Nick Prior, Motti Regev, Gareth Dylan Smith, Jacqueline Warwick and Heidi Westerlund have undoubtedly influenced and broadened our perspective on the concept of 'the double game of music'.

Our gratitude also extends to all members of the Manchester University Press team who have contributed to the publication of this book, especially Shannon Kneis and Laura Swift, as well as the anonymous reviewers employed by the publisher for their constructive challenge and assurance of quality. Furthermore, we would like to express our sincerest gratitude to the esteemed jazz musician and photographer, Mats Eilertsen, for his contribution in providing the striking and thought-provoking cover image.

Finally, we would like to acknowledge the contributions of all survey respondents and individuals who have allowed us to conduct interviews with and observations of them as part of our research. Their willingness to engage with our studies has greatly facilitated our knowledge development.

Introduction: the double game of music

Petter Dyndahl, Live Weider Ellefsen,
Anne Jordhus-Lier and Siw Graabræk Nielsen

Starting the game

Why does music mean so much to so many people? What do music educators want to pass on to their students? And who really wants to be a music teacher? According to data from a national survey of generalist student teachers specialising in music in a new five-year primary and lower secondary school teacher education programme in Norway (Nysæther *et al.*, 2021), the future music teachers in the Norwegian school seem to have both a very similar background as well as sharing a common belief in the importance of the subject of music for students:

> A major finding of this study is that generalist student music teachers appear strikingly similar in many ways. The majority of the student teachers are middle class, have Norwegian ethnicity and their immediate family works professionally with children and young people. Music has been a central part of their upbringing. They are motivated by the relational and performative aspects of teaching and learning and believe that the subject of music should focus on personal growth based on pupils' own needs and interests. As future music teachers, they aim for pupils to experience mastery and discover the joy of music. (2021: 45)

To even think that music could have other effects or be part of other relationships than those that point towards aesthetic expression, personal development and unifying cultural experiences and communities, seems far-fetched and difficult to take in. It is, so to speak, against the rules of the game. And that is perhaps how it was perceived in parts of the music education community when Anna Bull (2019) made her comprehensive study to examine contemporary associations between classical music and social class in the UK. Bull's study of four youth music groups within classical music, including a choir, two orchestras and an opera group, provides a rich picture of the varied and complex activities and experiences of the young musicians. But in addition to the participants' obvious interest in and commitment to rehearsing and playing the music, Bull clearly shows how bodily discipline and control characterise classical music; how classical music functions as a source of identification, helping to set the symbolic, cultural and economic boundaries of the middle classes to demarcate their space of privilege; how classical music practice is linked to increasing socio-economic inequalities in the UK; as well as how classical music is in various ways classed, gendered and racialised. In this way, the youth players do not only participate in an aesthetic game, but also in a social game about status, privileges and power. When the critique from the music education side fails to see that classical music's cultural practices actually cover several functions at the same time, it becomes a problem when it is assumed that Bull's agenda is to reduce or replace classical music's alleged nature and value with something completely different and indeed suspect:

> I have fundamental concerns about Bull's thesis, methodology, and conclusions. I fully accept that for many classical music devotees, part – perhaps all – of what classical music offers is a sense of 'exclusivity'. What I do not accept is that this sense of 'exclusivity' is what constitutes the totality of classical music's value for all people who engage in it. Nor do I accept that classical music directly engages any but a very small subsection of the middleclass. (Whale, 2022: 101)

> There is no question that the musical conventions that Bull articulates – 'seriousness', 'getting it right', 'moral virtue', 'discipline', and so on – may be linked to classical music. I believe, however, the author makes a serious error maintaining that the affirmation triggered by those conventions in people whose middle-class identity is underpinned by them captures the nature and the entirety of classical music's value. (104)

The problem arrives when one is only prepared to accept one game with one set of rules, when several games are actually played with different rules, different stakes and winnings, in the same place at the same time. Hence, the double game of music is the theme of this book.

Music matters, even more than one may believe or wish for

However, is it appropriate to think of the aesthetic, cultural, social and educational relationships with music in terms of a game? In any case, contributions from Bourdieu, Foucault, Goffman, Huizinga, Wittgenstein and other scholars who demonstrate the potential of the game analogue (see Chapter 1) suggest that, for social interaction, the metaphor of game might be particularly useful for investigating the dual character of what, on the one hand, may seem to be socially agreed upon, but on the other hand, may be hidden or require special analytical strategies to be exposed. This duality is particularly pronounced in Pierre Bourdieu's (1998) notion of *illusio* – i.e., players' belief and wholehearted involvement in the game. Indeed, the approach to studying games of music education used in this book leans heavily on Bourdieu's theories precisely because he recognises that there are several layers or dimensions to the playing of social games that all depend on each other to function effectively, truthfully and legitimately within their field.

This inclination towards investigating layers of game playing that are less obvious to the players themselves, or that players might even deny participating in, should not, however, be taken to indicate that these game levels are more real, more important or more fundamental than others. There is no need to question the reality or importance of the games of music (education) that the players themselves believe in, whether they concern the aesthetic and emotional musical experiences of performers and audiences, the carefree and playful musical interaction of children, the positive utilisation of music for social inclusion and/or change, the passionate dedication that teachers and students share when studying a genre or a piece of music or the genuine interest in scientific and academic musical inquiry.

In short, there is no question that *music matters*, as David J. Elliott and Marissa Silverman claim in their seminal book of the same title (2015). What could be added to their claim, however, is that music matters in complex and often contradictory ways that, to a certain extent, and precisely because of the participants' belief in and dedication to matters of music, tend to stay hidden from view if not continuously and strategically focused upon. Even then, participants might find them hard to accept. Media sociologist David Hesmondhalgh (2008) argues, for example, that there is a dominant conception of music, emotion and personal identity in sociologically informed analyses of music, which sees music primarily as an affirmative resource for active self-making:

> The dominant conception rightly emphasises the social nature of music and of self-identity, but if music is as imbricated with social processes as the dominant conception suggests, then it is hard to see how people's engagement with music can be so consistently positive in their effects, when we live in societies that are marked by inequality, exploitation and suffering. (Hesmondhalgh, 2008: 334)

Hesmondhalgh's critique strikes even better against dominant music educational trends and conceptions. It is therefore crucial to deal with this paradox by acknowledging that music cannot only have positive outcomes, but must necessarily also be part of conflicting historical, social and economic processes.

Elliott and Silverman's *Music Matters* maintains profound reflections and critical attitudes to many forms of music education and community music, persisting, for example, in seeing music education as something else and as more than a purely aesthetic matter; rather it is seen as comprising bodily and cultural fields of practice. Furthermore, and perhaps as a result of the above position, they assert that their own proposition of a *praxial* philosophy of music education is also a *normative* philosophy that aims to 'explain what musical, personal, and social understandings, abilities, dispositions, and values music education should develop' (2015: 13). However, when it comes to the social understandings and dispositions of music and music education, it may seem that the willingness to meet the normative ambition obscures the fact that both music and music education can also have quite different functions than those envisioned by Elliott and Silverman. Therefore, even though the authors refer to a critical sociologist such as Bourdieu when they distance themselves from the undue aestheticisation of music and the contention that listening to music entails a disengagement of the body (2015: 69), and instead maintain that musical experience is corporally rooted (2015: 301), they fail to accept that Bourdieu's social theory sees culture as an arena of conflict that in itself contributes to maintaining inequality and injustice in society. Similarly, they overlook the double character of the social games that Bourdieu describes, which facilitate but simultaneously also disguise the exchange and interchange of different forms of capital – in effect, normalising and authenticating the social hierarchies following from them.

With the notion of capital – social as well as economic and cultural – Bourdieu places emphasis on how social relations increase the ability of some well-placed players to advance their interests and to increase their power in and over the game. Social capital, for example, is 'the sum of the resources, actual or virtual, that accrue to an individual or a group by virtue of possessing a durable network of more or less institutionalised relationships of mutual acquaintance and recognition' (Bourdieu and Wacquant, 1992: 119). There is a fundamental and structural critique implied in Bourdieu's concept, which is left aside when Elliott and Silverman address the educational implications of (unequally) distributed social capital in *Music Matters*. While recognising the productivity of social capital as 'networks of resources that people have access to by working together, sharing common goals and experiences, and coming to care for one another' (2015: 383), the authors tend to neglect how capital, power and class structurally presuppose each other, trusting the effect of ethically sound professional conduct to neutralise possible pitfalls: 'Sometimes groups with social capital can (and unfortunately do) exclude more than they include. Also, sometimes it's difficult to be an "individual" when the strength of the group overpowers the individuals. Still, this is where ethical and educative teaching and learning need to be employed' (2015: 384f).

Elliott and Silverman's critical view of class reproduction is mainly related to two aspects. On the one hand, they claim (with reference to Bourdieu) that one specific concept of music – namely the aesthetic concept – is historically and institutionally class- and power-based (2015: 97) and should therefore be out-competed by their own praxial alternative. On the other hand, they seem to support the notion that socio-historical progress has eliminated some of the obstacles to, among other things, education and free choice of profession that were previously based on class, gender, race and ethnicity (see, e.g., 2015: 456f). Putting their faith in universal schooling based on the principles of universal accessibility, achievement and application, they leave the discussion of social class in favour of a critique of what are generally perceived as 'basic' subjects in education, advocating that schools should 'support the rich, cumulative, and enjoyable intercultural learning experiences that can be achieved when school music programs welcome children into a variety of musical praxes' (2015: 465).

Many music educators will intuitively sympathise with such an inclusive goal. For the critical sociologist, however, it may be difficult to accept that there is such a fundamental difference between 'the old world' and today. Indeed, for Bourdieu, it is rather a myth when modern Western societies boast that equal opportunities and a high degree of social mobility can be achieved through education. His work instead emphasises how social classes, especially the dominant and educated classes, preserve their social privileges across generations through the education system, as well as through cultural institutions and communities, although obviously this is achieved in more subtle ways today than before. This must therefore also apply to both school music programmes and music education in general, including music education research.

Moreover, in the early decades of the 2000s, some of the members of this research collective were influenced by the esteemed British popular music researcher and sociologist Simon Frith, who had identified aspects of Bourdieu's writings that underestimated the complexity and potential of popular music in comparison with classical music. Against this background, the objective was to establish the foundations for a more multifaceted approach to music education research, informed by cultural studies and sociology, which took into account the dual perspective advocated by Frith (see Dyndahl and Ellefsen, 2009, on which the subsequent section is largely based).

Towards a multifaceted approach to music education research

Frith (1996a) proposed that the sociology of culture, particularly in light of the influence of Bourdieu's *Distinction* (1984), had contributed to the consolidation of the notion that aesthetic ways of listening were social practices linked to what in Bourdieu's contemporary context was considered 'high culture'. Conversely, the cultural significance of popular music was explained and justified in terms of social functions and trivial needs for diversion and entertainment. It is evident that in early studies of youth culture and subcultures, such as Hebdige's (1979) comprehensive analysis of punk rock and the significance of style, there was a tendency to discuss these phenomena within a framework that primarily focused on social functions. This phenomenon was reflected in the attitudes of educators towards popular music, which for a considerable period of time were strongly influenced by approaches derived from critical theory, music sociology and media studies. These approaches mainly emphasised the significance of music for the development of identity and social belonging. In this way, the sociological doxa could contribute to maintaining the distinction between so-called high and low culture by insinuating that popular music fans do not engage in the same aesthetic listening and assessment as the classical audience. This distinction was further refined by the musicology of the time, which had developed a nuanced professional language for quality description and differentiation. However, Frith rejected such polarisation and asserted that 'all cultural life involves the constant activity of judging and differentiating' (1996a: 251). Therefore, when listening to popular music, we utilise our aesthetic capacity to make conscious and unconscious assessments of the music's merits and demerits. However, we also consider the social and cultural functions that popular music serves when we experience the emotional effects it imparts, or what dimensions of meaning are constituted in the relationships between music, people and context.

A significant aspect of Frith's argument was the dismantling of the dichotomy between aesthetic art music and functional popular music. In his reasoning, he maintained that the aesthetic and the functional are inextricably linked in the way we experience and construct meaning in popular music, in a manner analogous to the reception of classical music. In this way, Frith sought to justify what might be designated as 'aesthetic functionality' in musicological and – at our own expense – music educational approaches to any kind of music. Furthermore, he emphasised that aesthetic experiences in this multifaceted sense of the term only make sense 'by taking on both a subjective and a collective identity' (1996b: 109). Consequently, rather than conceiving of music as a mere passive mediator of pre-existing values and identities, Frith posits that identity is a process of initiation, formation and recognition that occurs within and in accordance with cultural practice, aesthetic assessment and musical appreciation:

> What I want to suggest, in other words, is not that social groups agree on values which are then expressed in their cultural activities (the assumption of the homology models) but that they only get to know themselves as groups (as particular organization of individual and social interests, of sameness and difference) through cultural activity, through aesthetic judgement. Making music isn't a way of expressing ideas; it is a way of living them. (1996b: 111)

Accordingly, individuals cannot be a self-constitutive 'doer behind the deed' (Butler, 2007: 195). Rather, identity processes must be understood as 'the "doer" is variably constructed in and through the deed' (195). Butler's understanding appears to be analogous to Foucault's (1997) concept of the subject's empowerment to control its relations with itself, while at the same time being constituted as a discursive subject by means of

> technologies of the self, which permit individuals to effect by their own means or with the help of others a certain number of operations on their bodies and souls, thoughts, conduct, and way of being, so as to transform themselves in order to attain a certain state of happiness, purity, wisdom, perfection, or immortality. (1997: 225)

Foucault posits that these practices are culturally constructed and represent ethical patterns of action that are both offered and imposed on us. At the same time, they are always dependent on other discursive technologies of power. Frith's perspective appears to align with this understanding, as musical practices constitute a specific aesthetic process for negotiating the self. This process allows us to test and transform available subject positions that constitute our identity and subjectivity, while also subjectivising us to the norms of a given discourse.

In other words, the aesthetic experience is discursively constituted as connections and relationships between the individual, the music and the social and cultural context in which the individual finds themselves. Consequently, music cannot be regarded as an autonomous, external object that generates meaning in itself. When we encounter music, we experience our subjectivity and cultural identity through aesthetic lenses. This may appear complex and contradictory, but in Frith's interpretation, the aesthetic experience connects us to the world in a manner that is simultaneously disconcerting and reassuring. The paradox is that the musical experience, which encompasses both aesthetic and functional aspects, constructs us socially and culturally, yet we experience it as if meaning and significance lie in the music itself, as inherent musical qualities or as the essence of music. To reiterate, Frith asserts that this phenomenon occurs in a similar manner regardless of whether the music in question is popular, classical or any other genre. In this perspective, Frith attempts to reclaim the concept of aesthetics, but without basing it on Kant's (1790/2007) critique of judgment and modernity's autonomous interpretation of aesthetic objects. Aesthetic experience is inherently subjective and collective, encompassing the experiences of both composers and performers, as well as listeners. As Frith (1996b: 114) maintains, music provides a means of understanding and navigating the world. Consequently, aesthetic processes cannot be considered 'pure' in the Kantian sense. Anything that appears to be purely aesthetic must necessarily also carry with it subjective and collective interests, including values, ontologies and identities.

Frith's arguments thus necessitate the deconstruction of the dichotomy between aesthetic autonomy and functional contextuality. Nevertheless, Derrida (1997) emphasised that his explanation of deconstruction implies a different concept from reconstruction. Deconstruction cannot be reduced to a strategically re-established and improved recognition of a given contradiction. In contrast, deconstruction is a process of building up and breaking down in parallel. The duality of interpretation implies that deconstruction is simultaneously situated within and beyond the discourse under consideration. The primary objective of deconstruction is not to eliminate the dichotomies through which we comprehend the world or to propose an alternative framework. Instead, it aims to contribute to our understanding of the intricate discursive formation in which it is embedded. Deconstruction can be defined as the analysis of all implicit assumptions and presuppositions that are embedded in historical, philosophical and ethical contexts pertaining to the discursive concepts and dichotomies in question. Concurrently, it entails the identification and acknowledgement of the significance of these phenomena in the uninterrupted negotiations about power, knowledge and meaning that have been and continue to be a constant feature of human history. In this regard, deconstruction does not represent a stabilising, 'reconstructed' endpoint for evolution. Hence, it is possible to acknowledge and dismiss Kantian aesthetics and instead attempt to perceive all music as aesthetically functional in the broadest, paradoxical sense of the term.

Nevertheless, it is essential to reiterate that this does not signify any diminution of music's aesthetic or cultural values. Conversely, this implies that music is accorded greater significance in shaping the identities of individuals within a social and cultural framework. By acknowledging subjectivity and cultural identity as processes of meaning-making rather than as reflections of an inner nature, music becomes more than a mere functional marker of either social belonging or cultural distancing. In contrast, music and music education are multifaceted aesthetic–functional games in which the construction and negotiation of cultural meaning, power and identity are exercised. It is similarly implausible to suggest that those engaged in the double game of music are cunning and two-faced players. In order for the game to be taken seriously and for its rules to be respected, it is necessary for players to have a firm belief in its meaning and importance.

In order to further explore these matters, which, based on what has been discussed so far, must accommodate aesthetic as well as functional or social aspects of music, it is necessary to consider them from a sociological perspective. This will allow us to understand how they can be both inclusive and exclusionary or marginalising. When viewed in the light of music education, the concepts of upbringing, teaching and learning can simultaneously be understood in terms of investments and expectations of return. It is therefore beneficial to utilise Bourdieuian theory, with the amendments, updates and clarifications made by a number of scholars, including Frith. The following chapters will thus attempt to examine a wide array of music education games, both theoretically and empirically.

The structure and content of the book

This book is composed of nine chapters. Despite the editorial and author collective's unified stance on the book's overarching concept and primary message, we have chosen to identify the individual authors of each chapter. Nevertheless, the objective is to present the book as a monograph rather than an anthology. Similarly, by employing and further exploring an established theoretical framework, the aim is to make the book interesting and accessible to an international readership, despite the empirical research being primarily focused on phenomena, practices, structures and institutions that are common to, but not exclusive to, the Nordic welfare state, with a particular focus on Norway. This is due to the fact that the book's empirical basis is firmly rooted in two comprehensive research projects, both of which were funded by the Research Council of Norway's funding scheme for independent projects (FRIPRO), as well as by the University of Inland Norway and the Norwegian Academy of Music. The projects are DYNAMUS – *The Social Dynamics of Musical Upbringing and Schooling in the Norwegian Welfare State*, 2018–2022, in which all the book's authors participated (see Chapter 2 for further insight into the project), which was preceded by the project *Musical Gentrification and Socio-Cultural Diversities*, 2013–2017 (see Chapter 3 for further details), conducted by a smaller selection of researchers (i.e., Dyndahl, Karlsen, Nielsen and Skårberg). Furthermore, we utilise findings from the researchers' independent research and international studies.

Chapter 1: The game metaphor

Chapter 1 examines the potential of the double game concept in music education, laying the groundwork for more detailed investigations in later chapters. It draws on Bourdieu's theories of cultural and social fields, games, players and capital to develop a theoretical framework for analysing music and music education as games. The text posits that games provide not only rules for participation but also the formation of knowledge, including game-specific truths, values and knowledge that have been agreed upon historically, socially and ethically. The game metaphor enables the discussion of how various games of music education and research are played, the forms of *illusio* that mask certain aspects and the analysis of structural differences affecting styles of play and participation. The game metaphor allows us to highlight the 'feel' of the game for favourably positioned participants and to explore the forms of capital that circulate and their distribution.

Furthermore, the metaphor of the game allows us to see actors as players in a social field. It illuminates how people engage in games to varying degrees of mastery. In music education, the games can be highly protected through methods such as auditions, participation costs, exclusive networks and power relations based on gender and class. These can result in the self-exclusion of some participants. Players, as investors, may invest different forms of capital in some games while neglecting others, contingent upon their total embodied capital shaped by their *habitus*. When the field of music education is conceptualised broadly, it becomes clear that there are numerous ways and roles for investors to invest.

The double game of music education entails two analytical levels. The term 'games' in plural represents multiple distinct social interactions with specific rules. The concept of the 'double game' in the singular represents a pervasive social structure that transcends the specific rules of individual games. The chapter delineates both levels, setting the stage for more detailed examinations in subsequent chapters.

Chapter 2: Democracy and inclusion: school(ed) music

This chapter examines the role of music games in the maintenance and challenge of the ideals, norms and socio-musical hierarchies associated with the welfare state. Music educational games are considered as practices of democratisation, in light of national curricula that require teachers to promote democratic core values, including inclusion, equality, social mobiity and respect for cultural diversity.

However, it is important to recognise that these educational games are situated within a cultural context and a symbolic, value-laden cultural economy. This cultural context determines the scope for participation and the forms of agency available to individuals based on their socio-economic and demographic position.

The chapter considers the Norwegian welfare state to be a double game. On the one hand, it performs as a society that is conscious of its egalitarian and social justice-orientated values, where players are assumed to reach a consensus about decisions and governing values through dialogue. Conversely, it performs as a game orientated towards self-preservation, which serves to perpetuate existing value hierarchies and power networks. Players position themselves within these structures in order to be recognised as players, thereby securing a fundamental belief in the state, its values and its strategies.

The chapter draws on research from the DYNAMUS project and similar studies to demonstrate how music education contributes to welfare work, presenting a positive picture of music as part of Norwegian schooling. However, it also highlights music education's role in stabilising and reproducing the values associated with the Norwegian welfare society, including the appropriation of potentially destabilising expressions.

Music education is distinguished by its inclusivity, incorporating new content and aiming to reach a broad audience. Nevertheless, the selection, adaptation or recontextualisation of music, driven by societal norms and values, can lead to exclusionary effects. The Norwegian welfare discourse emphasises the importance of listening to children's voices, music and expressions in the classroom. However, pupils' musical expressions are transformed, disciplined and shaped within the educational context by the social structures of meaning and power relations that govern the educational game. The integration of children's everyday musical games into the curriculum constrains potential forms of protest and chaos. Furthermore, the music curriculum largely reproduces established content and repertoires, subject to processes of gendering and 'genring' (Ellefsen, 2022).

Chapter 3: Social class and musical gentrification

Chapter 3 presents an approach to understanding the new meanings of social classes in late modern society through the lens of social class and musical gentrification. The updated concept of social class, based on both economic and cultural capital, is substantiated with the help of French economist Thomas Piketty and a Norwegian sociological research group.

The chapter also develops the concept of musical gentrification. This term refers to processes whereby music, musical practices and musical cultures of lower status become objects of acquisition by those in higher positions. This concept, adapted from urban geography and planning, helps to examine how musics that previously had a lower social, cultural and aesthetic status have become of interest to cultural actors of higher status. Musical gentrification can be observed when vernacular and popular music forms are explored by artists, educators and researchers, leading to aestheticisation, institutionalisation and academisation. Such processes can disrupt the original musical cultures and traditions and weaken or break some of the social and cultural ties to the musical cultures.

Using examples from higher music education, the chapter shows that while musical gentrification may appear to be a democratising process, it can also serve as a means of harvesting untapped cultural capital. At an institutional level, it can affirm and justify commitments to egalitarianism, tolerance and inclusivity. However, at an overarching social and cultural level, it confirms rather than changes the order of things and contributes to the discourse that obscures social class distinctions.

Finally, the chapter offers an intersectional perspective on social class and gender through the concept of musical genderfication (Nielsen, 2021). This concept refers to the production of gender norms and gendered divisions within social fields that also create hierarchies of 'high' and 'low' culture – both traditional and those that reuse established traditions in new guises, e.g., with the help of musical gentrification.

Chapter 4: Classification struggles: music education and genre

Chapter 4 addresses the crucial classification struggles inherent to contemporary Norwegian musical practices, particularly those pertaining to the concept of musical genres. The classification of

music according to genre is a fundamental aspect of musical education, commerce, politics, scientific enquiry and social interaction in
contemporary Western societies. Nevertheless, there are persuasive
arguments that challenge this view, suggesting that the significance
of genre has diminished. This is evident in the actions of artists who
assert their distinctiveness across or between musical boundaries
yet rely heavily on genre-based rhetoric to disseminate and promote
their music. The role and influence of genres in music educational
games can be discerned through the misrecognition of their impact,
where genres are so integral to these practices that the logic they
present is taken for granted.

This chapter employs a Bourdieuian approach to genres as actions,
building on the concept of 'classification struggles' as outlined by
Bourdieu (1984). This concept is used to examine the scientific production and organisation of knowledge in general, and to analyse
sociology as a field of classification in particular. This signifies that
the function of genre shifts from that of an educational (and analytical) instrument or corpus of material to that of an educational
(and analytical) practice. Genre is therefore regarded as a process
of genring, that is, a creative act of classification which establishes
the ontological effects of genres through discourse. It generates and
defines an intertextuality of cultural objects, which players simultaneously contest and accept as a given. In line with Ellefsen (2022),
the act of 'genring' entails the making of a discursive statement –
visual, verbal, gestural or otherwise – that contributes to the process of 'genrification' of cultural expressions, including those in the
domain of music and music education. Through the dual processes
of genring and identification, individuals categorise musical objects,
activities and other people within specific discourses, associating
them with particular identities, histories and expectations.

The practices designated as genring are examined through the
use of illustrative examples derived from the domains of music education in both compulsory and extracurricular schools of music
and arts, as well as from the music industry and broadcasting. It is
observed that genring may serve to obscure or to highlight aspects of
intersectionality. Gender is thus regarded as an act of interpretation
and classification, whereby acts of genring invariably occur within
and through discourses that are inherently gendered. Moreover,
genre is conceptualised as a process of subjectification, whereby

'childing' can be conceived of as specific instances of such actions which articulate certain musical practices and performances with each other, certain audiences, certain agendas and certain contexts.

Chapter 5: Musical parenting and the child as investment

Chapter 5 focuses on both levels of the game concept used in this book by looking at studies of musical parenting, distinguishing between those that emphasise the importance of music to achieve non-musical goals and those that focus primarily on children's musical development (Koops, 2020). Both can be interpreted as viewing the child as an investment with different social and/or cultural returns. However, Ilari (2018) has identified a significant limitation in much of the existing research in this area, namely that it has failed to consider the influence of 'parental conceptions of childhood and their associations to specific social and cultural groups in specific historical periods' (2018: 49). This serves as a useful reminder, which this chapter attempts to address by discussing late modern conceptions of childhood as well as parenting as social constructs in light of the book's overarching theoretical approaches, which include sociological perspectives on social class and intersectionality.

The chapter further explores the concept of 'intensive parenting' based on contributions from Faircloth (2014), Furedi (2002), Lee *et al.* (2010) and Hays (1996), as well as Lareau's (2011) concept of 'concerted cultivation'. In order to gain a deeper understanding of these concepts, both intersectional perspectives and Bourdieu's concepts of capital and *habitus* are employed. The argument put forth is that parental *habitus* enables the individual to comprehend society and that society, in turn, is embedded within the individual.

Two case studies are presented to illustrate these concepts. The first examines extracurricular municipal music and arts schools, where parents invest time, energy and money in their children's artistic activities and their own social status. The second case examines the music to which children have access in their everyday lives, where parents' decisions about appropriate and inappropriate music shape children's individual status and parents' social status. Both cases demonstrate the complex and multifaceted nature of musical parenting, which involves a number of simultaneous considerations.

Chapter 6: Children's games of music: play as investment

It is well documented that schooling reinforces social differences. But it seems harder to accept that the free play of day care, where children come as they are and play together as equals, might be a romanticised assumption. For good reasons, parents, educators, researchers, politicians and others who speak on behalf of children and have their best interests at heart want them to be free to play, to release and realise their innate capacities, to flourish and to experience flow, joy and self-worth. What is often overlooked is the doubleness of children's games. While the experience of being intensely and completely absorbed in the game in the here and now may be the meaning of it, there are social mechanisms in play that paradoxically regulate the disinterestedness of the experience, even in children's play, not least in relation to what it means to be a child of a particular (or not) gender and ethnicity and from a family with more or less accumulated resources and agency in terms of both material and symbolic capital (Bourdieu, 1986). Moreover, while the fields of education and upbringing are finally showing a greater awareness of the regulatory functions of gender and race, as discourses on education and upbringing, the circulation of capital in all its forms in children's play may be less visible.

The examples of play that we share in Chapter 6 show in different ways how musical agency and competence constitute symbolic capital for children in day care when they play. That is, their knowledge and ability to play in certain ways, musically, constitute a form of currency that they use to occupy legitimate and high-status positions in the play groups, to interact with each other, and that can be invested to gain future benefits. Indeed, it is a way of making important social distinctions between and within groups of friends.

Chapter 7: Public broadcasting: investments
in children and childed television music

Chapter 7 examines the historical function of children's television music within the context of the Norwegian welfare state. It considers the interpretation of the mandate of the Norwegian Broadcasting Corporation (NRK) and the exercise of its perception of the role of children's television music in conveying narratives that represent deep-seated socio-cultural values essential for the upbringing of children in a welfare state. As a public service broadcasting corporation, NRK is bound by a set of rules and regulations designed to meet the democratic, social and cultural needs of society, promote children's rights to expression and information, and protect children from harmful content. NRK occupies a position that is closely aligned with the overarching objectives of the Norwegian welfare state. Its mission is to disseminate societal norms and contribute to the education and upbringing of the nation's children.

Consequently, NRK occupies a pivotal role in the construction of narratives through the portrayal of onscreen characters, who are also regarded as active players in the welfare state game. The objective is to ensure that the onscreen narrative is perceived as credible by the child audience, who are also players in the same game, representing its rules, which may be taken for granted and appear to be almost invisible, with music playing a crucial role in storytelling.

The chapter commences with an account of the history of children's broadcasting in Norway, followed by an examination of the genre of children's music. The concept of 'childity' (Sjöberg, 2013) is then introduced as a means of examining the construction and recognition of music as children's music – that is to say, the process of becoming 'childed' – and the factors that facilitate such an interpretation.

The chapter then proceeds to analyses of selected children's television broadcasts involving music, with a view to examining how the music is constructed as childed and how it serves to reinforce key values associated with the welfare state, such as those pertaining to equal opportunities and the fostering of a sense of belonging. The chapter concludes with some reflections on the conditions for the double game of public broadcasting now and in the future.

Chapter 8: Talent and talentification

Chapter 8 concerns the complex perceptions of talent that exist in the field of media, the music industry and music education, and delves into how actors and institutions perform their roles and functions as players in the double game of talentification. Concepts of talent and musical talentification are discussed within the framework of music education in classical and folk music as well as in relation to social media and indigeneity, ethnicity and race in today's Norwegian society.

The concept and discourses of talent can be found across ages at all levels, from local amateur communities to global media events. They exist in all musical forms and genres, and they function as assessment and quality distinctions in everyday, commercial, educational and academic settings. This chapter explores these concepts from a critical, theoretically informed point of view, where talent does not by definition represent any fixed value or refer to the inherent characteristics of music, genres, styles of expression and the like. Instead, this chapter attempts to discern the common usages of the term talent from a corresponding perspective as given in Moore's (2002) critical approach to notions of authenticity as essentialist properties of something or someone. Contrary to this perception of authenticity, Moore investigates how or by what processes such characteristics have become firmly associated with what appears to be authentic. This analysis involves a de-essentialisation of the seemingly intrinsic qualities of authenticity, or, in our context, talent. Instead, it acknowledges that these features are attributed by historical, social and cultural processes, which can be described as processes of authentication, or, in this case, as processes of talentification.

Thus, the following questions to be asked in this chapter are: Who exercises or what causes the talentification of whom, and whose characteristics in which contexts and with which intentions and/or interests? These open the way to an exploration and scrutiny of musical talent and talentification in the light of the dual logic that otherwise pervades the book, and may also reveal that talentification is, in this respect, a double game.

Chapter 9: The double games of musical upbringing and schooling in the welfare state

Chapter 9 seeks to synthesise and theorise the double games of musical upbringing and schooling of the welfare state. This is done by examining the games related to music education and social class, gender, ethnicity, schooling, parenting, children's play, public broadcasting and the media, respectively. The chapter considers the distinctive and shared characteristics of these games in relation to the theoretical points of departure set forth in Chapter 1. By situating these games within the frameworks of the theorists presented throughout the book, this chapter also contributes to a more nuanced and theoretically informed understanding of the complex and often double-layered role of music in general.

The discussion also addresses the functions that the double games of music serve and the conditions under which they are played. Furthermore, the chapter considers the relationship between these games and the characteristics of the welfare state, exploring the insights they offer into the potential of music in contemporary society and their social, cultural and political significance. The discussion is predicated on the assumption of a cognitive dichotomy between the conviction in the purity of musical fields and the pervasiveness of socially constructed power. This is analogous to the Bourdieuian conceptualisation of a dual economy, comprising both material and symbolic assets and capitals. The objective of this chapter is to illustrate the potential of the approach presented in this book and to make a contribution to the field of music education sociology. Additionally, it seeks to provide insights that can inform neighbouring disciplines, including music sociology and cultural sociology, as well as the broader field of general sociology.

1

The game metaphor

*Live Weider Ellefsen, Petter Dyndahl, Anne
Jordhus-Lier and Siw Graabræk Nielsen*

Music [. . .] is the highest and purest expression of the facultas ludendi
[. . .] it is essentially a game, a contract valid within circumscribed
limits, serving no useful purpose but yielding pleasure, relaxation,
and an elevation of spirit. (Huizinga, 1944/1949: 187–188)

But it is just as true that a certain form of adherence to the game, of
belief in the game and the value of its stakes, which makes the game
worth the trouble of playing it, is the basis of the functioning of the
game. (Bourdieu, 1992/1996: 228)

Game and play

Life is a game, love is a game, language is a game. The game metaphor is frequently applied in academic and pop cultural discourse,
and by mathematicians and economists, as well as by philosophers,
historians and sociologists. Play theory and game theory have
developed as interdisciplinary fields of their own to explore the
meanings and analytical values of the game analogue. In aesthetics, notions of game and play constitute nodal points of meaning-
making when contemplating the nature of human engagement with
music and the other arts. And while the importance of games and
playing might be self-evident in the case of pedagogy and childhood
studies, in addition to the concepts' everyday meanings, they also
serve as metaphors in the discussion of broader issues of learning
and socialisation.

In *Homo Ludens*, Huizinga famously proposes that not only is
there a 'play-element' to culture, but that culture has been 'played

from the very beginning' (1944/1949: 46). Tracing social play and games across contexts and times, Huizinga demonstrates the significance of contest, what he calls *agon*, for social dynamics and development. His broad historical approach allows him to study the 'magic circles' (10) and/or 'sacred spots' (19) that the game-like qualities of social community life establish. Here, players temporarily accept that certain rules, goals and properties apply to themselves and their surroundings. Play/game – in German, *Spiel* – is also a central tenet in the aesthetics of Gadamer, where it serves to grant the artwork the status of an aesthetic event. As such, the artwork draws the participants out of the everyday and into its game-like, autonomous eventfulness. Gadamer makes the point that '[t]he players are not the subjects of play; instead play merely reaches presentation (*Darstellung*) through the players' (Gadamer, 1960/1989: 103). When playing, players are swept up in the game and reformed by its logic, thereby contributing to the constitution of the art/game event itself.

Within the field of sociology, Goffman's writings are littered with references to games and gamesters/gamers and players (see Goffman, 1969/1971, 1961/1972). Influenced by the symbolic interactionism of Mead and the emerging theories of games and economic behaviour (e.g., von Neumann and Morgenstern, 1944/2004), Goffman addresses the calculative, strategic aspects of human interaction in specific social settings. The game analogue enables Goffman to identify both basic and advanced moves, as well as movers, in social games of expression and information – whether in the fields of diplomacy and politics, in everyday social encounters and rituals or in educational and medical institutions. For Goffman, a game of social interaction is 'a field for fateful dramatic action, a plane of being, an engine of meaning, a world in itself, different from all other worlds except the ones generated when the same game is played at other times' (1961/1972: 25). Geertz taunted humanist scientists in general, and Goffman in particular, for their love of analogues such as 'game' and even 'drama' and 'text' (Geertz, 1980). He called for a more critical engagement with, and examination of, game 'imagery' in contemporary social theory. Geertz also noted the active role of the humanities in constructing the game-likeness of societies: 'As social theory turns from propulsive metaphors (the language of pistons) toward ludic ones (the language of pastimes), the humanities are connected to its arguments not in the fashion of sceptical bystanders but, as the source of its imagery, chargeable accomplices' (1980: 171).

As the title of this book implies, the following chapters concern themselves with games of music. Like Goffman, Geertz and other sociologists and social scientists, we explore the analytical potential of the game metaphor. Here, the game metaphor serves to investigate human interaction (strategic and otherwise) with and within music *education*, which is broadly understood as musical upbringing, schooling and socialisation. There is, however, a need to tread carefully and critically around powerful metaphors such as those of game, play and playing. Therefore, a considerable number of pages will indeed be dedicated to developing a sustainable and nuanced theoretical framework for treating music and music educational practices as games. Rather than thinking the analogue to be exhausted, this book contends that the notion of 'game' still has much to offer sociologically inspired music education research. The main reason for this can be illustrated by the two juxtaposed statements that open this chapter, from Huizinga and Bourdieu, respectively.

Huizinga (1944/1949) suggests that music is the purest expression of man's capacity for play. It serves no useful purpose other than yielding pleasure, relaxation and spiritual elevation. For Huizinga, musical play is also essentially a game. Music unfolds according to aesthetic rules and regulations that only make sense within the boundaries of the game itself. Although noting that musical play is driven by *agon* (contest), in that players (professional musicians, for example) compete to be master performers of the game, Huizinga sees musical play as an elevated, aesthetic game that takes place beyond and across other societal games. Musical play entails stepping out of real life. Furthermore, in existing beyond the severities of everyday life, games of music are immensely meaningful. The aesthetic game of pretence one steps into is transformative rather than trivial for the players involved.

Bourdieu, too, recognises that music is 'the "pure" art par excellence' (1984: 19). For Bourdieu, however, the notion of 'purity' is part and parcel of the value of music as a game – it is the basis of its functioning. The players' *belief* in the pure play of their game, understood as their adherence to the implicit values of its stakes, is what makes the game worth the trouble of playing (Bourdieu, 1990). This is the case in the artistic and literary fields, as well as in the educational, academic and political fields. This belief, which Bourdieu refers to as *illusio* (Bourdieu, 1992/1996: 227–228), can obscure other dynamics at play. For instance, participants often engage in strategic actions, make calculated investments to secure future rewards and compete to improve their positions within the game. Furthermore, and in keeping with the theoretical framework of Bourdieu, *illusio* – the belief in the game itself – masks the presence of structural differences in players' possibilities to participate. To the degree that the same games are available to all players (which might not be the case), the game-specific capital needed to play, including the players' socially and bodily constituted 'sense' of the game, is unequally distributed along axes that have to do with, among other things, class, education and gender.

The notion of game and interrelated theoretical concepts in Bourdieu's cultural sociology are central to the book's understanding of music educational practices and will be expanded upon subsequently, as well as in conjunction with other philosophical interpretations of game and play. For now, however, it is enough to conclude that the potential of the game analogue for music education research might reside in the diverse and perhaps also dichotomous meanings that are teased out by 'game' when used as a metaphor for musical interaction. These may concern distinctions between the pure and the impure (or 'disinterest' and 'interest', as aesthetic tradition would have it), between aesthetics and functionality (see, e.g., Frith, 1996a, 1996b), between reality and pretence and between artful play and social strategy. In the field of music education, however, the game metaphor might also enable an even broader discussion of how games of music, music education and, indeed, music education research are played. This includes investigations of which forms of *illusio* are involved in masking which aspects of the game, analysing the structural differences that enable different styles of play and participation, tracing the favourably positioned participants' feel or sense of the game and exploring the various forms of capital that circulate and how they are distributed.

Although Bourdieu certainly uses the game analogue generously in his various works (see Bourdieu, 1984, 1992/1996), the concept remains under-theorised in comparison to his more thoroughly developed analytical tools, such as *field*, *capital* and *habitus*. Inspired by Geertz's critique of sociological imagery and imagination in general (1980), as well as the further development and implicit critique of Bourdieu's terminology led by later scholars (see, e.g., Thornton, 1995; Peterson and Kern, 1996; Skeggs, 2004), this book aims to utilise the game analogue in an analytically nuanced and theoretically tenable way to provide insight into the complexity of music educational practice.

Games of truth and language

Games provide players with rules that outline the proper moves to make and roles to take. Furthermore, and in the words of Foucault, the game-specific rules produce game-specific truths. A game constitutes 'a set of procedures that lead to a certain result, which, on the basis of its principles and rules of procedure, may be considered valid or invalid, winning or losing' (Foucault, 2000a: 297). The validity of the *results* of games – indeed, the *truths* they tell – depends on the procedures that produce them. In other words, the rules by which the game is played determine what can be deemed valid, legitimate or successful. Consider, for example, the rules of television music talent shows, such as *Idol* and *The Voice*, and the truths they produce pertaining to notions of 'talent', 'quality' and 'age'. Taking the metaphor even further, consider the game of parenting a musical child, and the notions of 'love', 'motherhood', 'family' and 'success' that the socially established yet informal rules of parenting might produce. By providing participants with sets of rules, therefore, games also accumulate and manage game-specific truths concerning the meaning and value of objects, concepts and expressions, the relevance of certain topics and themes, the legitimacy of activities, relations and places and even hierarchies of previous performances and play scores (e.g., the success of certain musical talents related to their parents' strategies of investment).

Foucault used the notion of game metaphorically to illustrate his criticism of the traditional understanding of power as a state of hierarchically performed dominance. The game metaphor allowed him to forward a comprehension of power as a strategic game played across and between every level of the social fabric.

These are games of power 'in which some try to control the conduct of others, who in turn try to avoid allowing their conduct to be controlled or try to control the conduct of the others' (Foucault, 2000a: 299). Bourdieu, similarly, gives weight to the negotiations of powers and positions that games facilitate through their rules (explicit and implicit) for exchanging game-specific capital. In this, both Bourdieu and Foucault assert the material as well as relational aspects of game playing.

Relationality and materiality were also prime concerns of Wittgenstein in his *Philosophical Investigations*. Here, he introduced the notion of the language-game (*Sprachspiel*) to argue that 'the speaking of language is part of an activity, or a form of life' (1953/1986: 13). The meaning of words and utterances rise from and refer to objects, actions and relations in particular social settings, for example in the practice of a specific profession. In the communication between two builders at work, terms like 'blocks', 'slabs' and 'beams' are used as one builder directs the other to hand over specific elements. This simple interaction, Wittgenstein argues, constitutes a 'complete primitive language' (3).

We find similar language-games in the fields of music and education. Obvious examples include the piano masterclass, the recording studio session, the youth string orchestra rehearsal or the online K-pop fan forum, where the meaning of words and utterances (including non-verbal) is constituted in and through the specific material, discursive practices themselves. Language does not correspond to reality; reality creates language and language creates reality. Following contextually established procedures for interaction, words and utterances resemble moves in a game: 'The question "What is a word really?" is analogous to "What is a piece in chess?"' (Wittgenstein, 1953/1986: 47).

Wittgenstein's writings on the multifarious language-games of man challenged prevailing ideas about, and interest in, the creation of all-encompassing models of explanation. In this, he famously inspired Lyotard to announce the end of the grand narratives of modernism and structuralism. The postmodern condition would be recognised by emerging forms of rationality and a plurality of competing language-games (Lyotard, 1979/1984; see also Peters, 2020). Wittgenstein offered a radical critique of the traditional ambition of philosophy to hypothesise, theorise and explain. Instead, he argued that the task of philosophy is to investigate the workings of the language-games themselves:

> [Philosophical problems] are, of course, not empirical problems; they are solved, rather, by looking into the workings of our language, and that in such a way as to make us recognize those workings: *in despite of* an urge to misunderstand them. The problems are solved, not by giving new information, but by arranging what we have always known. Philosophy is a battle against the bewitchment of our intelligence by means of language. (Wittgenstein, 1953/1986: 47)

At least two methodological premises for research can be inferred from Wittgenstein's critique, which are of relevance for the discussion of music educational games presented in this book. Firstly, investigations into how the games of music education are played need to be concerned with the actual workings of the specific games under scrutiny, examining meaning as use (Wittgenstein, 1953/1986: 20). This involves observing how certain meanings are established by, and facilitate, certain actions. Music education is not one game but several games, which may operate by different logics and rules, reward different forms of play and participation and create different types of winners and losers.

Secondly, all research approaches represent language-games of their own. Wittgenstein pursued 'complete clarity' (Wittgenstein, 1953/1986: 51) in understanding language-games. As one gains insight into the workings of language-games, philosophical enigmas disappear, Wittgenstein believed. Clarity, however, seems to be constructed and produced within the self-same philosophical game that is seeking to reveal it, also in the case of Wittgenstein. This is what is implied by Foucault's notion of *truth games* (Foucault, 2000b) and in Bourdieu's descriptions of the expert games and players within the fields of art, academia and science (Bourdieu, 1992/1996). Furthermore, even when new truths are produced, they are revealed by following the procedures of already existing research games. They are secured by enacting relations of power and knowledge that have been established by previous players in previous games. Moreover, while the prime ambition and outcome of research games is the rearrangement of previous truths and the production of new ones, games of knowledge are also always games of social power, in the sense meant by Foucault and Bourdieu: they position people in relation to other people, the researchers as well as the researched.

Neither philosophical enigmas nor social power hierarchies will disappear as a result of the scholarly discussions presented in this book, nor is this the ambition of the authors. On the contrary, we acknowledge that this book, like music education research initiatives in general, represents an investment made by researchers participating in a double game: on the one hand, it is a game of scientific and philosophical curiosity and dedication towards true insight and improvement. On the other hand, it is a social, strategical and contextual game of truth and language, power and prestige. Both games matter – indeed, their significance is secured by their dependence upon each other for support, even when this interdependence is more or less hidden. We will explore this further, starting with an example of ostensibly inclusive music education.

According to Bourdieu, in a social formation, there will always be interrelational struggles for status, position and power. The inclusion of one thing requires the exclusion or marginalisation of something else – in the same way that if something or someone is given higher cultural value, something or someone else must be assigned lower value (these values will be explained in more detail as *cultural capital* further in this chapter). Even the now generally accepted aim of inclusive music education implies strong possibilities of new forms of social and cultural distinction. The concept of *musical gentrification* (Dyndahl et al., 2014) entails a further development of Bourdieu's views of the dynamics of power in society, which has been productively put to use in order to examine processes of inclusion and exclusion in music education (see also Dyndahl et al., 2017; Dyndahl et al., 2021).

Musical gentrification

Adapted and recontextualised from urban geography and city planning, the musical gentrification conceptual metaphor was coined to investigate popular music's introduction to, and, in turn, significant presence in, music academia (Dyndahl et al., 2017). It indicates that, from a certain point in the history of Scandinavian music education in general, as well as higher music education, it became increasingly attractive for students, teachers and researchers to include music, musical practices and musical cultures that previously had too low status to be considered relevant as teaching and research objects in this context. With academia gradually embracing popular music, one could believe that higher music education has been 'democratised' once and for all and that all kinds of music are now included in higher music education. In comparison to the overall dominant position previously held by Western classical music, an inclusive expansion has clearly taken place.

However, in the same way as urban gentrification is exercised by people with higher status than those who originally inhabited the neighbourhoods that become objects of new attraction, and therefore tend to expel the original residents, musical gentrification also has exclusionary or marginalising effects. For example, not all popular music genres and styles may be found attractive enough to be gentrified. Examining all Norwegian Master's theses and doctoral dissertations approved in any academic discipline of music throughout the century from 1912 to 2012, Dyndahl and colleagues (2017) noted that esteemed forms of jazz, rock and pop were well represented in the overall academic picture. At the opposite end of the scale was Scandinavian dance band music, which is a widespread music genre and cultural practice in Norway and Sweden, but which is often also interpreted as a stereotype of working-class culture and lifestyle. Equally important, moreover, is how popular music styles are included. By using sufficiently sophisticated theory and conceptual apparatus, it seems that almost any music – with a few exceptions, evidently – can be lifted to legitimate academic culture (Dyndahl *et al.*, 2017).

In these ways, musical gentrification processes lead to changes in the academic systems of classification, which implies that timehonoured hegemonies are set aside and replaced by new distinctions that are apparently disturbing the traditional balance between high and low culture. Also, the processes of academisation and institutionalisation of popular music can contribute to altering the characteristics of the musical communities as well as the music forms, practices and cultures that are subjected to gentrification, as Vestby found in his study of Norwegian country music (Vestby, 2017).

Double games of music education

The case of musical gentrification may serve as an indication of how much more complex and paradoxical the social, cultural and pedagogical games of music are, compared to what often emerges in normatively positive representations of music education's opportunities to advance and enrich individuals, culture and society (see Elliott and Silverman, 2015; Hesmondhalgh, 2008). In fact, one of the central findings from the Bourdieu-inspired study *Culture, Class, Distinction*, conducted by Bennett and colleagues (2009) in the UK, was that music 'is the most divided, contentious, cultural field of any that we examine and is central to our concern with probing contemporary cultural dynamics and tensions' (Bennett *et al.*, 2009: 75). By essentially just emphasising what is considered its positive possibilities, and shying away from the possibility that music matters because it lends itself so easily to procedures that exclude, violate, hinder and divide, for example, music educators may in fact reduce the overall power and meaning of music and of music education.

Against this background, it is a premise for this book that music and music educational practices matter precisely *because* of their complex and paradoxical game-like character. Games of music education are played strategically *and* improvisationally, for fun and for the win, for their aesthetic attraction and for the practical rewards they offer. Every game is a new game that may challenge existing structures of power and knowledge. At the same time, they are utterly dependent on socially and historically established power hierarchies to be played at all. Furthermore, the various logics and dimensions of game playing support and depend upon each other to create rules and regulations, good hands and bad hands and winners and losers within the realms of the game. Indeed, each game of music is realised not from one but from a plurality of rationales and possibilities, whose complexity is delimited only by the level of detail in the analysis we care to apply. Nevertheless, this book aims to describe, analyse and discuss a specific doubleness in the rationales of music educational game playing that pertains to the intertwinement of *symbolic* and *material* game-specific currencies and values.

In Bourdieu's theoretical take (1986), the social games people play – whether musical or academic, and whether belonging to the family sphere or the fields of profession – are supported by these two distinct but closely related economic dimensions or logics: the material and the symbolic (cultural and social) economy. Individually and in interaction, material and symbolic economies affect the preconditions for music upbringing, teaching and learning in today's society. As a social science, economics traditionally examines the production, distribution and consumption of goods and services, both at the micro and macro-economic levels, and it includes both public and private sectors. Of course, all these aspects affect music education in a wide range of ways, but we will start by focusing more closely on the symbolic economies, which will help to untangle the complexities of the double games of music as played in the fields of education.

The symbolic economies of music education

There are several economic terms in use in this book that are inspired by Bourdieu's capital theory (Bourdieu, 1986). These include (among others) *capital, investor, investment* and *yield*. Together with the notions of *field, game* and *distinction*, we will use them to explore the social dynamics of music educational game playing, the strategies of players who are invested in music education and the cultural, social and material hierarchies that their investments rely upon. We apply such terms to investigate the *symbolic economies* that govern how music educational games are played and by whom. Indeed, in exploring the symbolic as well as the material and economical sides of value – the social and cultural *capital* players invest and accrue when playing successfully and productively – the double character of music education *as* a game might become clearer. We will begin by outlining some of these central terms.

Classed currencies

With Bourdieu's and post-Bourdieuian approaches similar to the one taken in this book, the dynamics of society in general are understood as ongoing negotiations and exchanges of symbolic as well as economic forms of capital. Game-specific currencies enable players to strategically, intuitively and even unconsciously invest in the game to receive immediate or future rewards. In games of music education, such disposable currencies might include various forms of musical expertise and connoisseurship, instruments and technological equipment, job titles and positions, awards and grades, membership of communities or networks and experiences in specific knowledge traditions. It may also include family relations and traditions, a proper language, bearing and behaviour, time, dedication and passion, perceived originality and authenticity. Common to the different forms of capital that Bourdieu describes is that they might gain value when they are exchanged or converted into other forms of capital. Family relations (for example, coming from a family of recognised folk musicians) can be exchanged for awards and honours (a young folk fiddler with the right name participating in an audition or competition), which again might be exchanged for money (grants or scholarships).

The exchange rates and relationships between different forms of capital have changed throughout history and continue to change. Regardless, the distribution of capital itself in and across different domains – social, cultural and economic/material – keeps working to sustain a prevailing circuit of institutions, cultural artefacts and individual players. Cultural capital, for example (connoisseurship acquired through family connections and privilege), is likely to be designated in terms of objects and practices that are approved by the education system (grades and tests). This is again treated as a valuable currency by the privileged classes to secure the inheritance of privilege for new generations. Forms of social capital, such as friendships, memberships, status, prestige and attention, can serve the same function without being perceived as capital at all. Rather, they are perceived as personal or given qualities and rights that result from natural talent or hard work instead of inherited social relationships (for two excellent analyses of naturalised social capital, see Bull, 2019; Hall, 2018).

According to Bourdieu, networks of relationships are 'the product of investment strategies, individual or collective, consciously or unconsciously aimed at establishing or reproducing social relationships that are directly usable in the short or long term' (1986: 22). Investments in networks are therefore essential for gaining social capital. However, the importance of social and cultural investment history and background for success in the educational system, in working life and in terms of personal prosperity tends to be underestimated. This again leads to inherited social privileges being individualised and naturalised.

Symbolic economies in society are therefore misrecognised or even unrecognised forms of an economic logic that contributes to reproducing societal antagonisms. In the field of music education, symbolic capital (cultural and social) appears in the various guises of embodied, objectified or institutionalised properties. Embodied cultural capital, for example, may involve mastering and demonstrating appropriate behaviour as a musician, as a listener, as a teacher, as a student, as a connoisseur or as a fan. It could include anything from craftsmanship skills to elaborate terminologies, poses, hairstyles and tattoos. In an objectified form, it could be musical instruments, recordings and playlists, etc., but also fashion that shows affiliation with certain genres and styles. Institutionalised social capital generally involves academic or artistic titles and educational degrees but can also be made visible as participation in masterclasses, talent programmes, teaching and collaborating with renowned teachers or band members, etc.

Bourdieu's use of the term *cultural capital* has, however, received some criticism over the years, largely due to the rather static relationship he assigns to 'high' versus 'low' culture (cf. Bourdieu, 1984). In the 1990s, weighty arguments were presented that contributed to more nuanced sociological understandings of class-based cultural consumption and taste. With their empirically based concept of *cultural omnivorousness*, Peterson and collaborators showed how cultural expressions perceived as 'low' within the Bourdieuian framework could indeed serve as capital through the right *distinctive* practices (Peterson, 1992; Peterson and Kern, 1996; Peterson and Simkus, 1992). Thornton (1995) launched the concept of *subcultural* capital, which is clearly derived from Bourdieu's terminology but is based on her study of social, cultural and aesthetic distinctions in the British dance music club scene. In the subcultural context, 'hipness', for example, is a high-status form of capital that can be invested and exchanged into various popular cultural roles and occupations. In this way, Thornton claims, a Bourdieuian understanding of society is just as relevant at the micro as at the macro level. Her view is shared by Frith (1996a), who criticised

Bourdieu's overall high–low dichotomy and stated that popular culture itself contains similar spans: it always mirrors society at large in that similar social mechanisms as those described by Bourdieu at the macro level also apply in this specific (sub-)field.

These clarifications are important for this book as well. Indeed, due to reorientations provided by sociologically orientated scholars such as Peterson and Thornton, we find that the concept of symbolic capital remains one of the most effective for interpreting not only the social structures but also the social dynamics of music education, on both micro and macro levels of practice. The 'dynamics' of social fields and circumstances might, of course, vary considerably. What can be studied are certain forms of social dynamics as they play out in specific social fields at specific times in history. Bourdieu explored the social dynamics of his contemporary France, with its specific elite cultural institutions, agents and practices of consumption. In this book, the case in question is the social dynamics of musical upbringing and schooling in the Norwegian welfare state after World War II. In the following section, we therefore present a short, theoretically founded outline of this case, conceptualising it as a specific social field in which specific games of music education are taking place.

The music educational game field

In Bourdieu's (1984, 1992/1996) investigations of the social dynamics of societies, social space is divided into social *fields*, such as business, academia, education and the fields of art and cultural production. In sociologically orientated research, defining the field of interest is largely a methodological concern. However, for a field to function according to the theoretical premises that are outlined in this chapter, a degree of establishment and substantiality related to its practices and procedures must be identifiable. Music education certainly exhibits such a substantiality – historically as well as in its social complexity. Even if it obviously shares and celebrates stakes and rules governing the field of music as art and cultural production, the music educational game field also plays by its own rules, for its own stakes. This will become clear throughout this book's later chapters. For now, it is sufficient to observe, for

example, the enduring tradition of dividing higher music education into programmes and players committed to 'performance' and
'teaching', respectively, the institutionalisation and professionalisa-
tion of music education *research* specifically (with the establishment
of separate positions, networks, grants and journals), the range of
policy practices governing music education in schools (including
curricula and labour unions) and the veritable explosion of games
and players dedicated to and profiting from Internet-based musical learning. Furthermore, and in addition to these institutionalised
and/or explicitly articulated music educational games, the field of
music education offers more subtle games of musical teaching and
learning, such as the games of parenting, fandom, television and
radio entertainment, online music streaming, religious service, sport
events, nightclubbing and so on.

In the context of this book, music education is recognised as
a broad concept that includes music-related upbringing, teaching,
training, education, socialisation, acculturation/enculturation and/
or related terms. Nevertheless, we define our specific field of interest as *music education activities, practices and institutions that are
limited in time and space to post–World War II Scandinavia, with
an emphasis on Norwegian contemporary events, analyses and discussions.* Even more specifically, we emphasise music education
conditions that are linked to *interaction and mediation between
upbringing in the home and formal socialisation and educational
institutions.* In doing so, we recognise and allow for considerations
of the forms of informal and non-formal socialisation that take
place in all these contexts and, not least, in the interaction and friction between both the institutions and the degree of formalisation.

While all fields exercise a certain degree of autonomy from
each other in Bourdieu's understanding, they are also situated
within a broader social field of *power structures.* The practices
and procedures of the broader field of power support the seemingly autonomous or 'pure' (Bourdieu, 1992/1996) fields' practices
and procedures, albeit, perhaps, in hidden ways. As with the intertwinement of material and symbolic economies, the field of power
intertwines with the fields of music and education. It contributes to
a naturalisation of the ways in which music and education-specific
games are played and legitimises the music and education-specific
social hierarchies, stakes and rules that facilitate the playing. For

example, a music student's skilful entrepreneurial investments in certain relations, learning practices and social settings in order to succeed and profit during the course of their music studies might be seen as 'natural' expressions of musicality, passionate dedication and personal interest and suitability. In many cases, they certainly are. However, and this is central to the argument we present in this book, the successful and productive playing of music educational games is also always dependent upon support from the field of power – that is, from material, socio-economic structures and hierarchies and established social systems of privileges and rights. The sense of the game, as Bourdieu terms it, and the playfulness and skills shown by the entrepreneurial student-investor, are as accessible for them as the field of power allows. This entails that, for analyses of music educational games to be nuanced and informative, they must include analyses of power structures and hierarchies as they exist and change in relevant contexts.

In referring to double games in music education, we therefore argue that the music educational game field is a power field as well as a field of pure play, and that the two fields give each other strength even when they seem to be in contradiction:

> The degree of autonomy of the field may be measured by the importance of the effect of translation or of refraction which its specific logic imposes on external influences or commissions, and by the transforming, even transfiguring, effect it has on religious or political representations and the constraints of temporal powers. (Bourdieu, 1992/1996: 220)

Significantly for Bourdieu, the field of power is not precisely mirrored but *refracted* by the fields of art and cultural production (1992/1996: 220), or, in our case, the field of music education. The latter's autonomy is noticeable in the way in which power demands and logics *change* (while maintaining their relevance) according to field-specific demands and logics. This means, for example, that the logics of a national school music curriculum, which is produced and supported by the field of power through political procedures and hierarchies, might be refracted towards long-standing, field-specific discourses and practices (concerning specialisation, talent or quality, to mention a few) when operationalised as symbolic currency in a game of school music education, by knowledgeable and experienced players of music educational games. We will now look more closely at the players themselves, seeing them as *investors* who strategically, but also often tacitly and unconsciously, make *investments* to succeed in their games of interest.

Investors, investments and interests

The concepts of *investors*, *investments* and *interests* in games of music education allude to the long-term and strategic aspects of players' playfulness. This analytical idea entails, for example, seeing parents as *investors* in their children's musical upbringing. The time, energy and emotions they dedicate can be seen as *investments*. Similarly, their belief in the purity of their actions – performed to care for their children and coming from a true love of music – reflects their *interest* in the game of musical parenting.

Bourdieu's notion of the *habitus*, which refers to *embodied* forms of cultural capital (Bourdieu, 1990), is central to understanding the investors' roles and reasons, and this also applies in the field of music education. He describes the *habitus* as schemes of perception, thoughts and actions generated throughout the players' history of participating in and practising game playing (going to concerts with one's parents from an early age, for example, receiving piano lessons, singing together in the family car or performing on a stage). In a specific game, the *habitus* represents the active presence of past experiences and ensures that the players have the necessary feel or sense of the game being played. Indeed: 'It is because agents never know completely what they are doing that what they do has more sense than they know' (Bourdieu, 1990: 69). Good investors are able to perform the game's future – that is, they have an attuned anticipation of the development of the game (Bourdieu, 2024: 27). Their embodied or naturalised anticipation is achieved through repeated game playing – symbolically structuring encounters between the *habitus* and a given field, 'in fact, all actions performed in a structured space and time are immediately qualified symbolically and function as structural exercises through which practical mastery of the fundamental schemes is constituted' (Bourdieu, 1990: 75).

Participating in a youth string orchestra from an early age and growing up in a family that actively invests in such musical games cultivates in young players an intuitive sense of, and indeed a belief in, how to speak, behave, respond and anticipate outcomes within that context . It also teaches them how to position themselves legitimately and avoid negative attention within such and even similar games or, as Wittgenstein puts it (1953/1986), games that share a 'family resemblance' with string orchestra playing. Through different symbolically structuring encounters (with audiences, scores, conductors, older players, guest master performers, etc.), players accrue different amounts and forms of capital and come to be differently positioned for future investments. Conversely, in embodying different forms of capital and performing different investments, investors' *habitus* come to signify different social values and positions, as when an upper-middle-class entrepreneurial attitude and confident bearing is taken to indicate talent and capacity for deep and complex aesthetic devotion (cf. Bull, 2019).

As Bourdieu (1990: 72) outlines, 'the relation to the body is a fundamental dimension of the *habitus* that is inseparable from a relation to language and to time'. Also, the acquisition and embodiment of symbolic capital presupposes a personal cost, an investment in the 'socially constituted form of libido, libido sciendi, with all the privation, renunciation, and sacrifice that it may entail' (Bourdieu, 1986: 18). For example, the accumulation of cultural capital costs *time*, which must be personally, bodily invested. A parent's investment in time to ensure the transmission of economic to cultural capital in the form of a child's schooling (Bourdieu, 1986) might be crucial. However, the usable time possessed by players in the field of music education, such as parents, music students and researchers, may vary significantly. Furthermore, the *habitus* is subject to accumulation strategies even as an unconscious desire. Adhering to this desire, the players make 'investments in order to accrue value when [they] can conceive of a future in which that value can have a use' (Skeggs, 2004: 146), thereby socially qualifying their body for occupying present and future positions. Players who are born in the game have the feel for the game and are investing not where the profit is but where it will be next, like good tennis players who position themselves where the ball will be and not where it is (Bourdieu, 1998). The earlier that players enter the game, and the less they are aware of how they learn to invest, the greater their ignorance of what is quietly granted through their investments (Bourdieu, 1990). Put differently, the earlier players enter the game, the greater their ignorance of their own interests and investments in the field of power supporting the game.

Bourdieu refers to players' ignorance of their interest as *illusio*, describing it as a result of a relation of 'ontological complicity' (Bourdieu, 1998: 77) between mental structures and the objective structures of the social world. *Illusio* leads players to be drawn into a game and to (unconsciously) accept its rules (Bourdieu, 1998):

> *Illusio* is the fact of being caught up in the game, of believing the game is 'worth the candle', or, more simply, that playing is worth the effort. In fact, the word interest initially meant very precisely what I include under the notion of *illusio*, that is, the fact of attributing importance to a social game, the fact that what happens matters to those who are engaged in it, who are in the game. *Interest* is to 'be there', to participate, to admit that the game is worth playing and that the stakes created in and through the fact of playing are worth pursuing; it is to recognize the game and to recognize its stakes. (Bourdieu, 1998:. 76–77)

Illusio is a Latin word deriving from the root '*ludus*', meaning game/in-play. In his book *Homo Ludens*, Huizinga notes that, compared to the ancient Greeks' changing and heterogeneous terms for the play function, the Latin language only has the word '*ludus*' to cover the whole 'field of play'. Furthermore, '[t]he idea of "feigning" or "taking on the semblance of" seems to be uppermost', as noticeable in the compounds referring to the illusory and unreal aspects of *ludus*: *alluda*, *colludo* and *illudo* (Huizinga, 1944/1949: 35–36). Challenging the conceptual differences between pretence and persuasion, Bourdieu offers the concept of *illusio* as a way to understand players' complex interest in games and game playing. More loosely connected to the idea of intentionality than is the case with 'interest', *illusio* denotes a situation of being and believing in the game, taking it seriously and investing in it (Bourdieu and Wacquant, 1992).

Double games of music education: summing up

Summing up our use of the game analogue so far, we have enacted at least two different analytical levels when speaking of double games of music education being played.

On the one hand, we refer to games in the plural, meaning the variety of different, specific practices of established social inter-actions being played according to specific, established rules. As is the case with the 'field' metaphor, assigning practices the sta-tus of 'game' is largely a methodological concern. In this book, we are preoccupied with games that we find relevant for musical upbringing and schooling. To give a few examples, we consider formal music educational practices on higher as well as lower lev-els to constitute different games (even though they might adhere to many of the same rules). We also apply the game analogue to social practices such as the family, the music and television indus-tries and social media sites, where players follow the procedures of play and participation and invest their game-specific curren-cies and capacities to better position themselves within the social structures of the game.

On the other hand, we refer to the double game in the singular, thus invoking a general, social structure of interaction that we find to be operative regardless of the rules and regulations of particular games. The doubleness we refer to is the general symbiosis of mate-rial with symbolic currencies, the intertwinement of a subject field's heteronomous and autonomous relations and the larger power field and the overall *illusio* of disinterest – the players' belief in the autonomy of the game and the purity of its values hides the work-ings of power, class and status in deciding who wins and who loses. Bourdieu (1998: 88) writes that, if disinterestedness is sociologically possible, it is through 'the encounter between *habitus* predisposed to disinterestedness and the universes in which disinterestedness is rewarded'. The most typical of such universes are, in addition to the family and the economy of domestic exchanges, the fields of cul-tural production, such as the field of music. The doubleness we seek to investigate and untangle might therefore be particularly strong even in the field of music education, which overlaps considerably with the field of musical production in sharing many of the same institutions, expert players, areas of investment and so on.

The game analogue makes it possible to see the social agents of a field as players who (more or less masterfully) play the games that are available to them. Significantly, in the field of music education, these games might be highly protected, in the form, for example, of auditions or similar procedures of evaluation, participation costs, socially exclusive networks, ideas of authenticity and originality, as well as gendered, ethnic, racial and classed power relations that lead to participants excluding themselves at the outset. As investors, the players have the opportunity of investing – capital, time, energy and emotions – in some, but not other, games, all depending on their total embodied amount of capital – i.e., their *habitus*. When we conceptualise the field of music education in a broad sense, also including all aspects of informal socialisation and enculturation, there are nevertheless a multitude of variants of the investments investors choose to make. Similarly, there are a multitude of investor profiles and roles.

For the purposes of this book, we follow the play of some key investors in the field, choosing also to delve deeper into some of their key strategies of investment. However, in order to analyse the games of music education and the investments that keep them going on a macro scale, we see a need to expand the notion of player/ investor to also include entities such as institutions. For example, the Norwegian schools of music and arts are investors in local communities. They seek out new audiences and new recruits, aiming for future yields in the form of a strengthened and safer social position. The Norwegian welfare state has its interests in music education, which is believed to contribute to the upholding of democratic values such as inclusion and equality. The popular music industries and television broadcasting and/or streaming companies invest massively in children and young people's musical socialisation practices in order to increase their profits, and not only individual researchers of music education but also the research institutions themselves invest heavily in educational research.

The book employs the following categories of investor profiles or roles: the self/subject (teachers/learners/children/youth/parents), social institutions, institutions of music education, research institutions, policy institutions, the music and media industries, as well as the welfare state. Additionally, we examine a range of investment strategies based on empirical research that serves as the foundation for the discussions presented here. Indeed, the observation that these strategies are present in many of the different games we have studied provides a foundation for a more in-depth examination of the various paradoxes of power, status, class and so on that can be analysed and discussed within the double game of music. This is particularly pertinent given the presence of actual strategies in many of the different games that will be discussed in the following chapters.

2

Democracy and inclusion: school(ed) music

Live Weider Ellefsen, Anne Jordhus-Lier, Kari Marie Manum and Siw Graabræk Nielsen

Introduction

In the current political and educational climate of the Nordic states, high hopes seem to be invested in music education to promote democratic core values, such as inclusion and participation, (gender) equality and respect for cultural diversity. The Norwegian National Curriculum for Music (years 1–10), for example, calls for teachers and students to explore topics such as democracy and citizenship, gender roles and sexuality, and cultural understanding (Norwegian Directorate for Education and Training, 2020). Similarly, the curriculum framework for Norway's municipal schools of music and performing arts outlines the schools' role in contributing to inclusion, democratic participation and social mobility in Norwegian society (see, e.g., Norwegian Council for Schools of Music and Performing Arts, 2016), leaning heavily, for example, on discourses of diversity to emphasise its importance (Ellefsen and Karlsen, 2019; Jordhus-Lier, 2018; Karlsen and Nielsen, 2021).

The mandates and ambitions of both compulsory and extracurricular schooling are in line with much of the scholarly work on music education regarding discussions of matters of social justice (e.g., Benedict *et al.*, 2015; Hess, 2019). Educational games, however, like other social games, always take place within a culture and thus also within a symbolic and value-laden cultural economy (Bennett *et al.*, 2009; Bourdieu, 1984; Dyndahl and Ellefsen, 2009; Dyndahl *et al.*, 2014). The challenge is not only to secure general diversity and inclusion but also to deal with the complex cultural–economic value hierarchies that distribute possibilities of participation and forms of agency along certain socio-economic and demographic lines (see, e.g., Karlsen, 2017).

In asking, among other things, how the games of school music work to both sustain and challenge welfare state ideals, norms and socio-musical hierarchies, our overall objective in this chapter is to consider the complexity of curricular and extracurricular music educational games as democratising practices. We aim to show that music, as an educational welfare game, is inclusive in the sense that it includes new content and strives for a wide reach. At the same time, it has exclusionary effects; both selection and adaptation or recontextualisation are always taking place, and both are done on the basis of existing societal norms and values.

Democracy games

Democratic games of government take many forms and can be described in various ways, each emphasising different aspects of the purposes and functions of these games. This is also true of Norwegian democracy. Norwegian sociologist Øyen (1995) argues that what has become the Norwegian democratic welfare state is not only an economic and/or social and/or parliamentary solution to and result of various historical and political processes involving actors and institutions but also an actor and cultural institution in its own right, which holds and administers ideological principles and ways of thinking and organises the social system in a manner that is considered beneficial to these principles. The welfare state is an organisational approach and distribution model through which a society seeks to achieve certain goals that align with specific cultural values. However, like other cultural institutions – the family, the Church, the school – the welfare state eventually acquires the status of a value in itself and even begins to produce new, self-sustaining values (Øyen, 1995). The Norwegian society expresses these values through legislation, education and social interaction. Certain values are considered particularly Norwegian, and rituals and organisations are created to protect and perpetuate them. As organisations develop their own ideologies, it becomes difficult to distinguish between the original values and the organisational form itself. The welfare state is an example of this, having grown over the course of its history from a simple social policy measure, a rudimentary health service and a set of voluntary organisations into a complex and comprehensive structure.

Lijphart (2012) similarly acknowledges the variety of modern democracies in relation to systems of legislature and court, political parties and interest groups. Meanwhile, his authoritative text on patterns of democracy distinguishes between two main varieties: majoritarian and consensual democratic government models. The concept of majoritarianism pertains to rule by the majority, often resulting in the concentration of power within a single political party. It is characterised by competition and exclusivity. Consensus democracy, by contrast, aims to include as many people as possible in the decision-making process, promoting inclusivity, bargaining and compromise. It aims to maximise the size of decision-making majorities and disperse power (Lijphart, 2012). Following Lijphart's terminology and classifications, Norway is a consensus democracy where the executive power is dispersed in multiparty coalitions instead of being concentrated within one party in a two-party system. Furthermore, coordinated and corporatist interest groups are formally integrated into the decision-making process in an effort to achieve consensus or compromise (between different groups). In the Norwegian context, this could refer to the way labour unions, employers' associations and the government work together to negotiate policies that affect all parties, such as labour laws or wage agreements.

The Nordic democracies are commonly called 'social democracies', a term referring to a 'set of political beliefs, or a political ideology, created from a socialist tradition for political thought' (Thorsen, 2021: 7), as well as a 'theoretical and practical attempt to reconcile democracy with social justice through the use of state power' (Scruton, 2007: 642). The concept of the welfare state, in its Norwegian form, is closely linked to a strong state responsibility for allocating welfare benefits, and controversies surrounding the development of the welfare state tend to centre on just how extensive the public responsibility should be. The term 'welfare society', which has been in the government's vocabulary for several years, signals less state responsibility for welfare. It fits in well with the growing privatisation of the health, educational and social sectors and the ever-increasing transfer of welfare tasks to municipalities

(Øyen, 1995). Through the social democratic welfare state, benefits are distributed according to fundamental and cultural values concerning life and death, health, individuality and sociability, upbringing, care and schooling. Public funds allocated for care, free common education, the tax system and transfers from professionally active to inactive individuals all reflect such values and serve to minimise conflicts and perceptions of injustice in the Norwegian society.

Welfare state musical schooling and upbringing

Norway's industrial development and the consequent economic growth from World War II to the present has provided the country with some extraordinarily favourable conditions for shaping a welfare state and society that is conducive to optimal growth and development and positive social change, minimising social inequalities and enhancing social mobility. With a high degree of political stability, the Norwegian welfare state has facilitated an educational boom not only in science and technology but also in the humanities and arts and has provided universal public schooling, including free higher education. This has encouraged class advancement and also seems to have smoothed out steeper and more traditional social hierarchies. Regarding early childhood education and care, for example, it is worth noting that in 1950, 1.1 per cent of Norwegian school-age children attended kindergarten (Gulbrandsen, 2007), while in 2023, the proportion was 93.8 per cent of children aged zero to five years (Statistics Norway, 2024). Norway's Kindergarten Act, which includes a national framework curriculum, regulates kindergartens and applies to both private and public schools. Similarly, public schools, which take in over 95 per cent of all Norwegian pupils in years 1–10, are all subjected to the same national curriculum, as are private schools (Union of Education Norway, 2024).

As music is a compulsory subject in Norwegian primary and lower secondary education, this is where all Norwegian children presumably receive music education regardless of their social background and cultural interests. Since its inclusion in the Christian religious curriculum, which governed the first Norwegian attempt at broad public schooling (*Allmueskolen*, established by law in

1739), and throughout the school reforms of 1800 and 1900, the music subject has constituted an arena for the individual and social *Bildung* of Norwegian children (Varkøy, 2015) through music and beyond the training of specialised musical skills, aural or gestural. In its current form, as described in the national curriculum, the music subject includes educational aims and objectives concerning pupils' musicianship and performance skills but also their 'cultural understanding', 'health and life skills' and aspects of 'democracy and citizenship' (Norwegian Directorate for Education and Training, 2020).

In addition to the musical socialisation which takes place within the kindergarten and compulsory education system, the Norwegian society values having easy access to extracurricular or leisure-time music and arts education. Extracurricular music schools for children and adolescents were established in the 1960s in Norway with the aim to facilitate 'the best possible and most affordable music education to be given to as many children and young people as possible' (Hofsli *et al.*, 2013: 18). This phenomenon was further propelled by white papers in the early 1970s which especially emphasised the importance of versatile cultural self-activity taking place across 'social dividing lines as they often are more decisive than geographical distances' (St. meld. nr. 8, 1973–1974: 6, our translation). The 2023 Educational Act upholds this affirmative action by stating that the municipalities are obliged to offer 'a cultural school for children and young people, organised in connection with the school and cultural life' (§ 26–1, our translation). Furthermore, music education in Norway encompasses a wide range of upper secondary school programmes in music, dance and drama, as well as university and college courses, such as tertiary music teacher and musician training programmes, which include an increasing range of musical styles and genres.

Cultural participation as democratic play

For decades, Nordic cultural policy games have aimed to facilitate broad cultural participation across social groups and demographic borders (Sørensen, 2016). Of particular political interest, and as a means to reinforce welfare and democracy, has been to increase participation in groups that are assumed to be participating to a lesser degree than others and also to change patterns of cultural participation relating to, for example, gender, education, economic situation or place of living. Cultural participation, equated with welfare and well-being, then, is crucial to the broader project of building and bolstering the welfare state as musical and other aesthetic activities are believed to strengthen feelings of belonging and community, enhance people's quality of life, and thus their contentment, and foster communication skills, understanding and tolerance.

Viewed through a Bourdieuian lens, the logic of Norway's levelling cultural policy has been to break down patterns of distinction marked by barriers between traditionally 'high' and 'low' cultures by embarking on a 're-distinction' project aimed at reducing or eliminating the perceived articulation between taste preferences, cultural participation and social classes. Various political democratisation and inclusion initiatives – among them the heavily subsidised Norwegian extracurricular schools of music and arts, the system with state-employed county-based professional musicians (*Distriktsmusikerordningen*) and ç, a government-supported concert programme conducted at all schools in Norway that have signed up – have addressed the systematic differences in cultural accessibility and participation (*the cultural walking cane* representing a spin-off staging concerts in retirement homes). Indeed, throughout the decades, there has been a significant shift in traditional arts-related hierarchies. Popular culture is now more gentrified and musical tastes are more eclectic. Yet the blurring of highbrow and lowbrow cultural lines might not mean the end of dominant power structures; rather, as this book bears witness to, the dominant dynamics tend to persist through new forms of distinction (see Chapter 3). Indeed, the Norwegian society's preoccupation with cultural participation might contribute to what critics argue is the downside of consensus democracies: that they tend to downplay, even hide, antagonism and disagreement.

Consensus and government

In Lijphart's (2012) view, the strong community orientation and social consciousness of consensus democracies represent the 'kinder, gentler' (274), and indeed the preferred, democratic way of government. However, the crux of the system, Lijphart notes, is that it accepts majority rule only as a minimum requirement: decisions are reached through negotiations and face-to-face interactions for consensus and consolidation among interest parties at several levels of society (5). Seen from the bright side, this facilitates cooperative governance and the implementation of policies aimed at collective welfare and social equality and discourages the rather extreme political shifts and strong polarisation that can occur in a majority democracy. However, there is also a possibility that expectations of consensus will have the effect of discursively appropriating and even neutralising antagonistic attitudes between social and political oppositions. Laclau and Mouffe (2001) convincingly argue that modern democracies underestimate the antagonistic dimension that constitutes the political. Foucault's (1982) notion of 'governmentality' conveys how modern states, influenced by neoliberal ideals, govern by 'guiding the possibility of conduct' (789), and this effectively guides the self to make decisions which benefit the state by investing in and taking responsibility for one's own health, economy, education, love life, family relations, cultural participation, nature experiences and so on. In the words of Senellart, 'Governmentality is [. . .] the rationality immanent to the micro-powers, whatever the level of analysis being considered (parent-child relation, individual-public power, population-medicine, and so on)' (in Foucault, 2007: 389). Governmentality, then, as a technology of power, might contribute to glossing over discursive disagreement and even strife, (symbolic) violence and injustice.

In line with the analytical framework of this book, the Norwegian welfare state can be seen as a double game in itself which, on one hand, performs as a conscientious, egalitarian and social justice-orientated society where players presumably operate on a consensus basis about decisions and the values governing them. They reach agreements through continued dialogue, finding common platforms where every player may play according to their wishes, interests and needs. On the other hand, and persistently misrecognised, the Norwegian welfare state performs as a game which ultimately has self-preservation as its goal, like any other cultural game, alongside preserving the existing value hierarchies and power networks of the game. The power technology of governmentality rests upon the discursive, subjectivising phenomenon of players placing them-selves within these existing structures of their own accord to be recognised as players. In this sense, an overall form of consensus, a fundamental belief in the state, its values and its strategies, is secured at the outset.

Musical welfare work

As we will show in the following, music education plays a part in the same game. Indeed, music continues to occupy a small albeit enduring place in a curriculum that is gradually and steadily becom-ing more concerned with 'core' competencies related to digital skills, language and science, technology, engineering and mathematics (STEM) subjects indicates the potential of the aesthetics and arts of upkeeping, celebrating and strengthening existing social structures, perhaps largely due to people's belief in the purity of aesthetic play and its immunity to the influence of power concerns and economic interests. The fact that song and music have a place in Norwegian schools can thus be seen as a sign that music still performs a job for the welfare state. Music serves values that are also considered beneficial in the development of the future welfare state. It can, in various ways, be said to support the 'newer' values that the wel-fare state has produced through its development from the post-war period to the present.

The 2020 renewal of the national curriculum offers a good example. Here, the school subject of music is entrusted with ena-bling students to 'investigate how gender, gender roles and sexuality are presented in music and dance in the public sphere, and create expressions that challenge stereotypes' (Ministry of Education and Research, 2020: 7). Seemingly, the welfare state has confidence that music can provide a neutral ground for appropriating and perhaps even reaching a kind of consensus regarding a potentially hazardous topic, resituating it within the embrace of welfare education, thus legitimising and even normalising the discursive antagonisms with which it arrives. Situating the topic with twelve-year-olds, its con-troversy is smoothed over: challenging stereotypes is a child's game.

Similar tasks of reflecting upon gender and sexuality are laid (more and less implicitly) upon other school subjects. However, in these cases, pupils are excused from creative, productive, performative, bodily investigations into the topic. That creating expressions that challenge stereotypes falls on music might, of course, be mostly due to the performative, creative nature of the arts. However, physical education could constitute an arena just as fitting. Thus, an additional explanation for the fact that music is the trusted subject might be that the field of music education is considered a less risky field for playing around with gender stereotypes than, for instance, physical education or natural science or religion and ethics.

Indeed, in the contexts of comprehensive and extracurricular schooling, there seem to be particular expectations of music to fulfil the curricular ambitions of promoting democratic values and attitudes and thus realise the democratic ideals of welfare state schooling. If, or when, music 'works', it is believed to yield predominantly positive effects, not least concerning aspects of inclusion. We will discuss the justification for such a stance in the following sections, taking as our two main areas of analysis years 1–10 of Norwegian compulsory schooling and the Norwegian system of voluntary extracurricular music and arts education.

Compulsory schooling

The role of music in Norwegian compulsory schooling can be historically outlined as serving and supporting the Christian faith, national identity and moral behaviour of pupils (Jørgensen, 2001; Lund, 2010; Varkøy, 2015). Singing was traditionally the preferred and main activity, and the Christian religious curriculum aimed to cultivate pupils' piety, morality and devotion through psalm singing and voice training. Similar ambitions, albeit that gradually became more concerned with public enlightenment, national identity and specialised competence than religious upbringing, can be traced throughout the Norwegian school reforms of 1800 and 1900, which continued to trust in the uplifting and edifying potential of music in general and singing in particular to foster pupils' wholesomeness and sense of self, (national) community, democracy and responsibility. From the 1960s, playing instruments, composing, learning music theory and dancing were slowly introduced in Norwegian schooling, together with new styles of music, most notably popular music styles, children's repertoires and songs aiming to entertain more than to morally educate. Yet, as the current national curriculum for years 1–10 attests to, Norwegian compulsory schooling continues to place confidence in the positive, democratising and self-bolstering powers of music and musical activities. For example, the curriculum states that 'The sense of togetherness around music builds relationships between people, gives a sense of mastering and contributes to a positive self-image when the aesthetic and practical dimensions of music are in focus' (Ministry of Education and Research, 2020: 3). Furthermore, 'in music, the interdisciplinary topic of democracy and citizenship refers to the pupils developing knowledge about how music can be an important democratic resource' (3).

Such beliefs, enshrined as they are in curricular legislation, suggest that a formal musical upbringing potentially realises the crucial governmental ambitions of raising wholesome, socially dedicated Norwegian citizens through inclusive, democratic musical practice. This belief in the purely democratising and self-bolstering function of socio-musical interaction is never as obvious as in seasonal, festive or ritual school gatherings, which typically include pupils singing in unison, most often to a backing track. Here, community and belonging are celebrated in songs dedicated to the school, the district or the nation. Norway is a sparsely populated, outstretched country, where people's commitment to place and space is essential to maintaining infrastructure and production. In the Norwegian welfare state narrative, locality is nationality. Solidarity, friendship and positive self-esteem are also attitudes that are rehearsed in school assembly singing activities, with songs written for and on behalf of children. The texts demand positive engagement from the children for a better future. A bonus effect is that the children's emotional and empathic capacities, as enacted in the songs, represent the success of the welfare state, the societal order and structure that these children know is safe and stable. Children in the welfare state have opportunities, rights and influence. At the same time, one could ask whether group singing contributes to an ideological shrouding of children's lack of real political influence on their own future. The same mechanism is in play when the singing insists on conditions of friendship, community and respect in the school environment. Institutionally anchored and musically strong group

statements assuring that everyone is friends and that no one is bul-
lied could render invisible and even disown pupils' experiences of
the opposite. A similar minimisation of children's and youth's complex identities and emotional lives is risked when the group singing
demands from the children to 'be who you are' at all times, and to
'know what makes you unique'. Furthermore, the assembly singing
channels children's need for the chaotic and carnivalesque into con-
trollable, playback-governed unison singing practice, which veils
the chaos and extreme expressions. Having attended gatherings
with a hundred children happily sing-shouting lyrics that challenge
both school behaviour and grown-up educational authority, it is
easy to think of school group singing as a kind of controlled blow-
out – an approved power critique that, all in all, stabilises, rather
than undermines, school discourse and welfare state education.

Like in the other Nordic countries, popular music was already
included in Norwegian school music education in the late 1960s
and early 1970s (Karlsen and Väkevä, 2012), and it has formed a
significant part of such education ever since. One might even claim
that popular music and its related practices and value systems today
have a hegemonic status in school music education (Dyndahl and
Nielsen, 2014) and that there exists a certain popular music canon
in schools comprising 'easy-to-play pop and rock songs' (Georgii-
Hemming and Westvall, 2010: 24). Popular music's inclusion in
the curriculum has been regarded as a way to bring young people's
'own music' into music education as well as an inherently democratic and creative approach to school music education (Green,
2002; Kallio and Väkevä, 2017). Similarly, for pupils, bringing
'their own music' is a starting point for socially just, inclusive music
education (Karlsen, 2014). In the double game of music education,
however, the stakes are high, and strategies must be considered for
their usefulness in the social field of power as well as the aesthetic
field of play. When pupils bring 'their' music, they must consider
what is proper for the game as it is, and they might easily choose
the lowest common (musical) multiple – that is, mainstream music
– that is socially pre-negotiated and thus socially safe. There are
many forms of music that can be characterised as the students'
own that thus do not enter the classroom, perhaps especially for
groups that are already marginalised, such as students from immigrant backgrounds. Assuming that this form of music education

acts democratically is thus a total fallacy; rather, it might work to homogenise and is based on a perception of 'youth' as a musically uniform group. The music subject effectively absorbs and didacticises children's and adolescents' cultural expressions. While the world of children and young people is acknowledged, this same world is thus recontextualised within existing knowledge and power structures. It gives children and youth an outlet for engagement but simultaneously controls chaos and protest and makes children's real lack of influence invisible.

The DYNAMUS research project and similar studies have also shown school music to be highly gendered (for the Nordic context, see, e.g., Blix and Ellefsen, Källén and Onsrud in the anthology *Gender Issues in Scandinavian Music Education: From Stereotypes to Multiple Possibilities*, edited by Onsrud *et al.*, 2021). The DYNAMUS research project's investigation into the music of the Norwegian compulsory music classroom shows that some styles and traditions included in the curriculum, particularly rock music and classical genres, are completely dominated by male artists, producers, performers and composers. Indeed, all the music examples collected in the study – a total of over 2,500 examples of music used for music educational purposes in Norwegian years 1–10 classrooms in 2019–2020 – show the whole sample to be male-dominated, even when prioritising emphasising the presence of women wherever possible, such as in coding the musical example 'female' when the educational emphasis is on the artist rather than, for example, a group of producers or a composer.

Furthermore, school music education emerges as a thoroughly 'genred' practice. Genring is an analytical concept coined by Ellefsen (2022) as a contribution to the DYNAMUS research project. By genring, we mean categorisation processes where teachers, students and others recognise and sort musical expressions by associating music with music, music with people and people with people, thereby also drawing on and contributing to the reinforcement of cultural, aesthetic and social value hierarchies (see more about this in Chapter 4). In Norwegian compulsory music education, genring works in three distinctive ways. First, the teachers tend to organise their teaching thematically over genres. Second, certain repertoires of music are used for certain learning activities; the teachers do not do the same things with rock, art music, film music, blues, rap and folk music. Third, the overall choice of music is genred: some types and forms of music receive more attention than others.

In addition to being gendered and genred, school music in Norway is a gentrified and gentrifying practice. From a historical perspective, it is easy to see how the school gentrifies music – from having no status, popular music is today dominating school music in Norway. Songs that, for previous owners, used to represent resistance and defiance function today more like school anthems. Similarly, Internet memes perhaps lose their critical potential for childish chaos and protest when well-meaning teachers include them in an attempt to recognise the children's culture and needs. Rap lyrics are composed to engage with topics like friendship, inclusion, peace and environmentalism. The critical potential of art music is rarely explored; rather, teachers focus on composer biographies or dance/ movement and listening. Finally, the music subject continues to be governed by the performance and specialisation traditions of music as an art field (which Bourdieu describes as a self-regulating professional field of art and cultural production). For example, music teachers adjust the demands of the national curricula to fit with existing canonised and legitimised approaches and understandings in the (art) field of music. The DYNAMUS research project shows how discourses about specialisation and quality continue to regulate aspects of the music subject (Ellefsen *et al.*, 2023). Compared to previous surveys (which, to a lesser extent, capture low job percentages), a higher number of teachers in the DYNAMUS survey's sample have a solid music education. The national survey carried out in the project also shows that the teachers with the highest education are most likely to implement a specialised music subject, understood as activities that require a higher degree of specialised skills from the students. Following Bourdieu, this could be interpreted as the influence of curricula, everyday culture and economic interests being refracted towards, and recontextualised within, an ostensibly autonomous professional and artistic field of music by actors who already hold privileged positions in this field.

To offer a preliminary conclusion, compulsory school music education in Norway today is practised in a field of tension where children's autonomy and voices are encouraged and even venerated but are still subjected to educational cultivation within the regulating frames of schooling. Indeed, the institutionalisation of childhood and youth seems to be a distinctive (but not necessarily deliberate) strategy that changed the music subject in the years following World War II. One could even term it a 'colonising' of children's lifeworlds. Furthermore, the music subject's historically anchored functions concerning the solidification and celebration of Norwegian identity, faith and behaviour still seem to apply. The music subject is also democratising in the sense that it works to stabilise and reproduce the Norwegian welfare society's values by efficiently appropriating expressions with the potential to destabilise. Musics are gentrified – each one made an object of acquisition for compulsory school music education – through didactic facilitation. Explicitly or implicitly, gender is practised alongside this musical regenring for educational purposes, strengthening the process and facilitating its gentrification.

It is important to the Norwegian welfare discourse that children's own voices, own musics and own expressions are heard in the classroom. When music educators take children's and adolescents' lifeworlds as their point of departure, they support and recognise the pupils' musicianship. At the same time, the pupils' expressions are changed, disciplined and shaped within the educational context by and within the social structures of meaning and the relations of power that the educational institution governs. There are, therefore, more sides to democratising music education than inclusion.

Extracurricular music education: the municipal schools of music and arts

The development of the Norwegian municipal music and art schools can be described as an organic and locally driven process which has given rise to schools with somewhat different profiles and different mandates (Bjørnsen, 2012). One could also see this extracurricular education system as a result of targeted political and advocacy work, as the Norwegian Council for Schools of Music and Performing Arts (2016) does in its own organisational report (see also NOU 2013:4). The schools of music and arts have attracted ever-increasing political attention, and the curriculum framework plan for them can be said to be a direct result of this political commitment as it outlines the schools' role in contributing to inclusion, democratic participation and social mobility in Norwegian society (Norwegian Council for Schools of Music and Performing Arts, 2016).

Although the premises of social and cultural inclusion in public extracurricular music education are enacted by law, several analyses of the schools' curriculum framework(s) have identified discursive acts of closure especially regarding the existence of certain patterns of social and cultural domination in favour of middle-class and elite cultures (Ellefsen and Karlsen, 2019; Jordhus-Lier, 2018; Karlsen and Nielsen, 2021). Further, in examining the schools, Karlsen and colleagues (2024) refer to certain acts of social and cultural closure within the schools' teaching practices as 'cultural mismatches' between the headmaster, music teachers, parents and pupils – discrepancies between 'the cultural world conceptions of headmasters and music teachers on the one hand, and the cultural world and logics lived-in by the interviewed parents and their children on the other' (9). One significant mismatch concerns whether it is important for the schools to offer courses based on the homeland music of immigrant minority groups – 'a course dismissed as unnecessary by the headmaster, but experienced as valuable by the parents' and the teacher (10). Such cultural mismatches may operate as soft elimination processes within the schools that may prove difficult to change (Bourdieu and Champagne, 1992). However, it is important to display how the kinds of doubleness in the inclusion/exclusion games in the schools of music and arts involve 'seemingly contradictory and irreconcilable forces working both for and against their own policy at once' (Karlsen and Nielsen, 2021: 39), and we will do so in the following.

Most children and youth (about 87 per cent) do not participate in these schools at all (Berge *et al.*, 2019), and children from the working class make up a particularly large part of this group of non-participating children. Thus, this form of non-participation represents an even more abrupt or brutal form of social and cultural elimination in Norwegian society that also challenges these schools' role in the democratising practices in the music educational games of the welfare state. Words such as 'inclusion' and 'diversity' are commonly used in white papers, reports and strategic documents (e.g., Dugstadutvalget, 1989; Eikemoutvalget, 1999; Meld. St. 18, 2020–2021; St. meld. nr. 39, 2002–2003). However, what is actually meant by those terms, who is to be included and how are not given. Should we aim for a diversity of art forms, genres, cultures or teachers and students in terms of gender, ethnicity, cultural background or social class? Diversity in the schools of music and arts can be understood in at least two ways: as diversity among students and as diversity of content and activities. We can also speak of diversity among the teachers. All of this is connected. If we are aiming for a diverse student group, there is a need for diversity in the teaching content and thus a diversity of teachers who can teach this varied content.

The lack of clarity within the word 'diversity' in combination with the importance of a municipal school being both diverse and inclusive could lead to the term being used politically and strategically. One example is a document compiled by the Norwegian Council for Schools of Music and Performing Arts (2021) titled a 'Strategic Plan for In-depth Learning with Diversity', where diversity is expressed only as geographical diversity, focusing on collaboration at an institutional level to be able to offer depth/talent development programmes regardless of where in Norway the students live. This is a good thing in many ways, but is it enough to focus only on geography when aiming for 'in-depth learning with diversity'? Is it really inclusive when nothing changes in relation to, for instance, the teaching content, methods and genres and musical styles represented? A double game is thus played, which could be more or less hidden, where the school appears inclusive, but there are other factors working against this which have not been addressed, for instance, concerning class and cultural background. Another paradox, so to speak, is that without the class structure in the society but also within the school, the school of music and arts would not be a democracy project. There would not be a need to address inclusive practices and projects. The non-inclusivity of the school feeds the inclusive work. This points, however, to the need for addressing and shedding light on the non-inclusive practices, and addressing the games being played is therefore a contribution.

Schools of music and arts for everyone?

The aim of schools of music and arts to be for everyone is stated by, e.g., the Council for Schools of Music and Performing Arts (Norsk kulturskoleråd, n.d.). It is, in many ways, also an expectation of an institution developing alongside the growth of the Norwegian welfare state. The schools are publicly financed, constituting a reason for them to strive to be for everyone, because can a society accept using tax money on something which is only for a few? It is not necessarily the number of people participating that is relevant but rather whether the school is open to everyone who wants to be part of it. The aim of being open to all, regardless of class and economic or cultural background, could thus be seen to constitute the ground for legitimisation. However, the school contains exclusionary traits, where middle-class children are represented to a higher degree than working-class children (Berge *et al.*, 2019; Jordhus-Lier *et al.*, 2023; Karlsen *et al.*, 2024; Nielsen *et al.*, 2023b). Many of the schools' activities are permeated by a conservatoire discourse and a type of school discourse in which progression is central and where middle-class ideals are strong. A certain cultural capital is required to know about the schools and to consider sending one's children to one. According to Berge and colleagues (2019), the school of music and arts is 'Norway's best kept secret'. From an interview study with teachers and headteachers, we see that the majority of parents whose children attend schools of music and arts are 'resourceful and bright parents' with higher education and a 'cultural background', having 'leisure time competence', meaning knowing how organised leisure activities for children function and what is available (Jordhus-Lier and Nielsen, 2025). They are also quite attentive and engaged in their parenting style (Nielsen *et al.*, 2023b). The Norwegian and Swedish schools of music and arts are quite similar, and Jeppsson and Lindgren (2018) observe that the typical school of music and arts' student is a Swedish-born girl with well-educated parents. Their findings support cultural reproduction theory, and building on Bourdieu, they find a strong connection between middle-class *habitus* and a 'school of music and arts-appropriate habitus', where the middle-class parents and students to a larger degree 'fit' the practices and cultures within the school of music and arts (Jeppsson and Lindgren, 2018).

As discussed, these schools focus on being inclusive. However, their facilitation of accessibility, both practically and financially, for children with physical and psychological challenges, children from immigrant backgrounds and children from lower socio-economic strata is paradoxical when the schools are still not open to everyone because of the cultural structure that permeates the institution and the families' cultural capital and opportunities for succeeding in the school system. There is thus a risk in believing that all children have opportunities to participate in these schools and that non-participating children simply do not want to be part of it, with the consequence that the fundamental issues underpinning non-participation remain undetected.

Progression or 'just for fun'?

A school of music and arts offers both an extracurricular leisure activity for children and youth to play music, socialise and have fun and also a school where the aim is to learn, among other things, to play an instrument, for which self-effort is expected to achieve progression. These two ways of understanding the school's mandate and mission can easily conflict, as addressed by Berge and colleagues (2019), Jordhus-Lier (2018) and Jordhus-Lier and Nielsen (2025). Progression is, in many ways, embedded in the concept of education, and having fun increases one's motivation to learn. Thus, there will always be a duality connected to progression and having fun. However, what makes compulsory schooling and extracurricular activities, such as those offered at schools of music and arts, different is the institution's (stated) aim and mission. Compulsory schooling in the welfare state should, for instance, as stated in the Education Act § 1–1, 'give the pupils and apprentices historical and cultural insight' and 'help to increase the knowledge and understanding of the national cultural heritage and our common international cultural traditions', where the students should 'develop knowledge, skills and attitudes so that they can master their lives and can take part in working life and society' (Norwegian Education Act, 2023). Extracurricular activities are things that children can participate in if they want to, if they think they sound like fun. Moreover, we would argue that playing music is fun, but ideas of progression, mastery and development are central to music teaching in the schools of music and arts, visible both in the curriculum framework (Norwegian Council for Schools of Music and Performing Arts, 2016; Karlsen and Nielsen, 2021) and the teaching practices (Jordhus-Lier *et al.*, 2023). Therefore, we could state that there is a double game being played here, where the music activities, on one hand, are an education practice aimed at progression and development in playing an instrument and, on the other hand, leisure activities which can be participated in just for the fun of doing so. These two games could be played at the same time, but there is also a risk that the players (the teachers, students or parents) are unaware of the doubleness and believe they are playing one game while also, or instead, are playing another. In short, they could be in it for the fun but have to play the game of progression and development.

Inclusion of various popular music genres

Through the DYNAMUS research project, which explored the kinds of music being offered in schools of music and arts, we know that popular music is well integrated in these schools, and it forms a large part of the educational content offered alongside classical music (Jordhus-Lier *et al.*, 2021; Nielsen *et al.*, 2023a). As such, the schools of music and arts seem to represent an institution that is inclusive of emerging musical genres and that different popular musical genres are assigned value as relevant educational content. At the same time, interviews with parents and music teachers offer examples of teaching practices that include a 'hidden' intolerance for the students' taste in music within the popular music genre. Quite resignedly, an interviewed parent stated how important it was that the students – her son being one of them – at least once in a while 'were allowed to play what they enjoyed the most' (Karlsen *et al.*, 2024: 281) – namely, heavy metal music – within the school. However, the teacher proudly uttered how he, as a trained jazz musician, had formulated an unstated learning goal for the student to guide the student's taste in popular music away from the metal genre to jazz/improvised music instead, as musical cultural competence in the latter is considered more legitimate. In this respect, the teacher seemed to disregard the student's taste in music by deeming it 'not refined enough', 'not good enough' as well as 'not relevant enough' for the student to be investing in to develop the relevant skills and knowledge necessary for qualifying for music education at the upper secondary and/or higher education level. In playing this kind of game, stating the noblest intention of caring for the student's musical future, the music teacher's introduction of this neoliberal perspective on the relevance of educational investments in public extracurricular schools fits a pattern of social and cultural domination in favour of the successfully gentrified popular music genres of the middle class. It also suggests that although the schools of music and arts make 'a conscious effort to cater to and welcome a more demographically varied student body' (Jordhus-Lier *et al.*, 2021: 11), strong exclusionary forces still work against this policy (Karlsen and Nielsen, 2021).

A 'democratising' double game

Music education as part of Norwegian schooling is unquestionably a democratising practice. As an extracurricular offering as well as a mandatory school subject, it must provide Norwegian children and youth with equal possibilities for learning and experiencing music and instil in them the skills and attitudes valued by the welfare democracy, such as tolerance, empathy, cultural understanding and critical thinking. Music education in Norway embraces new content, recognises children's and adolescents' voices and musical cultures and facilitates student participation in and lifelong learning of music. As a game, it is played for pure pedagogical purposes to educate competent, free, creative, self-secure, healthy individuals and citizens.

Meanwhile, Norwegian music education is democratising in the additional sense that it educates for a particular political and cultural system of values, distribution principles, power positions and social hierarchies. It educates citizens of the democracy to take responsibility for and accept the values applied to them, the distribution principles they are subjected to, the social identity taxonomies available to them and the power/knowledge structures surrounding and embracing them. Thus, it works to stabilise and reproduce the Norwegian welfare society's values, including by efficiently appropriating expressions that have the potential to destabilise. In school assemblies, social challenges, such as bullying and racism, environmental issues, poverty and war, are handled in songs that, by insisting that children have agency, also conceal the fact that the children might lack real influence and are in vulnerable positions. The possible critical potential of children's protest and the chaos offered by Internet memes and questionable rap lyrics is moderated when everyday musical games are incorporated into the curriculum by sympathetic teachers. Musical expression is schooled, disciplined and gentrified – made an 'object of acquisition' (Dyndahl *et al.*, 2014) for compulsory and extracurricular music education – through didactic facilitation. Furthermore, the music subject already largely reproduces canonised content and repertoires, which are both subject to processes of gendering and genring (Ellefsen, 2022). There is always a selection, and the selection is made on the basis of the existing norms and values in the society.

Thus, the game of music education in the Norwegian welfare state has misrecognised sides to it which nonetheless have a significant impact on how the game plays out as an assumedly democratising practice. One of the paradoxes that emerge when looking specifically for the interaction between recognised, appreciated ways of playing and misrecognised rules, regulations and play strategies is the 'informalised formality' of the Norwegian education system, at both the micro and macro levels. For example, the Norwegian schools of music and art rely on pupils' participation and entrepreneurial construction of knowledge across additional informal educational practices to fulfil the ambitions of the curriculum's learning objectives (Ellefsen and Karlsen, 2019).

Similarly, upper secondary programmes in music not only encourage but heavily depend upon pupils' entrepreneurial, musical activities beyond their formal education to secure the programmes' continued relevance and quality (Ellefsen, 2014). Entrepreneurial playfulness, however, is regulated and created by the pupils' *habitus* – the result of specific forms of socialisation and upbringing that occurs at the intersections of, among other things, class, gender and ethnicity. Thus, the productive exchange of learning experiences that Norwegian welfare state education assumes to happen within and across school and leisure practices is discursively governed in a highly material sense, with and through the pupils' bodies, and therefore not necessarily 'productive' for all, in ways that generate exchangeable gaming capital.

In the context of this duality, expectations of pure pleasure and fun also govern leisure culture and informal music making to the extent that they hide or at least overshadow the enactment of other power/knowledge structures. Meanwhile, exhibiting an ability to pursue leisure in a fun, pleasurable, effortless, carefree way means exhibiting valuable symbolic capital, Bourdieu (2000) insists:

> In fact, unless a special effort is made, 'free time' does not readily escape from the logic of investment in 'things to do', which even when it does not go as far as the explicit concern to 'succeed in one's holidays', according to the precepts of the women's magazines, prolongs the competition for the accumulation of symbolic capital in various forms. (209)

In line with this, and from an investment perspective, when parents, on behalf of themselves and their children, invest in leisure activity game playing, they can expect as its outcome symbolic capital in the form of leisure capacity – that is, the ability to play 'as if' free of *illusio* and free of preoccupation with the future. Significantly as well, when investing in formal educational games, children and youth's learned playfulness, their capacity to act 'as if' comes to their aid when entrepreneurial strategies are required of them or when they are expected to exhibit a pure dedication to musical pleasure and fun.

In general, players' capacity to play the double game of music education 'as if' this duality is irrelevant or non-existent conceals the fact that music education can never be 'pure' practice. The notion of inclusion in music education is particularly interesting and indeed symptomatic in this regard. In recent decades, inclusion has become an increasingly fashionable and valued ideal in political and educational thinking. Contemporary accounts of 'the excluded' encompass numerous categories, such as gender, social class, ethnicity, religion, sexuality and (dis)ability. However, as with other democratic ideals, the state of inclusion is something to be constantly striven for but never completed or located anywhere in reality. In this sense, the notion of inclusion refers to a utopian state and functions as a transcendent ideal.

The reason why the inclusion narrative about music is so prevalent among educational policymakers, musicians and music teachers today may be the view of art and aesthetics in Western philosophy – namely, the presumed autonomy of art and music. In this tradition, music is seen as a medium capable of expressing a transcendent, utopian state that serves as a form of resistance to the prevailing social order. At the political level, this narrative depoliticises music: the discourse of inclusion makes music education appear neutral and pure. Meanwhile, and paradoxically, when music is prescribed as a tool for educational inclusion, it becomes highly politicised again. In other words, music (education) is assumed to offer the potential to criticise and resist the field of power and its power/knowledge relations and also to play a central role as an actor in the same field of power through the same power/knowledge relations. Certainly, this game demands of its players the ability to play 'as if'.

This is perhaps truly the most productive, ethical and sustainable way to play. 'As if' Norwegian welfare state cultural practices in general and music education practices in particular are aesthetic games which nevertheless allow for specific, targeted political inclusion work. Undoubtedly, democratising strategies justified by the remarkable capacity of music to educate the whole human being, facilitate communication and tolerance and bring together people in social rituals and communities – all due to its aesthetic nature – have been successful in Norway and continue to work their magic. However, the supposed aesthetic state of play can have various functions in a consensus society: idealised and explicit but also misrecognised. Indeed, as we have argued above, the belief in music's inclusive powers, as a neutral aesthetic game, makes music education a perfect game for quiet government.

Popkewitz and Gustafson (2002) claim that music education is 'less a field of practices about the pedagogy of music and more as a set of practices that make children legible and administrable' (89). Criticising the use of standardisation within music education in the United States and thinking about such use as an 'alchemy', they contend that 'the alchemy reconfigures the sensitivities and awarenesses of the field of music to make the child's "soul" the site of administration' (Popkewitz and Gustafson, 2002: 80). Norwegian educational traditions practise standardisation to a lesser degree. Yet music education is certainly an arena for administering children's 'souls' – their identity, personal development, understanding, self-image, emotions, expressivity and creativity (Norwegian Directorate for Education and Training, 2020). Therefore, it also applies to Norwegian games of music when Friedrich and colleagues (2010) point to the following:

> efforts to develop democratic schools have moved along particular rules and standards of 'reasoning' even when expressed through different ideological and paradigmatic lines. From attempts to make a democratic education to critical pedagogy, different approaches overlap in their historical construction of the reason of schooling: designing society by designing the child. (571)

Biesta (2013) could be said to hold a similar view in his multidimensional understanding of education as qualification, socialisation and subjectification. In line with his Rancière-inspired 'anti-sociology', Biesta sees qualification and socialisation as society's instrumentalist 'pressure' on the subject. Thus, in presenting a seemingly holistic, balanced and inclusive model of education, Biesta nevertheless stresses the importance of subjectification for individual growth and formation. However, by failing to consider the social and cultural preconditions for processes of subjectification that are assumed to entail the growth and formation of the individual in full, his preferred educational ideal seems to emphasise forms of education and upbringing tailored to the children of the elite (Dyndahl, 2021). Such a pedagogy – including music pedagogy, as we find it, for example, in forms of informal music education – will favour those who are already qualified and socialised into the musical and music pedagogical codes (and *habitus*) that justify the rather elitist subject formation that Biesta maintains (Dyndahl, 2021).

Music education is a complex and multidimensional double game, and since all players in one way or another play by their *illusio* – that is, their unconscious belief in the process, value and indeed the sheer existence of the game – the players' awareness of the complexity and multidimensionality might be severely limited (and this certainly includes the awareness of music education researchers). Game awareness – our sense of how the game is, has, can and could be played – is crucial, critical even, for us to be able to participate at all. However, the degrees to which our awareness is directed towards complexity and intertwinement may vary. Indeed, we have argued that neglecting to consider the full spectrum of economies which run the game is part of the music educational field *illusio*. Game awareness, then, could be theorised in two layers: the field's awareness of its own pure and valued existence – *illusio* – and the field's meta-awareness of its own existence in the complex intertwinement with a field of power through symbolic and material economic capital relations.

Our immersion in the game and the *illusio* by which we play make it complicated to engage in meta-reflections about the self-same immersion. Nevertheless, we urge teachers, politicians, musicians, parents, students and researchers alike to at least recognise that a double game is being played, and, when encountering one-sided assumptions concerning the full force of school musical inclusiveness and democratising capacities, critically and analytically employ this awareness to question the nuances in and the reach and sustainability of such claims. With this appeal, we do not undermine the power of music. Quite the contrary: we are convinced that when accepting and raising field awareness of the double game of music education, the political, educational, artistic and ethical importance of music and music education is impossible to ignore.

3

Social class and musical gentrification

Petter Dyndahl, Sidsel Karlsen and Siw Graabræk Nielsen

Introduction

The concept and understanding of social and economic class have undergone considerable expansion since their constitution as a crucial aspect of Marx's (1867) historical materialism and critique of the political economy of capitalism. For Marx, class is a strictly economic concept defined by the relationship to the means of production. Some – specifically, the capitalist class – acquire ownership and, in turn, find their counterpart in the working class, who must sell their labour to this capitalist class or bourgeoisie for a wage – albeit in a relationship of exploitation where the wage has a lower price than the result of the labour input is worth – and this discrepancy constitutes a surplus value or profit.

Weber (1922/2013), however, argues that the stratification of society is a result of the combined influences of economic class, social position and respect in relation to societal, cultural and religious factors, and the power that different social groups possess and can exercise. He thus considers both the social status attached to certain professions considered prestigious, for example, due to academic credentials, and the lack of status or prestige associated with other professions.

By combining and continuing elements from both Marx and Weber, Bourdieu (1984) develops an elevated understanding of what social class entails at both the collective and individual levels, not least by introducing new dimensions to the concept of capital. In addition to the fact that material or economic capital obviously still means a lot, Bourdieu (1986) introduces social capital or the importance of social connections and networks, as well as cultural capital, which becomes particularly significant in this context. This capital is laid out in three typical variations – namely, embodied (e.g., long-lasting dispositions of the mind and body), objectified (e.g., cultural goods, like books, paintings and musical instruments) and institutionalised (e.g., educational degrees and qualifications) forms of cultural capital (Bourdieu, 1986: 243).

While Marxist analysis traditionally concentrates on the main opposition between the capitalist and working classes, Bourdieu mostly focuses on the dominant class or elite, the middle classes and the dominated or working class. In principle, all three can again be divided into three fractions based on whether they are mainly defined by economic or cultural capital or a combination of both.

This way of analysing social dynamics according to both horizontal and vertical distinctions has been continued by significant recent and contemporary social and cultural researchers. For example, research groups associated with French economist Thomas Piketty have conducted international, comparative studies on major political shifts among both the economic and cultural elites of Western democracies (Gethin *et al.*, 2021; Piketty, 2018). In Norway as well, larger studies on elite and upper-class self-concepts in an apparently egalitarian society have been carried out using a similar approach (see, e.g., Korsnes *et al.*, 2014). The desire and willingness to debate and update Bourdieu's conceptual framework to fit contemporary society can also be found in cultural sociological contributions that particularly emphasise the significance of music, beginning with Peterson's (1992) concept of cultural omnivorousness and Thornton's (1995) research on subcultural capital, which have been followed, criticised and revised by many others.

Against this background, one might perceive social class, given its aforementioned potential for diverse and nuanced perspectives on social theory and development, as a useful concept for both critical and productive discussions about music and music education in relation to today's politics, society, education and culture. Indeed, in her assessment of the current state of sociological theory within music education, Karlsen (2021) identifies Bourdieu as the most prominently featured theorist among the publications she examined. However, she also observes that a 'strong focus on music education practice and applicability which suggests an understanding of music education sociology as a mainly educational field' (Karlsen,

2021: 147) consistently characterises the material. Karlsen therefore draws the following conclusion:

> The emphasis on practice and applicability and the subsequent relative absence of theory creation and theorization can be interpreted as a collective lack of an elevating and positively distinctive academic disinterest. By focusing on the practical necessities of our disciplinary world, we simultaneously position ourselves away from the elite (of academia), if transferring understandings from Bourdieu's conceptual world of the structuring of social class. (148)

Bates (2019) takes a slightly different approach in examining music education research publications with social class in mind, compared to the widespread research focus on race in particular. He claims that music education researchers tend to elide social class concerns, yet they seem far more willing to pay attention to other social issues. He supports this argument by pointing out that in a wide array of international handbooks of music education and social justice as well as diversity and marginalisation, entire chapters are devoted to race, ethnicity, sexuality, gender and ability, while no contributions specifically or systematically treat class issues. If social class is mentioned at all, it is usually put in an intersectional context with some of the aforementioned topics.

As a conceivable extension of this, one can also find explicit resistance to being concerned with cultural sociology and social class within certain, not insignificant, fields of music education in academia and scholarly journals:

> One of the other problems with the fixation on *music education as culture*, then, is that class issues tend to dominate the conversation. Over 30 years ago Vulliamy (1984) cautioned about the dangers of 'concentrat[ing] on social class at the expense of other variables such as age, sex/gender, and race/ethnicity'. (Mantie, 2023: 126)

In order to further discuss how such tendencies and proclamations should be interpreted in the context of the double game perspective of this book, we will proceed to the following sections, in which we will explore the relationships between music education and social class from different angles and especially with reference to the concept of 'musical gentrification'. This concept was extensively presented and operationalised in the research project *Musical Gentrification and Socio-Cultural Diversities* (2013–2018), a collaborative endeavour between several of the authors of this book (see Dyndahl *et al.*, 2014, 2017, 2021).

Social class and classed dispositions and strategies in the Norwegian society

Norway is known as one of the Nordic welfare states with a stable and even prosperous economy and income and wealth distributions that are more equal than in many other countries, even comparable ones. This situation is partly due to the discovery of oil in the North Sea in the 1960s, the subsequent establishment of the Norwegian oil industry and the legislation connected to this source of enormous economic wealth, which largely prevents the private exploitation of the oil fields and allows the nation state to maintain control of the economic outcome and distribute this revenue for the good of its citizens. However, the establishment of the Norwegian welfare state as such happened much earlier. It can be traced back to political processes and decision-making in the early 1900s, which advanced rapidly after World War II.

For the purpose of our explorations in this chapter, perhaps the most important institution to mention in this regard is the Norwegian body distributing student loans and grants for a wide range of types of education, *Lånekassen*. This institution was founded in 1947 and today supports students economically in entering, among other things, upper secondary school, vocational school, folk high schools and, not least, universities and university colleges, both nationally and abroad. It can therefore be regarded as the post-war period's monumental state investment in the nation's institutional or educational cultural capital, which was expected, in the next phase, to yield a financial return. The establishment of *Lånekassen* allowed access to higher education across social class backgrounds for the post-war generations, consequently spurring an until-then unknown higher education participation rate among these cohorts.

Although upward social mobility caused by higher incomes seems to have increased quite steadily in Norway since the 1930s (Salvanes, 2017), social class origin has somehow retained its status as the primary factor influencing whether an individual will invest in higher education. In a discussion of whether the so-called talent reserve of the working class has already been exploited or even used up, Hansen (2011) shows that the parents' and even the grandparents' level of education and class position strongly influence individuals' educational paths both at the upper secondary school level and beyond. Even when achieving the same grades and results, young people make different choices depending on where they are socially situated, and students from higher class backgrounds are far more likely to enrol in higher education than their working-class counterparts. Even in the seemingly egalitarian state of Norway, then, the educational system contributes to social class reproduction and consequently to social closure. Recently, reports have revealed that other forms of social inequality are on the rise as well (see, e.g., Goldblatt *et al.*, 2023).

Perhaps due to the popular belief that social class-related differences in Norwegian society were almost extinct, for many years, social class was not high on the agendas of Norwegian researchers, regardless of discipline. In the past decade, however, important contributions have been made in this regard, focusing on the elite (Korsnes *et al.*, 2014), the middle classes (Sakslind *et al.*, 2018) and, most recently, the working class (Ljunggren and Hansen, 2021). Following this, empirical studies on the impact of social class in Norwegian (and Nordic) music education have been rare since the field's establishment in the mid-1990s; indeed, there is a general lack of published studies or even conference papers focusing on this topic. Our previous collaborative work, showcased in the anthology *Musical Gentrification: Popular Music, Distinction and Social Mobility* (Dyndahl *et al.*, 2021), marks one of the exceptions in this regard.

Sociologists Hansen and colleagues (Hansen *et al.*, 2009; Hansen *et al.*, 2014; Hansen and Ljunggren, 2021) have, through several empirical investigations of capital distribution in Norwegian society, developed and refined an analytical tool for class analysis named the *Oslo Register Data Class Scheme* (the ORDC-model). The ORDC-model positions different professions in various social classes according to their related type and volume of capital. The distribution of various types of capital is illustrated vertically, based on the volume of capital, as well as horizontally, based on the type of capital accumulated (e.g., cultural and/or economic) (Hansen *et al.*, 2009: 26–27). As mentioned in the introduction to this chapter, the three different horizontal class fractions are referred to as the cultural, economic and balanced fractions, which are only specified for the upper classes/elite and the upper and lower middle classes of the population. The economic fraction of these classes is made up of those professions which require larger volumes of economic capital than cultural capital (e.g., managers in business and finance), and in order to make a hierarchical division between the upper classes/elite and the middle classes within this economic fraction, the criterion of private ownership is added to the model. Further, the professions with larger volumes of cultural than economic capital comprise the cultural fraction (e.g., artists and academics). The middle or balanced fraction amounts to those professions (e.g., lawyers and doctors) with large volumes of both economic (in the form of high incomes) and cultural capital (in the form of educational degrees and qualifications) (Hansen and Ljunggren, 2021: 38). In this model, the working class (skilled and unskilled workers as well as welfare recipients/those living on welfare transfers) occupies the position below the lower middle classes, while people in the primary industries (e.g., farmers, fishermen and forest workers) are not given a fixed class position since this group may comprise both workers and owners of land and of profitable enterprises (Hansen and Ljunggren, 2021: 40).

In investigating how the ORDC-model would position different professions related to the Norwegian music education context, Dyndahl (2024: 160) notes that 'professors, researchers, and leading musicians, for example, will belong to the cultural elite; teachers with a BA or MA degree, musicians in entertainment, and the like are placed in the cultural upper-middle class; while primary school teachers and early childhood teachers belong to the cultural lower-middle class'. He also points to the fact that when the competence requirements for primary school teachers changed to a master's degree in 2022, there would, in the future, be 'a tendency for teachers in the Nordic school systems to become an increasingly homogeneous group in terms of social class' (160). In surveying today's student music teachers in the new Norwegian generalist teacher education, Nysæther and colleagues (2021: 45) find 'that generalist student music teachers appear strikingly similar in many ways. The majority of the student teachers are middle class, have Norwegian ethnicity and their immediate family works professionally with children and young people'. This situation and the development towards even less social diversity within the teaching profession may represent a serious challenge with regard to social closure in music education, especially since we know how the impact of social class helps to explain 'how some social groups are better than others in navigating our highly competitive and complex social world' (Brook *et al.*, 2020: 111), with 'social groups' here referring to the elite and upper-middle classes.

For the lower social classes, engaging in relevant leisure-time activities to accumulate valuable cultural capital (Lareau, 2011; Nielsen *et al.*, 2023a), or making the proper/correct choices in upper secondary school to be able to enter higher education (Berg, 2021), has, for some time, been central to preparing for children's upward social mobility. However, several studies have shown how students from the working class (may) meet obstacles within educational institutions, given that they do not know how to play 'the educational game' in as sophisticated a manner as students from the upper-middle classes or the elites (e.g., Reay, 2017; Skeggs, 2004). Bourdieu and Champagne (1992: 72) refer to these types of processes as a form of soft elimination (versus brutal elimination, which refers to being denied access), continuously being performed within the school system to maintain society's social structure. This kind of social closure is related to the fact that higher education is a limited resource upon which the value of higher education in society rests (Hansen and Ljunggren, 2021: 41).

As mentioned earlier, the skilled and unskilled workers as well as those living on welfare transfers make up the working class in the Norwegian society, and according to Hansen and Ljunggren (2021: 47–48), they comprise nearly 45 per cent of the population between the ages of thirty-five and fifty, with males in this group outnumbering females. The welfare recipients constitute a considerable part of the working class (about 10 per cent), and there is a valid classed relationship between class background/ class position (e.g., skilled and unskilled workers) and becoming a welfare recipient (52). Further, in 2017, people from immigrant backgrounds made up about 20 per cent of the working class and thus formed a minority group within the working class. Hansen and Ljunggren emphasise that '[t]hough this minority is signifi-cant, it is clearly not the case that the working class in Norway is now primarily made up of people with an immigrant background' (54, our translation).

As hinted at previously, only a minority of people from a work-ing-class background may experience upward social mobility in Norwegian society. In investigating such mobility between 2003 and 2017, Hansen and Uvaag (2021) identify that an increasing proportion of people from a working-class background expe-rienced intra-generational mobility into the middle class and the elite (about 20 per cent of females and about 25 per cent of males) in 2017. Therefore, the odds of gaining an elite position are both overwhelmingly in favour of people from higher class backgrounds and, it seems, of males. The researchers attribute these findings to differences in access to higher education. That is, the impact of higher education on intra-generational mobility depends both on the length of study programmes accessed (e.g., BA, MA or PhD) as well as the study programmes' levels of status, where students from a working-class background tend to choose the shortest and less prestigious ones. However, for both male and female students, 'there are large and systematic differences in educational achieve-ments related to different social classes' (74). Even within the same types of education, a working-class background still negatively marks the odds for achieving middle and upper-class positions. This process is also highly gendered. First, males in skilled professions (e.g., electricians and plumbers) may experience upward mobility by gradually holding managerial positions within these professions or by becoming self-employed with a high income, and thus becom-ing part of the upper-middle class, albeit within the economic or balanced fraction. Second, Hansen and Uvaag find that few females access this specific 'channel of mobility' (87) since these professions are still highly male-dominated. Instead, working-class females tend to rely on higher education to make a short-range career leap into the lower middle class (e.g., as social workers, nurses or teachers). Their upward mobility 'distance' in the classed society often then becomes shorter than that of males. Overall, the belief in emphasising access to education as a means of securing social mobility for the working class is weakened, and this also means that most working-class parents do not succeed in making successful educational investments for their children. Thus, the disposition of the working class seems to be characterised by social closure with limited strategies for social mobility through acquiring cultural capital (e.g., education, cultural goods) but with more accessible/available strategies within the economic fraction.

The general characteristics of the Norwegian middle class have been investigated relatively recently (Sakslind *et al.*, 2018), and in this chapter, we will especially emphasise the findings related to education and the significance of culture in middle-class lives. As mentioned, even within the Norwegian welfare state, the educational system works as an instrument of social class reproduction. Thus, it should come as no surprise that enrolment in higher education constitutes an important part of the middle-class value system, including in Norway. The length and status of the education also matter, but not as much as they do, for example, for middle-class citizens in the UK. A feature of the economic system quite specific to Norway is, however, that higher education, and even the length of such education, does not necessarily yield any substantial individual economic benefits. Rather, 'Norway is the country [among the thirty Organisation for Economic Co-operation and Development (OECD) countries] where education gives the least remuneration, salary-wise' (Sakslind *et al.*, 2018: 118, our translation). This does not mean, however, that education is insignificant for achieving or retaining one's (middle) class position but rather that its importance lies perhaps mostly in the social and cultural capital it brings. Even though Norwegian middle-class citizens are aware of their elevated class position, they tend to downplay their own place in the social hierarchy and instead nurture an *illusio* of themselves as 'ordinary' and 'commonplace'. Egalitarianism then seems to be one of the core values of the Norwegian middle class, and according to sociologists Sakslind and colleagues (2018: 129), '[e]galitarian values are being mobilized in social practice to counteract existing hierarchies, and they appear as an important part of the system of "boundary blurring"'.

A similar kind of hierarchical indistinctness seems to characterise the Norwegian middle class's cultural taste. While a small segment clearly prefers so-called bourgeois or avant-garde culture, most middle-class people seem to be drawn to a variety of cultural expressions, whether within a frame of more 'serious culture', such as quality literature, jazz and movies by renowned filmmakers, or within a broader frame of lighter entertainment or a combination of the two. Thus, the overarching ideal of cultural preferences seems to be an omnivorous one where legitimacy is gained through the ability to produce a certain kind of cultural relaxedness. In line with this, there is also a tendency to minimise the distinctive aspects of culture, and an expressed ambivalence connected to acknowledging both 'cultural and knowledge-related hierarchies' (Sakslind *et al.*, 2018: 93). An important disposition then, if perhaps not a conscious strategy, seems to be for the Norwegian middle class to blur or try to dissolve the boundaries that separate them from the lower classes, and even to draw on the discourse of egalitarianism to conceal the attributes that allow them to compete in the social game.

A similar, blurred social game is found within the elite positions in Norwegian society, where the acceptance of an elite position is legitimised by referring to one's own outstanding skills and competencies – 'I did it with my own two hands' – in spite of obvious economic, social and cultural privileges. Therefore, Korsnes *et al.* (2014) find that the elites in all three fractions downplay the crucial impact that high volumes of inherited capital have on their own elite positioning. On the contrary, the elites are marked by self-recruitment and elite circulation, and the economic elite stands out in particular with its wealth, largely based on inherited economic capital, in addition to its segregated places of residence ('Golden ghettos') (Andersen and Ljunggren, 2014). However, family dynasties are also found within the professional and cultural elite, where 'the next generation not only inherits the institutionalized cultural capital, but also the *specific type* of this form of capital' (Hjellbrekke and Korsnes, 2014: 63). Having parents who are lawyers also marks the level of income among the next generation of lawyers (Hansen and Strømme, 2014). As such, upper-class/elite families put their economic, cultural and social resources to work to prevent their children from experiencing downward social mobility. Thus, the importance of parental resources for the children's life chances persists (Hansen and Uvaag, 2021; Nielsen *et al.*, 2023a).

In line with this, Trulsson (2015) has conducted an interesting study on how families from an immigrant background in Sweden have attempted to reclaim their middle to upper-class status from their country of origin by investing in extracurricular music education for the next generation. If the children potentially gain greater cultural capital in this way, the families hope to achieve what Trulsson describes as 'class remobility' (see Chapter 5 for further details).

Musical gentrification as a vehicle for social positioning

A common saying is that everything was better or at least clearer before. Although this is incorrect in most cases or, at best, an over-simplification, there is perhaps a grain of truth in the fact that at the time when Bourdieu (1984) was conducting his major correspondence analyses of the French society – i.e., in the 1960s and 1970s – there was greater consensus about what forms of cultural taste were considered good and bad. Moreover, these distinctions were quite firmly linked to different social classes, who also expressed unmistakably opposing political preferences and interests.

However, changes were gradually taking place across the Western world in terms of such distinctions and how they were expressed. In the US, for example, Peterson and colleagues (Peterson, 1992; Peterson and Simkus, 1992; Peterson and Kern, 1996) found that there had been major changes in the musical taste of the cultural elite over the course of a decade. While in the 1980s they had reported a preference for opera and classical music, surveys in the 1990s showed that large sections of the middle to upper classes now also recognised music that had previously provided low cultural capital, such as popular music. Peterson thus coined the aforementioned term 'cultural omnivorousness' as a characteristic of the new, apparently open-minded, tolerant and inclusive mindset towards cultural consumption among those who had previously practised a more exclusive, distinguishing relationship with music and other cultural expressions. Not surprisingly, a certain cultural omnivorousness also seems to be a distinct feature of the Norwegian middle and upper classes, as shown previously.

Piketty and colleagues (Gethin *et al.*, 2021; Piketty, 2018), for their part, have uncovered gradual but altogether very significant political shifts that took place during the entire post-war period among both the economic and cultural elites of the 21 countries commonly referred to as Western democracies, including France, the UK and the US, as well as Norway and the Nordic countries. Obviously inspired by Bourdieu, Piketty (2018) draws an analytical line between the economic and cultural divisions of the elite, which he respectively designates as 'merchants' and 'Brahmins', the latter named after the traditional Hindu caste of priests, teachers and intellectuals in general. In the first phase of the post-war period, there was a political alliance between the economically and culturally orientated elite fractions, with both groups mainly voting for conservative parties, while the working class traditionally voted for left-wing parties. Later, the picture changed significantly. Today, the researchers have found evidence to claim that while 'the merchant right' has maintained its traditional voting pattern, the highly educated 'Brahmin left' has emerged as a voter group that consistently gives twice as many votes to left-wing as right-wing parties in most Western democracies. At the same time, large sections of the working class are drifting towards the right – among other things, towards right-wing populist, and in some countries, radical right-wing parties. According to Piketty, this is part of the explanation for why people with low incomes and little education stand adamantly against the cultural elite when it supports liberal values related to issues concerning cultural diversity, immigration and globalisation, while not sharing an interest in economic redistribution with the working class.

In such a perspective, practices of cultural omnivorousness can be said to form a clear marker for the new Brahmin left, and in the extension of this, our concept of musical gentrification can be seen as both an aggregate and a result of this development. As a metaphor, musical gentrification is obviously derived from gentrification as it has long been a phenomenon in the architectural, demographic and socio-economic transformations of urban geography and city planning. A particular characteristic is that homes, buildings and areas that previously had an industrial and/or working-class character have been given a new attraction, status and pricing, with all that this implies for both inclusion and exclusion. In an early definition of the concept of musical gentrification, we therefore emphasise 'complex processes with both inclusionary and exclusionary outcomes, by which musics, musical practices, and musical cultures of relatively lower status are made to be objects of acquisition by subjects who inhabit higher or more powerful positions' (Dyndahl *et al.*, 2014: 54; Dyndahl *et al.*, 2021). We further argue that 'these processes strongly contribute to changing the characteristics of particular musical communities as well as the musics, practices, and cultures that are subjected to gentrification' (Dyndahl *et al.*, 2014: 54). Based on further research, particularly within higher music education and research, we have placed increased emphasis on the fact that musical gentrification is not only about which music is included or excluded but just as much about how the gentrification is conducted (Dyndahl *et al.*, 2014, 2017, 2021). Depending on the kind of conceptual apparatus and the theoretical and methodological frameworks in which it is enclosed, almost any form of music can achieve increased cultural capital value. In this way, it is analogous to urban gentrification, whereby former working-class homes and neighbourhoods gain increased value and status through attention and investment from the affluent classes. Musical gentrification can similarly provide academic legitimacy, and thereby cultural capital, to musics that were not justified in a similar way. In this way, such processes also affect the gradually more dynamic systems of classification (Bourdieu and Wacquant, 1992: 7) within music academia – that is, what kind of music is believed to be worthy of research and teaching at a given time.

If we follow the gentrification of popular music, since we have research evidence to say something about when, how, by whom, why and what kind of popular music has been included in Norwegian higher education and research through examining all master's theses and doctoral dissertations approved in any academic discipline of music throughout the century from 1912 to 2012 (Dyndahl *et al.*, 2017), we can point to several outcomes and issues regarding these extensive processes.

The obvious academisation has already been mentioned, but in addition to legitimising popular music for education and research, it leads to opportunities for academic positions, scholarships and careers. A related result is the institutionalisation of popular music not only in educational institutions and programmes but also within the public sphere as such. A striking example from Norwegian cultural policy is that during the period 1995–2012, the government built up a funding scheme for what was assumed would become the country's leading cultural festivals – so-called hub festivals – which, at the end of the period, included twelve music festivals representing various genres. Probably as expected, it started with a couple of festivals mainly focused on classical music but eventually expanded to include contemporary classical music, church music, folk music, Sámi and Indigenous music, multicultural music, jazz, blues, rock and country music. Despite all the controversies surrounding the inclusion of the latter genre in particular (see Vestby, 2021), then Minister of Culture Anniken Huitfeldt of the Labour Party found a reason to claim that the genre discrimination in Norwegian cultural policy was now in the past (Ministry of Culture, 2011) – a highly debatable assertion.

A consequence of the state funding and cultural policy programming of festivals in the field of popular music was that they were faced with demands for artistic quality and innovation. This form of aestheticisation of popular music and festivals, which might rather be characterised by a hedonistic party atmosphere than by a devout, seated listening culture, created predictable distinctions between different audience groups. Nevertheless, it can also be argued that through a noticeable change in the function of popular music towards being considered aesthetically high-value, it has gained entry into fields that were previously unthinkable, for example, public arenas, such as the celebration of the Nobel Peace Prize laureates, royal weddings and funerals, as well as commemorative and consolation concerts for national traumas, such as acts of terrorism – all duly covered by the media.

It may seem reasonable to summarise the ever-increasing academisation, institutionalisation and aestheticisation of popular music into an overarching belief in these tendencies being predominantly inclusive and democratic. However, we must maintain that musical gentrification is a double game that is about both inclusion and exclusion. The genre discrimination has never ended; there are still music festivals whose main genre never gained status as a hub festival. Although many popular music genres are included in education and research and receive public and political attention and support, there are also several that are consistently marginalised or excluded from both music education and cultural policy. A telling example is Scandinavian dance band music, which is a very popular music genre across generations in Norway and Sweden but has an unequivocal connection to the working class and what is perceived as simple-minded vernacular taste.

Musical gentrification as such contributes to a symbolic economy that helps perpetuate inequality in society, including by assigning and devaluing cultural capital. Thus, it can function as a vehicle for social positioning, for individual players, for social groups and classes, as well as for institutions. Bourdieu (1977: 86) refers to *habitus* as 'a subjective but not individual system of internalised structures, schemes of perception, conception, and action common to all members of the same group or class' and further explains how this creates a practical sense that becomes a strategic expression of agency. The practical sense is linked to accumulated insights into how constellations of symbolic power are configured, allowing players to position themselves strategically in the prevailing discourse and social field. In line with this, Foucault (1980) reflects on how power is woven into the field as a kind of network or a web into which the players are also woven, both as people against whom power is exercised and as 'vehicles of power' themselves:

> Power is employed and exercised through a net-like organisation. And not only do individuals circulate between its threads; they are always in the position of simultaneously undergoing and exercising this power. They are not only its inert or consenting target; they are always also the elements of its articulation. In other words, individuals are the vehicles of power, not its point of application. (98)

A similar double logic comes to the surface in our understanding of strategic social positioning, which encompasses the entire continuum from consciously deliberate actions to embodied dispositions originating in the preconscious *habitus* as well as the *illusio* of the game. By means of the musical gentrification concept, we seek to focus on how this is performed by the gentrifying players, who carry out strategic actions to accumulate cultural capital in new, unspoiled fields and/or exercise the practical sense according to the habitual preparedness that is intuitively experienced as adequate for the situation. In this context, it is also valuable to reflect upon how the practical sense is developed and expressed and about what class dispositions underlie or oppose staying within or breaking out of given cultural realms, as it may be interesting to pursue Lahire's (2003: 329) argument that 'social agents have developed a broad array of dispositions, each of which owes its availability, composition, and force to the socialization process in which it was acquired'. We will explore these issues in more detail in the next section.

Music academia gentrified: collective and individual games of power

As mentioned in the preceding section, a decade ago we carried out an investigation of the gentrification of popular music that took place within Norwegian master's theses and doctoral dissertations in music from 1974, when the first thesis that made such a genre connection was approved, up to 2012 (Dyndahl *et al.*, 2017). In that context, we also investigated which institutions and gatekeepers were the most central in these processes. We found that three Norwegian institutions were paramount in the processes of gentrifying popular music: two university music departments and one music conservatory. We also found that at the national level, a total of seventy professors had been involved as supervisors in this field. However, it became apparent that some were far more active than others, in that only eleven professors had supervised 57.2 per cent of these works, and of these, ten were male and one was female. To get an impression of how a few of the most central players have reflected and acted, we will therefore take a closer look at four of these, all of whom are males and have held positions within the aforementioned three most influential institutions within the musical gentrification of popular music in Norway. In terms of age, the interviewees span a couple of generations that have been professionally active in the field from the 1970s to the 2020s. They also have different musical, cultural, social and geographical backgrounds.

Being the one among those interviewed who had supervised the most master's theses in total, as well as the most in popular music, one supervisor apparently derived his justification for contributing to the introduction of new genres from the students' involvement in and commitment to multifarious kinds of popular music:

> After all, I have had the attitude towards students who have come and asked at the beginning of their master's, and I have listened to them: 'Yes, that's fine. If you want to go for this, I'll look into those things, but give me some good reasons why you're passionate about this field'. [. . .] And, then I have accepted anything as long as there has been some commitment. [. . .] ideas that I initially thought were a bit of crap myself. (Interviewee 5)

Coming from a vernacular musical background himself, where the music in the family and the local community was perhaps neither recognised as being on par with esteemed popular nor what was perceived at the time as 'proper' Norwegian folk music (e.g., by the Norwegian Broadcasting Corporation) has possibly made this interviewee's *habitus* particularly predisposed to openness to musical forms that fall outside established music academia. Moreover, he eventually met several people from a similar background in the music department, and a special research interest in musics that few others had shown an academic interest in was allowed to grow and prosper. Paired with the practical sense of finding space for the students' personal music and research interests, the interviewee undertook the responsibility of introducing or developing methodological and theoretical approaches relevant for analysing the specific forms of popular music in question, and thereby contributed to the academisation of the popular music genre within the institution:

Interviewer: Because it is an important part of the supervisor's role? To academise this music?

Interviewee 5: Yes, absolutely! To get it approved and let him [the student] get credit for it. Otherwise, there might be a semi-classical examiner just stating that 'this is just some crap'.

At the same time, such a disposition could prove suitable as a more or less conscious strategy on which to build one's own academic career. Two other interviewees recounted professional life stories in which musical gentrification as a phenomenon seemed to be the warp of the weave that came to be their personal academic careers. Yet both emphasised that the gentrified music did not originally come through their own efforts; it came with the students and the students' interests and aspirations:

They [the students] have had that ability to simply write about what they want to write about and often they have chosen either their favourite artist or, in some cases, the artist they dislike the most, and ended up liking them because of the study. (Interviewee 8)

Even before popular music had officially entered music academia, it was present, as one of the interviewees emphasised. It was there since the students had popular music backgrounds but were forced to study classical music, since that was the only option. Even then, this interviewee made personal efforts to acknowledge these students' competence in his teaching as well as through the topics he chose for his own academic writing.

The interviewees described here had supervised many popular music-related student works but perhaps had not always sought out this area consciously. One of them described it as a mere coincidence that he came to supervise such master's theses in the early days, when popular music made its way into Norwegian music academia:

Interviewee 2: [Names of two colleagues] took everything, in a way, that others did not want [to supervise].

Interviewer: [The topics] that nobody else wanted? Mm. Those that were outside the mainstream?

Interviewee 2: Yes, and well, actually, so did I [. . .] I do not remember everything, but [. . .] some wrote about feminism and music, some wrote about jazz.

A more conscious, deliberate approach can be detected in terms of what the interviewees chose as topics for their own research. Although popular music was described in the interviews as 'the Other' entering music departments in these early days, it also came with new theoretical perspectives, money and possibilities for forging successful, individual academic careers. Whereas researching popular music challenged the dominant paradigms and the hegemony of Western classical music, it also brought about a world of theory that was 'the new thing', academically speaking:

Popular music studies have been composed of people who have built much of the work on the theories of cultural studies which have come about [as] – which are very unsettling. These are approaches and ideologies that shake establishments up. Popular music has been the unruly partner in almost all cases. (Interviewee 8)

Although establishments were shaken, taking on new theoretical landscapes also brought respect and appreciation, and collaboration with colleagues from other fields became a crucial part of this expansion. One of the interviewees described a situation in which researching popular music in collaboration with another researcher led to receiving a grant. This not only allowed for extensive research activity because of the money but it also opened doors to new theory and to learning how to use theory in an expansive way:

That was really important to me, because [name of collaborator] was a huge theoretician [. . .] he was very good at analysing and very creative in his use of theory. I learned a lot from that, and we were very early in using [a particular form of theory] in the field of music, and it really increased my awareness. (Interviewee 2)

In looking back at the development of the popular music research field, the interviewees acknowledged that it has *become* a field in its own right, both in the universities in which they have worked and internationally. One of them described this development as 'astronomical' and as something he consciously sought out and has been quite instrumental in making happen. Another interviewee might not have been as instrumental in this development but described the leadership roles he had taken on over the years and through which he had had the power to exercise a heavy influence as opportunities that just happened to come his way:

I have not taken these positions because I really *wanted* them [. . .] I take my turn [. . .] [being a leader] is a shitty job, I was not [. . .] really interested in positions of leadership [. . .] but I have been thinking that, okay, if I take on this shitty job, then one is also allowed to promote one's own agenda. (Interviewee 2)

Thus, a certain level of disinterest once again came to not only serve this interviewee's individual career but also the phenomenon of academic musical gentrification more generally.

Yet another interviewee emphasised the central role that music teacher education and the discipline of music education had played in including genres other than classical music at the institutional level. From the early 1980s, the interviewee's institution had experienced that well-qualified applicants for music teacher education often had musical backgrounds in popular music and jazz:

> Could we continue to only admit classical students when we gradu-ally saw how many there were who belonged to a completely dif-ferent tradition, and who we knew would become fine teachers in school? Should we shut them out of the programme just because they played so and so? (Interviewee 4)

The situation culminated in the professional community informally using its role as gatekeeper to open the door slightly:

> So, in the music education department [. . .] We realised that it was not right to continue like this. We weren't pop musicians ourselves. But it was so obvious that we had to react. So, we started very little at the beginning of the 80s actually, letting a few in, without making a big deal of it, so to speak [. . .] So that process, I would say, was essentially internally managed. It was we who ran the programme who recognised that we must do something here. And, of course, we were backed up by the students who were admitted and stuff like that. (Interviewee 4)

One result of this practice was that it quickly became so popular among the new type of students that a quota system had to be introduced to ensure that students from a classical background also entered the programme. Over time, a considerable number of music education master's theses were also produced with connections to popular music in which, however, the music genre often constituted the teaching content or activity area rather than an object of analy-sis in itself. Eventually, the conservatory-like institution also estab-lished performance programmes in jazz and improvised music as well as folk music, for which music education must therefore be regarded as a kind of institutional door opener.

However, genre-wise gentrification via music education was anticipated in a far more formal way in Sweden a decade ear-lier, when in 1971, the culturally, educationally and politically

committed musicologist Jan Ling initiated SÄMUS[1] at the University
of Gothenburg. This was an experimental scheme in music teacher
education that included jazz, folk music, pop and rock. Here, a
coherent interplay between music education as a potential field of
action, education policy and academic activism comes into view
(Olsson, 1993; Tagg, 1997).

This approach was echoed in Norway, where a small group of
particularly dedicated teachers at the Trøndelag Music Conservatory
took advantage of the opportunity that arose when the institution,
which in the late 1970s experienced a drop in student recruitment
and consequently received poorer funding, was forced to seek initiatives that would attract more students. Led by a music theory
teacher, who was also a significant jazz musician, they formed an
alliance with the then Ministry of Church Affairs and Education,
in which the State Secretary happened to be a jazz aficionado and
succeeded in establishing a pilot project in music teacher education
with an emphasis on jazz in 1979 (Bjørklund and Aksdal, 2012;
Dyndahl, 2015). The pilot project soon became a permanent programme, with a gradually increasing focus on jazz performance
rather than teacher education. Thus, compared to the preceding
examples, it is probably fair to state that music education has been
more of a means to an end and not an end in itself in this case.
Notwithstanding this fact, the jazz programme is probably the best-
known and perhaps the most important institution for jazz education in Norway today. In 1996, the conservatory became part
of the Norwegian University of Science and Technology (NTNU),
which is the largest university in the country, and, for a substantial
period, the jazz programme and its professors have been promoted
as a flagship for the institution, alongside its scientific Nobel Prize
laureates, accounting for a prominent part of the way NTNU has
represented itself to the outside world (Midling, 2014).

In sum, the presented interviews and examples indicate that there
has been a step-by-step gentrification of popular music from a state
of being the Other to becoming a naturalised, even celebrated, part
of higher music education in Norway. Music academics have acted
as players – some as veritable activists, others in more reluctant yet
powerful positions of leadership – in this game, on behalf of students but also in pursuit of their own interests. What is intuitively
initiated or consciously intended can be discussed in terms of, on

one hand, habitual dispositions and, on the other hand, deliberate strategies. As a double game, musical gentrification is probably being played out simultaneously along the entire axis of belief and conviction. Moreover, musical gentrification is about institutional concerns and needs, if we look at it one way, resulting from the ubiquitous neoliberal market orientation and competition that have increasingly dominated higher education. However, if we look at it another way, the need for development and change is also related to the detraditionalisation of classical music, which has suffered a loss of naturalness, meaning that what becomes naturalised as the *illusio* instead is that everything – including musical genres – should be negotiated. Accordingly, in the perspective of musical gentrification, this allows the institutions to appear as more or less open-minded, tolerant and inclusive regarding, among other things, aesthetic and cultural diversity, thereby distinguishing them from the caricature of the formerly exclusive – and exclusionary – music conservatory. In that way, they act in accord with the late modern principles of social and cultural distinction described by Piketty (2018), but in this context, it is important to emphasise that musical gentrification refers to a double game of both inclusion and exclusion, and previous hierarchies and forms of establishment tend to survive and re-emerge in new, more subtle forms.

Many of the examples above, not least our own investigation of the musical gentrification of popular music in Norwegian higher education, are linked to postgraduate education and research. Regarding the impact of higher education on social mobility in Norway, we refer to findings cited earlier in the chapter indicating that it depends both on the lengths of study programmes and the programmes' levels of status (Hansen and Uvaag, 2021). In such a perspective, students from a working-class background tend to choose the shortest and less prestigious programmes, while getting a higher education degree, in which both the length and status of the education matter, represents an important part of middle-class values (Sakslind *et al.*, 2018).

In addition, there are at least three other factors that make musical gentrification a perfect match for the needs of the cultural middle class and elite. First, higher education provides a relatively poorer financial than cultural and social payoff in Norway compared to many other countries. This means that it is proportionately more profitable to invest in higher education for the cultural fraction of the middle and upper classes than for the economic one. Second, the Norwegian cultural elite (or wannabe elite) like to adorn themselves with an egalitarian and unsnobbish disposition, especially when it comes to omnivorous cultural taste and consumption (Sakslind *et al.*, 2018). Third, contributing to musical gentrification can convey a sense of people being particularly tolerant and open-minded with a will for cultural diversity and inclusion – not unlike Piketty's (2018) description of the Brahmin left, to which many from the cultural middle class and elite belong or wish to belong. Musical gentrification can thus support the belief that one is partaking in an exalted cultural game that may, however, be at odds with being inclusive in the full sense of the word. This applies to ethnicity and race in addition to social class since it seems paradoxical that the apparently positive interest in cultural and musical diversities has, to a very small degree, led to a correspondingly broad representation among students and faculty members in Norwegian higher music education and research.

When Bennett and colleagues (2009) discuss possible limitations of Peterson's (1992) concept of cultural omnivorousness in their replication study of Bourdieu's (1984) *Distinction*, situated in a more recent British context, they find that the omnivorous appetite is not bottomless. Instead, it is often characterised by what they term as 'cognate musical forms' (Bennett *et al.*, 2009: 77). A recurrent example of such a relationship is between opera, classical music and jazz, forms of music that do not necessarily have any direct musical or genre-related kinship, but which have a somewhat similar status, sociologically speaking, in the sense that they may provide roughly the same amount of cultural capital in their respective fields. In this regard, jazz is in itself a very interesting example, which throughout its history of just over a hundred years has been associated with both folk music and popular music as well as art music. This has led to racial, functional, sociological and other implications but has also resulted in the fact that today, jazz is among the absolute most attractive, and exclusive, study programmes in Norwegian higher education overall. The aestheticised, academic and institutionalised dealing with and access to jazz can thereby offer some of the same status that classical forms of music have usually provided.

However, we have already mentioned that musical gentrification is not only about what kind of music is gentrified but just as much about how it is conducted. In a critical study on the SÄMUS programme from the 1970s, Olsson (1993) shows, for example, how the inclusion of folk music, jazz and popular music took place on the premises of art music and the classical conservatory tradition, with their definitions of soloist and ensemble repertoire, formats of classical works, stylistic periods and the like. Nevertheless, over time, we see a clear tendency for a selection of popular musical genres to be transformed into kinds of cognate forms in the academic sense. This is largely connected to the fact that popular music studies have acted as an important driving force for reorientation and further development of the theoretical basis for music academia, as was also highlighted by some of the interviewees discussed. Popular music without an obvious genre or stylistic relationship can thus be perceived and operationalised as cognate, as it forms part of a discursive theory formation, for example, associated with gender studies, critical race studies, post-humanism or ecomusicology, to name a few recent variants. In these efforts, there is undoubtedly a strong urge to constantly include new perspectives in music (education) research. At the same time, it obviously also involves mutually contesting and excluding each other's contributions in the struggles that Bourdieu (1988) claims characterise both the individual *Homo Academicus* and the common academic *illusio*. However, the power exercised and the status achieved are often hidden in double games, which is not least reflected in the gendered dimension of musical gentrification.

The paradox of hiding one's power: achieving (gendered) status in (musical) society

The collected empirical material from the aforementioned comprehensive study of a century of Norwegian master's theses and doctoral dissertations in music shows an almost surprisingly equal gender balance between female-authored (827 theses, 48.8 per cent) and male-authored outputs (866 theses, 51.1 per cent) (Dyndahl *et al.*, 2017). Nonetheless, there are some interesting gender differences to be found and analysed. First and foremost, as indicated in the previous section, there are large gender differences in terms of the role of academic supervisor, gatekeeper or tastemaker, with 84.8 per cent of the output being supervised by male and 15.2 per cent by female professors. In addition, concerning authorship related to genres and approaches, some clear differences emerge.

An interesting path to follow is certain shifts in patterns of gendered dominance. For example, such a shift becomes apparent within the academic interest in classical music. From the 1920s to 1983, there was a clear preponderance of male researchers in this field. In 1984, there was a sudden gender balance, and from then on, until 2012, female academics were increasingly studying and researching classical music (Nielsen, 2021). This becomes particularly interesting if we compare it to the fact that the academic gentrification of popular music was gaining momentum from the 1980s. Research interest in this genre was strongly male-dominated throughout the entirety of the investigated period with an overall amount of 63.1 per cent male authorship versus 36.9 per cent female. Similar tendencies towards gendered dominance shifts can be found in other areas besides classical music. For example, from the first thesis published in 1965, on a topic that can be categorised as pedagogical or therapeutic forms and uses of music, until 1997, male authors dominated this particular area. Then from 1997 until 2012, the number of female authors increased, while the opposite was true for male authors.

On one hand, this may suggest that in choosing to concentrate on Western classical music and on pedagogical and therapeutic aspects, female authors did not assume the roles of pioneers or gentrifiers that became available with the advent of popular music in music academia. Instead, they filled the space left vacant when male academics seized that opportunity. On the other hand, Nielsen (2021), inspired by van den Berg's (2011) definition of 'genderfication' as processes that intersect class and gender with urban gentrification, has presented the notion of 'musical genderfication'. This implies that music academia, 'through its inbuilt processes of musical gentrification [. . .] does not only produce a social space for affluent and omnivorous users; within the same space it also produces specific and gender-hegemonic collective expectations which largely determine men and women's career paths and possibilities' (Nielsen, 2021: 114).

Also building on Bourdieu's (2001) *Masculine Domination*, Nielsen (2021) further argues that gendered norms are produced through the exercise of a certain 'double standard' (Bourdieu, 2001: 60), according to which the performance of similar tasks may be assigned a different status depending on whether they are performed by males or females:

> Not only can a man stoop without degrading himself to certain tasks that are socially defined as inferior (not least because it is unthinkable that a man should perform them), but the same tasks may be noble and difficult, when performed by men, or insignificant and imperceptible, easy and futile, when performed by women. (Bourdieu, 2001: 60)

Through such processes, an *illusio* of masculinity as some kind of 'nobility' may become established in the academic field (Bourdieu, 2001: 56), in which male students are allowed to differentiate themselves from female students by how they go about undertaking tasks 'inasmuch as it is based on a form of recognition of domination, [which] tends to reinforce the established relation of symbolic domination' (59). Therefore, stereotypically speaking, when male students instinctively pursue their pre-existing music interest (or, just as often, fandom), it would be perceived as a noble action to include underprivileged forms of music in academic settings, whereas the female disposition to care seems intuitively or habitually directed towards educational and therapeutic needs or an impulse to cherish the endangered greatness of classical music. However, to contradict the stereotypes somewhat, we also detected an empirical inclination for the gender dominance within popular music gentrification to be slightly shaken. Until 2004, the initiative to introduce new popular music subgenres and styles belonged to male academics, but from then until 2012, we found that female authors increasingly acted as pioneers of new styles and thereby challenged the male dominance in this respect – in so far as it did not shift the imbalance of the overall picture. Whether this was due to a tendency towards gender equality or was an expression of a certain feminisation of popular music research, similar to what was found regarding classical music and others, remains to be further explored. With Bourdieu (2001), one would have to question whether the doxa of music academia and the predominantly male supervisors were ready to overcome what he describes as a pervasive fear of feminisation: 'The most striking example of this *permanence in and through change* is the fact that positions which become feminized are either already devalued [. . .] or declining, their devaluation being intensified, in a snowball effect, by desertion of the men which it helped to induce' (91).

Looking at the field of Nordic music education research in particular, Karlsen (2025) observes that there has been exponential growth in the number of female faculty members, including full professors, within the field. At the same time, Nordic music education has expanded its area of research interest, not least owing to the fact that several of the expansions have been initiated and carried out by female researchers. However, even if this 'could be interpreted as the dominated taking up space within the quite newly formed field of opinion, pushing back doxa and aiming to carve out professional contexts which could also inhabit female academics' (Karlsen, 2025: 384), Karlsen summarises that 'even though research fields can be changed with regard to their gendered composition, this does not necessarily alter the broader gender dynamics underpinning them' (2025: 386). Anyway, the perspectives on boundary work (Lamont, 1992), as well as on musical genderfication, imply a dynamic and broader concept of musical gentrification at the intersection of gender and social class.

Keeping the gender aspects in mind, the way musical gentrification has been operationalised as a critical concept in this context is essentially about exploring the search for and investment of cultural capital from new sources, while distinctions between what has been perceived as high and low culture have simultaneously been blurred. The musical gentrification processes can therefore easily be interpreted as inclusive and democratising. Nevertheless, in late modern Western capitalism, we can, with the help of Piketty's (2018) analyses, see tendencies that traditional relationships between, on one hand, politics and political parties, and on the other hand, the distribution of economic and cultural power, have become unclear and confusing. In Norway and the Nordic countries, political discourses on social class have long been pushed into the background or, alternatively, have been conducted by proxy. In a situation where the political discussion about power and the distribution of economic capital takes place in ways that become less transparent, Bourdieu

(1986) argues that cultural capital gains increased importance for the reproduction of a social system that keeps its structural assumptions hidden:

> Thus the more the official transmission of capital is prevented or hindered, the more the effects of the clandestine circulation of capital in the form of cultural capital become determinant in the reproduction of the social structure. As an instrument of reproduction capable of disguising its own function, the scope of the educational system tends to increase, and together with this increase is the unification of the market in social qualifications which gives rights to occupy rare positions. (Bourdieu, 1986: 254–255)

In this connection, Bourdieu (1984) points to artists in particular, who can function as 'cultural intermediaries' or those who are in a position to add value to new objects and practices. In music education and academia, it seems obvious that those practising musical gentrification fulfil a corresponding role. The apparent democratisation of musics that have previously been accorded little importance and low status even though they are important to many, not least ordinary people, must be seen in light of this. It can contribute to a narrative conveying that, when it comes to music, we are all the same. In that way, it helps to make social class and class differences unimportant or invisible. The most effective way to reproduce a class society is probably to pretend it does not exist.

In British sociology, the Bourdieuian concept of cultural intermediaries has been used to explain the alleged declining significance of social class. Savage and Bennett (2005) criticise this interpretation and argue that Bourdieu, in contrast, 'was interested in the role played by such groups as the bearers of new forms of cultural capital, in reshaping class relations' (3). The critical objective of the musical gentrification concept is exactly the same: to examine the role played by gentrifiers as initiators and mediators of *new forms of cultural capital*, with the result that class relations tend to be *reshaped*. Thus, regardless of the motivation, the state and society's investment in higher music education and research represents a (capital-)logical step towards updating and reproducing the social system, including its class structure. Having said that, it is important to underline that the game has a double nature, and the dual logic still diffuses even though the players may have subversive intentions and harbour a deep belief – or *illusio* – that they are contributing to – and investing in – something quite different, or more precisely, they may to some extent but not solely.

Note

1 SÄMUS – *Särskild Ämnesutbildning i Musik* [Special Subject Education in Music] was an experimental activity regarding music teacher training that took place during the years 1971–1978 at the Swedish Universities of Gothenburg (from 1971), Malmö (from 1973) and Piteå (from 1976).

4

Classification struggles: music education and genre

Live Weider Ellefsen, Anne Jordhus-Lier and Ingeborg Lunde

Introduction

The classifying subjects who classify the properties and practices of others, or their own, are also classifiable objects which classify themselves (in the eyes of others) by appropriating practices and properties that are already classified (as vulgar or distinguished, high or low, heavy or light etc. – in other words, in the last analysis, as popular or bourgeois) according to their probable distribution between groups that are themselves classified. (Bourdieu, 1984: 482)

Bourdieu's (1984) investigation of the social dynamics of his contemporary French society reveals that music constitutes a particularly vital, 'radical', even, form of negotiation of the social world (19). Central to such negotiations, according to Bourdieu, is the practice of classification – that is, the procedures and struggles through which people interpret and understand their social realities, relations and opportunities. By means of establishing differences and emphasising distinctions, classification practices are employed to categorise subjects as well as objects and selves as well as others. Furthermore, classification struggles might proceed and unfold covertly, in ways and forms misrecognised by the classifying subjects themselves, even while reinforcing symbolic yet powerful value hierarchies.

This chapter addresses classification struggles which we find to be crucial for games of music as played in contemporary Norwegian society – namely, those struggling by and with the concept of musical *genres*. Undeniably, there are compelling discourses arguing quite the opposite – that genre has ceased to matter. Artists assert their unique position across or between borders; critics and connoisseurs claim an omnivorous taste predicated on quality rather than likes and dislikes; and educational institutions attempt to allure potential students by promoting courses and programmes that allow for crossover or even genreless musicianship. Yet artists heavily depend upon genre rhetoric to distribute and promote their music; there are genre-related limits to connoisseurs' and critiques' tastes; and higher music education might be seen to accessorise more than innovate with genrelessness (Ski-Berg, 2023). Indeed, the presence and importance of genres in Norwegian music educational games can be inferred by the sheer misrecognition of their influence. Genres are so central to these practices that the logic they present is taken for granted. They are not seen not as discursive constructs, but as universals, even though we are fully aware that genres are created, emerge and eventually fade away. In a sense, they have no other function than a descriptive one, acting as neutral labels for actual musical expressions in the present.

Genre as social action

Certainly, the dynamics of social fields and circumstances might vary considerably, including in the ongoing classification struggles. What can be studied are certain forms of social dynamics as they play out in specific social fields at specific times in history. Bourdieu's exploration of the social dynamics of France in the 1960s and 1970s includes the specific elite cultural institutions, agents, practices of consumption and classification struggles. In the DYNAMUS research project, which has largely informed this book, we investigated the social dynamics of musical upbringing and schooling in the Norwegian welfare state after World War II. Undoubtedly, Norwegian musical upbringing and schooling constitute a case that differs greatly from music education in France, the United States or Brazil. Social democratic welfare policies and beneficial economic conditions have ensured free public education at all educational levels. Over 95 per cent of Norwegian pupils are attending public primary and secondary schools (Union of Education Norway, 2024). Private schools are also subsidised and obliged to follow the same national core curriculum for years 1–13 that public schools do. Music is a mandatory subject in the first ten years and an elective programme in the last three. Furthermore, all municipalities are obliged to offer extracurricular and state-subsidised art and music education (see Chapter 2).

However, as games of music work, they rely on mechanisms and strategies of meaning-making that operate beyond the formal, non-formal and informal (Folkestad, 2006) Norwegian music educational practices discussed in this book. This is certainly the case for classification struggles over musical genres. Genre-based classification is central to music educational, commercial, political, scientific and everyday social game playing in contemporary Western societies. Higher music education institutions follow the logic and rhetoric of musical genres in organising and labelling their courses and content and, indeed, even in categorising students and teachers within the logics of musical genres (Ski-Berg, 2023; Wahlberg, 2020). Global music industries and digital streaming services practise and encourage elaborate and multi-layered genre hierarchies which also connect and articulate music with consumer markets (see, e.g., Frith, 2000, on the world music industry; Johansson *et al.*, 2018, on streaming music practices and cultures; Bull, 2019, on classical music as a classed cultural repertoire). Researchers in the fields of musicology, music education, music theory and music sociology apply pre-defined genre categories in investigating cultural expressions and consumption (Bennett *et al.*, 2009; Dyndahl *et al.*, 2017; Faber *et al.*, 2012; Peterson, 1992) or in mapping out patterns of participation and value-laden social structures (Dyndahl *et al.*, 2017; Ellefsen, 2014; Georgii-Hemming and Westvall, 2010; Wahlberg, 2020).

Recognising the widespread practice of genre-related classification in the art fields, Fabbri (1982), Miller (1984), English (2011) and Brackett (2016), among others, have come to understand genres as socio-discursive and media-specific events or practices rather than formulas and pre-defined templates for meaning-making. They are created for certain purposes, evolve in specific cultural and economic contexts, and their aesthetic and functional aspects constitute a double game where the two dimensions of play are exceedingly difficult to separate from each other. Miller (1984), writing from within rhetorical genre theory, advocates an understanding of genre grounded in rhetorical practice, that is, 'in the conventions of discourse that a society establishes as ways of "acting together"' (163). Miller further argues that genre as social action 'acquires meaning from situation and from the social context in which that situation arose' (163).

   In 1980, Derrida wrote in 'The law of genre' that while no text can be genreless, individual texts participate in rather than belong to genres. Furthermore, he held genre citations to be disruptive anomalies rather than clean repetitions, meaning that when participating in a genre, a text simultaneously undermines it. In addition, building on and contributing to making Bakhtin's ideas known to a European audience, Kristeva developed the concept of intertextuality to investigate how individual texts come to be – their structurisation – rather than interpreting their autonomous structure. Intertextuality is 'a mosaic of quotations; any text is the absorption and transformation of another' (Kristeva, 1969/1986: 37). Bourdieu's seminal study on social distinction was published in English in 1984, demonstrating how cultural classification – of subjects as well as objects – in the various fields of French society serves to uphold hierarchical societal power structures. According to Bourdieu, through classification and consumption, forms of symbolic as well as economic capital are produced and traded, and the producing and trading agents in the fields achieve their status and legitimacy. Miller's (1984) stance, too, implies that the role of genres in everyday social dynamics extends beyond serving as simple schemata for communication: 'what we learn when we learn a genre is not just a pattern of forms or even a method of achieving our own ends. We learn, more importantly, what ends we may have' (165). Indeed, Miller holds that genres provide people not only with tools to achieve particular ends but with knowledge of what those ends might entail: accounting for something, apologising to someone, eulogising, recommending and so on (165). Furthermore, we might add, they provide people with knowledge of who can eulogise and recommend what and in what ways.

   A compatible perspective on genre is offered by English (2011) in one of very few explorations into the educational possibilities that open up when seeing genre as social action rather than examining only genre characteristics. She tasks her students with regenring a text (e.g., by recontextualising an academic essay as a phone-in radio debate) and investigates how disciplinary knowledge is represented and experienced and how material dimensions (representation) interact with social dimensions (agency and identity). Rather than teaching the features of a genre, understood as 'what it looks like', English's educational ambition is for students to reflect on how genre-related 'features' practically force authors to construct meaning in certain ways (200). In suggesting educational engagement with regenring, English also criticises the fields of rhetoric and genre theory for being preoccupied with how audiences and users perceive genre based on structural and compositional features, constituents and elements. She argues that in research as in education, one tends to focus on what genres *contain* rather than on what they *do*. A similar critique could indeed be directed towards music.

As a discursive resource, genre mediates between the social and the material, English (2011) holds, and in doing so, they orient students towards being and acting in particular ways:

> In the most simple way that I can, I want to suggest that genres configure the participants as being a particular kind of participant. . . . the student is oriented towards a particular discursive identity which derives from the way in which the institutional interactions frame the experience. (89)

In an even more radical critique, Bull (2019) goes a long way to consider the social and aesthetic power of the classical music genre in young people's lives, describing how children and youth choir and orchestral musicians are orientated towards particular classed and gendered ways of being and doing, intellectually and bodily, in and through the music they play. She argues convincingly that children's and youth's classical musicking, as she finds it at her research sites, contributes to reproducing social hierarchies related to class, gender and economy. She sees this as a challenge that socially responsive music educators urgently need to meet. What makes Bull's critique radical, however, is that she locates the safeguarding of middle-class privilege not only in classical music (educational) practices but also in the aesthetics of the music itself – what makes the music beautiful and pleasurable. This leads her to argue that the only way classical music can be claimed by a wider audience, and resignified, is if we endeavour to open up or even disrupt the aesthetics.

Classical music genres themselves do the boundary-drawing work that keeps most young people outside the middle class from participating. The barriers to wider participation are inextricable from what creates beauty in the classical music tradition and thus cannot be removed without making fundamental changes to the culture of practice. Therefore, we need to be questioning ideas of quality, beauty, authority, interpretation, authenticity and talent in addition to the educational approaches and social forms of organisation. We must mobilise a radical meaning of access that also renegotiates the meaning of excellence.

There is considerable depth to English's and Bull's suggestions that genres configure students in certain ways and orient them towards certain actions, and we will elaborate upon the implications of this point of view subsequently. For now, we take from the aforementioned that genres are thoroughly discursive. They are constructed by people to make meaning in and of the social, and they therefore also carry meaning produced within certain social constellations of knowledge and power where subjects and objects are positioned in relation to each other. Musical 'events', to use Fabbri's (1982) terminology, participate in a range of different past, present and future discursive genre formations (Brackett, 2016), and it is our creative classification of that participation which enables us to utilise genre in the various social games we play. Thus conceptualised, it becomes incredibly interesting and valuable to understand the cultural work that genres do and, indeed, the concept of genre itself and its implications and uses for human interaction and meaning-making.

Genring

In this chapter, we go deeper into understanding genres as actions. We conceptually shift the idea of genre from an educational (and analytical) tool, or content, to an educational (and analytical) practice. Genre, we suggest, could productively be comprehended as acts of genring – that is, acts of creative classification that discursively establish the ontological effects of genres. It creates and shapes an intertextuality of cultural objects over which players struggle, simultaneously implying that it was always there. Following

Ellefsen (2022), to genre is to make a discursive statement – visual, verbal, gestural or otherwise – that contributes to the genrification of cultural expressions, such as in music and music education:

> genring refers to productive acts of temporary interpretation and signification, in which existing classification systems and genre categories in the social are operationalized and (re)negotiated. Given that people understand themselves in and through classification processes, the meaning-making procedure of genring unavoidably also includes and operationalizes existing social positions, relations, and identities. (57)

In the field of music education, genring is certainly a common strategy for associating music with music, music with people and people with people for educational or artistic purposes. By genring musical events, activities, identities and contexts and relating them to each other, players of music educational games, for example, enable desired learning contents, situations and outcomes. Musical genring, then, is a classification struggle that renders objects, subjects and social relations in the fields of music meaningful and, with them, the genrifying subjects themselves. Through the double play of genring, people identify and make value judgements about musical objects, activities and other people by placing them within certain discourses and tying them to specific identities, histories and expectations. Thus, they are able to identify, historicise and know what is to be expected from their own participation in the game (Ellefsen, 2021).

Furthermore, the intertextual (and educational) game of genring is played by creating differences and distinctions as much as similarities. Through genring, musical expressions are (re)defined, ranked in hierarchies, compared and distinguished from each other also by being associated with certain cultural practices, contexts and identities. It is a form of distinction that classifies people and music according to each other in the same classification system. To genre is to make and maintain differences (and thus also similarities) in the social as well as the musical. Thereby, genring can maintain and/or challenge prevailing cultural distinctions in the fields of music and music education – distinctions that support existing social power networks. A corresponding feature is that the production and maintenance of symbolic capital in society largely take place through players' distinctions – practices where actors implement capital in ways that highlight differences (and thus similarities).

Classification struggles

In using the term 'classification struggles', Bourdieu (1984) refers to the scientific production and organisation of knowledge in general and to sociology as a game of classification in particular. Furthermore, distinguishing between practical and academic, or reputedly 'objective', classification, he argues that scientific classification games habitually risk melding or confusing the two. Consequently, (disciplinary) knowledge categories which follow from struggles not only to understand but also to master, gain the upper hand, win, achieve status and earn material and symbolic capital and power – that is, to play the game properly – appear to be naturally occurring instances and events. Similarly, the classification procedure itself seems more of a practical concern than a contest between investors (institutions, disciplines, research communities), where scientific investments are expected to yield symbolic as well as economic capital. Following this way of thinking, the same naturalising effect can be found in everyday social knowledge games. Conflating what are practical means of communication about illness and health, art and music, gender and sex, education and upbringing, with scientifically and/or disciplinary authorised classifications, like Attention-Deficit/Hyperactivity Disorder (ADHD) and migraine, musicality and talent, transgender and transsexual, digital and hybrid learning, naturalise and universalise terms and ideas without taking into consideration the struggles through which they have been produced.

Classification struggles, then, are scientific as well as everyday negotiations and competitions to know, interpret, judge and communicate about the world, and thus they also always involve a struggle over material and symbolic capital – that is, power. Moreover, these struggles divide and define groups of people, classifying others and selves, articulating relationships and belongings as well as objects and events. In the processes of classification, statements, texts, artworks and musical expressions are associated and dissociated not only with/from each other or with past and future others but also with/from social practices and contexts, groups and identities, possibilities and impossibilities.

Classification struggles in games of art and music, but even education and science, are characterised by the performance of 'taste', Bourdieu (1984) holds, of making distinctions concerning what one does/likes/is, as opposed to what one does not/dislikes/is *not* (but which others do/like/are). Taste 'functions as a sort of social orientation, a "sense of one's place", guiding the occupants of a given place in social space towards the social positions adjusted to their properties, and towards the practices or goods which befit the occupants of that position' (Bourdieu, 1984: 465). Moreover, one's taste for – that is, one's capability for and disposition towards – certain procedures and objects of distinction and not others are socially conditioned: 'the classificatory schemes which underlie agents' practical relationship to their condition and the representation they have of it are themselves the product of that condition . . . Position in the classification struggle depends on position in the class structure' (484). This means that different systems of classification are available for different games and groups of people. The practice of taste is a skill that enables players to identify and name something compliant with themselves. It entails recognising the worth and meaning of socially established categories and knowing which ones are available to whom, which applies to oneself and in what ways, in what contexts and to what ends. Put differently, exhibiting and performing taste entails naming and classifying the world according to categories which also, simultaneously, entails naming and classifying ourselves. Moreover, this skill – or 'sense' – of practical classification is rooted in *habitus* (Bourdieu, 1990).

Bourdieu links the conditional context for and the potential impact of distinctions to *habitus*, the physically embodied social agency of agents, which he primarily sees as a function of class and socio-economic upbringing. While we find the importance of players' socio-economic backgrounds to be misrecognised in the Norwegian welfare state games of music education, we also recognise that their dispositions of classification, their practical sense, are conditioned through multiple discursive engagements within a complex field of different forms of symbolic capital. Whatever the form of its constitution, however, *habitus* provides players with a set of dispositions on the basis of which they carry out classification in practice, intuitively and rationally. 'The schemes of the *habitus*, the primary forms of classification, owe their specific efficacy to the fact that they function below the level of consciousness and language, beyond the reach of introspective scrutiny or control by the will' (Bourdieu, 1984: 466). Furthermore, individual and collective classification struggles are closely tied to people's strategies and struggles to claim social and cultural capital for themselves and thus achieve legitimate positions within relevant social contexts. Both social and cultural forms of capital, according to Bourdieu, can be institutionalised as educational qualifications and titles and converted to economic capital.

Against this backdrop, when players of music educational games, be they individuals or institutions, operationalise the idea of musical genre to know, interpret, judge and communicate about music and musical activities, courses and contents, learning traditions and performance history, they engage in classification struggles over material and symbolic capital – that is, over power and positions within the social. In habitually misrecognising the struggle itself, believing that one's classification acts entail a practical organisation and representation of the aesthetic world rather than the active creation of it, players play a double game where the apparent autonomy of the musical game conceals its dependence upon and contribution to the social game of capital and power. This is what secures the significance of genring, as a form of socio-musical classification, in enacting and maintaining the contemporary social dynamics and classed subject positions.

The classifying subjects

As previous chapters have shown, players of music educational games invest deeply and dedicatedly in their game: time, energy, money, emotions, exercise and discipline. Consciously or unconsciously, and according to their capacity and capital, they invest with the aim of drawing a surplus from the game: to be acknowledged as a player, to acquire additional skills, to position themselves favourably among other players, to gain ground, to raise and earn more capital. Returning to the opening quote of this chapter, perhaps without recognising it, when 'classifying the properties and practices of others, or their own', the players 'turn themselves into classifiable objects' (Bourdieu, 1984: 482), and it is precisely their appropriation of existing classifications that gives them away as certain kinds of players.

Who, then, are the active, skilful players of music educational games? Who are the classifying – genring – subjects who appropriate existing genre categories to classify the properties and practices of others, thereby also turning themselves into classifiable objects? Insisting on the capillary distribution and enactment of power/knowledge relations, Foucault's answer would be that classification happens in all day-to-day human interaction – as a conduct upon other people's conduct (Foucault, 1982: 789), a positioning of the subject in relation to other subject positions, a leading of meaning and knowledge along or across other strands of meaning and knowledge. Genring, then, is a discursive, performative phenomenon practised in all the myriad power/knowledge relations of society. In contrast to Foucault's acknowledgement that power/knowledge tends to stiffen in certain networks, Bourdieu is more insistent on the authority and influence of some classifying players over others and the uneven distribution of the possibilities to play. Genring, for these influential players, provides them with an opportunity to create new distinctions and thus to revitalise existing, for them beneficial, hierarchies. Particularly influential music educational game players in this regard would include elite players, such as politicians, scholars, renowned artists, critics, higher educational institutions and programmes, media and media personalities.

Genring school music

Genre is a nodal point of knowledge construction in music education and, in Norwegian educational settings, it commonly also defines a disciplinary domain and topic of study – 'genre theory/musical styles/musical periods and styles' – as well as a specific form of competence – 'genre knowledge/understanding musical styles' (Ellefsen, 2022; for more about the Norwegian compulsory school system, see Chapter 2). In a survey research study carried out in 2019–2020, Ellefsen and colleagues invited state-employed teachers

in Norwegian compulsory music education years 1–10 to describe
the music subject at their school, their most recent music lesson
and their favourite musics and activities for educational use. The
survey did not employ the concept of genre, and in asking specifically about 'the music you and your pupils listened to, sang, played
and created', the survey design did not require teachers to describe
the 'style' or 'type' of music used in lessons and lesson activities or
to situate the music within 'traditions' or 'periods'. Even so, the
teachers' answers included both genre and genre-related terminology when offering examples of music, describing and justifying
activities, and explaining the structures and objectives of the music
subject. Indeed, based on the teachers' responses, genre and terms
associated with the concept seem to constitute an arena of disciplinary knowledge in itself in Norwegian compulsory music education.

First, genre is a nodal point of knowledge construction that also
serves to define a disciplinary domain and topic of study, which
the teachers referred to as 'genre theory' (in Norwegian, *sjanger-
lære*), as well as a specific form of competence, 'genre knowledge'
(*sjangerforståelse*). Second, a range of genre-related terms and concepts are operationalised as educational activities and objectives:
the pupils are 'learning about blues', 'listening to an example of
bebop', 'dancing to pop songs from *Just Dance*' and 'writing rap
lyrics'. Third, examples of music are articulated together with
generic terminology to support historical narratives (rock history,
the history of blues), political and ideological narratives (the music
industry, rap as opposition, African American identities in music)
and biographical narratives (the life and works of the composer,
your 'own' music and what it means to you).

The teachers answering the survey invariably employed generic
terminology, and they used the word 'genre' as if its meaning were
self-evident, undisputed and referring to existing, identifiable phenomena in music. For the teachers, genre was an ontological rather
than an epistemological concern, and only to a small degree did
their statements indicate an educational focus on the processes that
name and establish a genre rather than the characteristics of an
established genre. That is, an interest in the genrifying processes that
identify and organise power/knowledge in music and music education was missing in the empirical material produced by the survey. Even when the topic of education was described, for example,

as 'music and society' or 'music as industry', a regard for genring as a technology for producing and distributing music was lacking. Rather, the survey material analysed indicated that a main function of genre, in the context of Norwegian compulsory music education, is to facilitate the listing and learning of criteria or characteristics for delimiting some musical expressions from others, with the educational aim of enabling students to identify and categorise music as a musical competency in itself. Furthermore, the main purpose for which this function is put to use is the telling of music historical narratives, including the rehearsal of canonised musical expressions, events and artists. Notably, the music historical narratives supported by generic terminology are also social history. Genres are seen to represent identifiable and traceable traditions with socially anchored histories, commonly situated in particular places in the world, with particular key persons, important events and, most significantly, particular examples. This is the fourth main task of genre in the analysed material: serving as a frame of reference for displaying and praising the quality and significance of particular works and composers/artists. Lastly, but of significant importance, judging by the teachers' descriptions, the concept of genre provides standards of reference and comparison when students compose and perform music: rap lyrics or rhythms, 'stev' (short Norwegian folk verse), grunge, pop choreography or rock music. In view of the teachers' practices (as evident from the survey results), we suggest that the concept of genre constitutes an educational technology for producing knowledge as well as a topic of knowledge in music. This is why a turn of minds towards genring instead of genre might be relevant when researching music education as well as when teaching music.

Genring practices in municipal schools of music and arts

Within the municipal schools of music and arts, the players play the game of genring at various levels. At a personal level, music teachers draw distinctions between genres to identify themselves as specialists, both as musicians and teachers. This is thus connected to both their professional and personal identities and is inscribed in their *habitus*, providing them with a set of dispositions accumulated from their socialisation into established practices and cultures within the field of music and musical training when they themselves started learning music, often at a young age. Jordhus-Lier (2018), in her study on music teachers' professional identities, finds genre to be related to how the teachers define their competence, where they make distinctions mainly between classical, popular and Norwegian folk music. Genring their competence within a narrow or broad set of musical styles and genres is seen to be connected to whether teacher competence is articulated by the versatility or specialisation discourse, where the findings indicate that the teachers define themselves as having a larger repertoire of genres when teaching than when performing music (Jordhus-Lier, 2018). Something quite similar is seen among teachers in a later survey study (Nielsen *et al.*, 2023a), where the teachers define themselves as more versatile in connection to genre when teaching than when they describe their backgrounds. This is especially evident in favour of popular music genres.

A question related to the defining function of teachers' genring, however, concerns what lies within the teachers' genring practices. When they express versatility in connection to genres when teaching, what does this imply when connected to, for instance, teaching methods and interpretation practices? In other words, what do the students and their parents see as the possibilities of music making? The teaching practices define what counts as musical meaning, which is incorporated into the students' *habitus* and thus contributes to practices being reproduced. One example of this is the ways in which the teachers in the survey study reported working with teaching content, where working towards established musical goals (in contrast to open-ended musical goals where improvisation, exploring the instrument and making new arrangements are central) is the most prominent way (Jordhus-Lier *et al.*, 2023). This could indicate the presence of traditions and methods associated with the classical genre (as described in, e.g., Bull, 2019) when (seemingly) teaching within other genres. There is thus a double game being played where the students and the teachers believe they are teaching/learning/playing music within a breadth of genres when the practices, to a great extent, are grounded in the classical music tradition.

We also find examples of genring at an institutional level within the schools of music and arts field, where the practice of genring is performed in at least two ways, which could be seen as opposing each other. The first is connected to the school's stated vision of being for all (Norsk kulturskoleråd, n.d.), where the school can be understood as legitimising itself as a publicly financed institution within the welfare state by promoting the idea of being for everyone and thus purporting to offer activities within a wide range of genres – or even being a 'genre-less' institution. A national survey among the headteachers at schools of music and arts (Jordhus-Lier *et al.*, 2021) provides examples of headteachers asserting that they do not label music and that 'talking about genres does not "make any sense to them"' when asked to describe their school's development in the last ten years connected to, for instance, genre. Further, both headteachers and teachers report that planning the selection of teaching content (but not always the actual selection of it) is connected to, among other things, the students' wishes (Jordhus-Lier *et al.*, 2021; Jordhus-Lier *et al.*, 2023; Nielsen *et al.*, 2023a). When seeing this in relation to how some headteachers report 'rising above' the practice of genring, it can be understood as a strategy for being a more inclusive school. However, genring is a discursive practice which is ubiquitous in our society and, thus, also among headteachers, teachers, students and parents in schools of music and arts. When making decisions about the kind of music to be played or taught, one participates in the act of genring. Is the idea of being 'genre-less' thus an attainable goal or is it a game being played to legitimise a welfare state institution? A consequence of playing this game is also the danger of underplaying the significance of music in people's lives, because for most people, it actually matters which music they listen to, both as a positive resource and, in more complex and contradictory ways (Hesmondhalgh, 2008), in connection to feelings, identity and identification processes.

While investing in being 'genre-less', the school also divides the students by genre. To apply for piano lessons at, for instance, Oslo kulturskole, the largest school of music and arts in Norway, one must choose between 'piano classical' and 'piano/keyboard, pop, rock and jazz' (Oslo kulturskole, n.d.). The same goes for saxophone lessons. Furthermore, if one wants to learn violin, one must choose between playing classical or Norwegian folk music. If one is interested in playing the drums, one must choose between 'drums', 'versatile drums' and 'mirthangam' (Indian drum). If one is already a student, one can apply for the extra offering of 'improvisation' (Oslo kulturskole, n.d.); in other words, this is something one cannot expect to focus on in the regular music lessons in which one is already participating. Oslo kulturskole is an example of how these schools make distinctions by making new students choose not only between instruments but also between musical styles and genres. The schools thus participate in constructing frames for teaching and learning. This is even more widespread in connection to the depth programme[1] at these schools. Schools of a certain size often oblige students to choose between 'classical' and 'popular' music when applying for a place in the depth programme. This is in line with how talent development programmes and higher music education institutions distinguish between genres and programmes – and as a consequence of that, between students. Thus, the educational pathway builds upon the game(s) of genring, where both people (such as teachers and students), but also institutions, are players (see, e.g., Ski-Berg, 2023). It thus seems as if there is a double game being played, where both preaching genre breadth and being 'genre-less' are central, and which contributes to maintaining distinctions between ways of playing and learning music which designate children and youth in often mutually exclusive ways/groups.

Academisation, institutionalisation and musical gen(t)rification

As the previous examples evince, teachers' use of the genre concept and generic terminology enables knowledge, communication and learning in everyday educational practices. It facilitates the working and establishment of (specific) networks of power/knowledge relations at a discursive micro level. Operationalising genre in educational and academic activities, however, also facilitates the practice of power/knowledge relations at discursive meso- and meta-levels and serves to legitimise, ritualise and institutionalise knowledge, ways of teaching and learning knowledge and ways of organising the dissemination and practice of knowledge. Indeed, in higher music education, genres may serve to provide the identity, profile, focus and political legitimacy necessary to succeed as an institution of higher music education, and as such constitute the educational institutions and programmes themselves. As with

genring in general, the genring of educational institutions and programmes involves making distinctions by enacting differences. In
investigating the 'folk and world music' programmes within higher
music education in Sweden, Wahlberg (2020) shows how students
and teachers, in interviews and in educational situations, emphasise the differences between programmes for performing, teaching
and learning 'Western art music', 'jazz music' and 'folk and world
music', thereby constituting the qualities and characteristics of
the latter. The continuous discursive work that goes into genring
an educational programme as 'folk and world music', for example, also entails emphasising and performing 'difference' related to
musical and social origin, geography, people, culture and lifestyle:

> [The] co-construction of tradition, place, and identity turn out to be
> characteristic of the construction of uniformity within FWM [folk and
> world music] in HME [higher music education] . . . Representations
> are made through actions of place-fixation and imaginary geogra-
> phies, and by presenting identities in fixed ways through difference-
> making systems. . . . The construction of place is also used to form a
> 'we' with the audience, and narratives of imaginary places are part of
> the way that the educational area legitimizes itself in relation to the
> FWM industry, in which place is consumed to meet the alleged needs
> of a western middle-class audience. (Wahlberg, 2020: 164)

Furthermore, Wahlberg's research reveals that the genring of a 'folk
and world music' field of study takes place within a larger frame
of already 'fully genrified' programmes in 'Western art music', to
paraphrase Altman (1999). Indeed, the implicit and explicit genring
of higher music education as the study of Western art music in the
conservatoire tradition has been so thorough, systematic and widespread that it, for a while, seemed to have succeeded in achieving
synonymy with the study of music itself. However, from being a
domain almost exclusively concerned with practising and learning
the traditions of Western art music, higher music education today
seems to be more multifariously genred in several aspects and at
several levels.

In examining the academisation of popular music in higher
music education in Norway, Dyndahl and colleagues (2017) note
that 'the inclusion of popular music into higher music education

in Norway has been increasing on an ever-steepening and ever-broadening path' (439). In surveying the entire body of master's theses and doctoral dissertations in any academic music discipline from 1912 to 2012, they find a considerable expansion of academic interest in forms of popular music beginning with the first thesis on modern/contemporary jazz submitted to the University of Oslo in 1974. Dyndahl and colleagues (2014) situate the study within an overall Bourdieuian theoretical framework, adding to that their own concept of musical gentrification – processes by which 'musics, musical practices, and musical cultures of relatively lower status are made to be objects of acquisition by subjects who inhabit higher or more powerful positions' (54). Thus framed, and from a historical perspective, the appropriation of popular music for academic study can be understood as a process that turns music previously considered to have little academic value into high-value objects by skilful academic consumption. Such a display of popular music connoisseurship combined with theoretical finesse fits favourably with contemporary performances of elite omnivorousness in musical taste, as opposed to a (presumably) culturally impeded 'univore' taste (of the working class). Therefore, it also serves individual as well as institutional needs for acquiring symbolic capital to maintain and reinforce legitimate positions within high-status social contexts.

One way of investigating gentrification more closely may be to examine the genring that, we suggest, is at the heart of the process. Gentrification can be said to operate through genrification. The successful incorporation of subordinate (lower) cultural expressions into dominant (higher) culture is contingent on the creative identification of the expression in relation to other expressions, its use in relation to other uses, its association with contexts and practices and groups in relation to other contexts and practices and groups. It entails a skilful regenring of the expression that prepares it for its new context – a regenring that assigns to the expression certain frames of understanding, or emphasises certain aesthetic features, or strengthens the relation to certain other expressions, artists or contexts. Genring, then, prepares the ground for gentrification. By this, we mean that it renders music gentrifiable, for example, by placing it in existing historical narratives or educational canons, by subtly adjusting performance and sound to fit within a new (educational) context, or by forging affiliations with already accepted proponents. Indeed, when music previously regarded as lowbrow and of lesser status is regenred by artists, educators or researchers, 'what characterises the original musical traditions and cultures may be disturbed, and some of the social and cultural ties to the musical cultures in question can be weakened or even broken for some of the initial participants' (Dyndahl *et al.*, 2014: 53). Such creative acts of verbal, musical and/or material distinction and differentiation might even render the gentrified music all but unrecognisable to its original users or, if not, reduce its original distinctive function for this group.

Subjectivation games

Bourdieu's studies on taste and social distinction (1984, 1992/1996) operate on genre logics to show how the art field overlaps with the field of power to constitute a particularly intensive and dynamic area of day-to-day struggles over positions, identities and agency. Indeed, Bourdieu finds genres to be vital to the performance of taste in music and to the day-to-day struggles over positions, relations and understandings. Genres are cultural artefacts that can be consumed according to one's sense of place. To understand more profoundly the implications of genred classification struggles for the players themselves, however, including how genring defines and divides individuals and groups of people as well as objects and expressions, we extend our perspective beyond Bourdieuian sociology to include the concept of discursive subjectivation, as explicated by Foucault and, later, Butler.

Referring to Bourdieu and Wacquant (1992), Dyndahl (2021) notes the active, creative role of social agents within a field or, we might say, players within a game. Players, who are bearers of capital, actively orient themselves towards a conservation or subversion of capital distribution; they are not mechanically pushed and pulled by external forces. Though more concerned with discursive 'push and pull' and less with creative agency, Butler (1997), drawing on Foucault, adopts a similar perspective on the discursive subjects' powers: 'Power acts on the subject in at least two ways: first, as what makes the subject possible, the condition of its possibility and its formative occasion, and second, as what is taken up and

reiterated in the subject's "own" acting' (14). When enacting discursive genre categories on musics, musical actions, musicians, self
and others, we are exercising power. We are subjects of power in
the sense that '"of" connotes both "belonging to" and "wielding"
[power]' (14). Butler thus adds to Foucault's insistence on the active
and productive character of what he calls 'power/knowledge'.
Butler's concept of performativity concerns how subjects practise
and experience themselves as gendered – or, we might add, genred – in daily life. Performativity is 'the reiterative and citational
practice by which discourse produces the effects that it names . . .
that reiterative power of discourse to produce the phenomena that
it regulates and constrains' (Butler, 1993: 2). Genring is a performative, discursive practice in the sense that it produces and establishes
ontological effects not only of genres but also of people, audiences
and subjectivities. To wield power/knowledge, the player must sub-
mit to already available power/knowledge relations. In genred classification struggles, genred subjectivities come to be.

Ellefsen (2014) presents the following scene to introduce her eth-
nographically inspired study on everyday life in a Norwegian upper
secondary music programme:

> Oliver: 'Do I really have to stand like this?! Looking like I have a
> knife in my back? Seriously, I will quit playing the fiddle if this is how
> I have to stand!' The young musician arches his back and shoots out
> his chest, peering down his nose at the fiddle resting on his shoulder.
> His teacher laughs. Picking up his own fiddle, he plays a mock-virtu-
> oso classical cadenza, nose pointing upwards, throwing his long hair
> backwards with the final high strokes. (1)

For the purpose of this chapter, this scene serves to illustrate the
very material, physical genring of subjects as well as objects in
music education. In a friendly atmosphere, the teacher and student
are striving towards the common goal of mastering the folk fiddle
and its repertoire. In doing so, they perform cultural values and
distinctions related to the music, the instrument and the identities
and actions that may be associated with it. Seemingly, the teacher
and student cooperate in making distinctions between what characterises folk musicians like themselves and the airs and graces of
the classical violinist. In responding, adapting and contributing

to the ongoing genring of himself, his teacher, their instruments, their music and their bodies, Oliver constitutes the situation as a meaningful practice while at the same time constituting himself as a meaningful subject. Moreover, by vigorously resisting what appears to be a mild disciplining of his subjectivity, both physically and intellectually, he engages in serious negotiations concerning the who-to-be and what-to-do of music and music education, with bodily behaviour and posture being of crucial importance (Ellefsen, 2014).

From a point of view aligned with discourse theory and perform-ativity theory, then, we can see the enactment of classification, the practice of distinction that Bourdieu (1984) addresses in his inves-tigation of taste, as a power technology characteristic of the game played. This is also how we understand the concept of genring: it is a technology of power/knowledge that drives music educational games by rendering objects and subjects understandable within existing discourses of classification, and also for the genring sub-jects themselves. The power supported and supported by the genri-fying act resides beyond the player and their immediate strategies of play. This is because genring sets in motion a whole material field of existing power relations (Foucault, 1969/2010). The act of genring positions the genrifying subject within these existing power struc-tures (Ellefsen, 2022). Furthermore, the performative force of the genrifying act, done by oneself, a critic, teacher, fan, parent, insti-tution or researcher, depends not so much on the conscious inten-tion as on discursive iterability and citation. This means that when listening to a streaming service or using a digital teaching resource with backing tracks, players might assign what they hear to a con-text, associating it with certain bodies and identities, feelings and ambitions, groups and places, all without necessarily invoking the name of a genre.

Genred intersections

The influence of gender studies on the field of educational research has made it possible to see gender as an act of interpretation and clas-sification – that is, *to gender* – as well as the discursive result of such an act. The intertwinement of discourses of genre with those of gender in music and music education has been thoroughly documented, including in recent studies in the Norwegian and Scandinavian school contexts (see, e.g., Blix and Ellefsen, Källén, and Onsrud in the anthology *Gender Issues in Scandinavian Music Education: From Stereotypes to Multiple Possibilities*, edited by Onsrud *et al.*, 2021). It might well be the case that acts of genring always take place in and through discourses that are already gendered. If so, to genre is always also to reiterate gender – to gender – in one way or another.

However, as Hall already argued in 1996, identities are 'points of suture' between self and discourse. They are 'never singular but multiply constructed across different, often intersecting and antagonistic, discourses, practices and positions' (Hall, 1996: 4). Subjectivity, then, gendered or otherwise, is a site for discourse to temporarily settle through the needlework of genring and similar subjectivising procedures. Revisiting the folk fiddle lesson mentioned, Oliver and his teacher are hailed by a range of discursive performatives, implying a similar range of discursively available identities relating to age, nationality, ethnicity, class, musicianship, gender and master–apprentice practices. In the situation described, genring facilitates the navigation – indeed, the 'suturing' – in a field of points and possibilities.

Crenshaw (1991) coined the term intersectionality to disrupt tendencies to see race and gender as exclusive and separable (1244) and to provide a metaphor for 'mediating the tension between assertions of multiple identity and the ongoing necessity of group politics' (1296). Intersectionality is basically a prism, as Crenshaw later emphasised in an interview with *Time*:

> for seeing the way in which various forms of inequality often operate together and exacerbate each other. We tend to talk about race inequality as separate from inequality based on gender, class, sexuality or immigrant status. What's often missing is how some people are subject to all of these, and the experience is not just the sum of its parts. (Steinmetz, 2020)

In the double games of music and music education, genring may work both to obscure and to make visible aspects of intersectionality. In addition to the classifications advanced by Crenshaw, these may also concern professions and positions in music education and the music industries, as well as identities related to tradition and nationality, age, religious beliefs and practices, ethnicity, family situation, (dis)ability and so on.

A salient case to consider in this regard is the Norwegian TV show *Stjernekamp* (Battle of the stars). A live broadcasted family entertainment success that entered its eleventh season in 2023, *Stjernekamp* challenges high-profile vocalists to compete against one another in a variety of predefined musical genres. Throughout the seasons, the show has introduced hip-hop and rap, opera, folk, rock, musical, country, electronic dance music, Sámi joik (a traditional Sámi form of melodic chanting with deep cultural and spiritual significance), hymns, reggae and a range of other genres for the participants to master and perform. In each episode, a carefully chosen genre connoisseur and exponent is provided to lead the artists through unfamiliar genre territory. By votes phoned in by the audience, the contestants advance or are eliminated from episode to episode. The participants' backgrounds and experiences are captivatingly narrated through the series as they relate to each one's career, family history and relations, ethnicity and nationality, religious beliefs, illnesses and troubles, age, sexuality, gender, musicianship and professional experiences, musical preferences, capabilities and weaknesses. Thus, the genrification of each artist's performance in each episode includes not only their voice and vocal techniques, their musicianship and stylistic connoisseurship, outfits and dance moves but also the more or less strategic and more or less conscious consideration of their gender, age, ethnicity, family, sexuality, class and religion by the producers, mentors, judges and audience of the series. This, again, might entail that when the votes are cast, gender, age, ethnicity, etc., intersect to constitute the value, authenticity and persuasiveness of the performance. Indeed, critics have commented that there seems to be a certain pattern to the show where more senior age and darker coloured skin lead to earlier elimination from the show.

'Childing' music, 'childed' subjectivities

In understanding genre as subjectivising social action, 'childing' can be conceived of as particular instances of such actions which articulate certain musical practices and performances with each other, certain audiences, certain agendas and certain contexts. As Chapter 7 discusses at length, the concept of 'children's music' is complex, and as a genre, its aesthetic and functional aspects reach far beyond musical features. Indeed, children's music can be described as a conglomerate of genring processes that identify and establish a 'childed-ness' with music when occurring as practices with, by and for children. What keeps the genre of children's music together and makes it recognisable and distinguishable as children's music is the associated childed-ness of the aural, visual, material, social and cultural aspects of the music. This entails a procedure of genring where the child, as both a philosophical idea and a human individual, is granted the position of both imagined audience and active contributor. In this process, children are seen as both receivers and producers of music and musical cultures. Social and cultural conceptions of what children are, then, are part of the genring procedures. In short, acts of childing music add profound aspects to the subtle system of classification and meaning-making.

Parents, teachers, artists, streaming services, cultural workers, researchers, priests and politicians alike partake in the childing of music, by all accounts with children's interest (and education) in mind. Conversely, in terms of genring and as ways of 'acting together' (Miller, 1984), even young children are active, skilful players in the games of music education and upbringing. Vestad (2013) describes how children contribute to discourses in which music acquires meaning in early childhood education programmes and family homes. As a matter of fact, Vestad argues, children's status as legitimate producers of musical cultures and as experts of their own lives seems to enable classifications on the grounds that children's mere interest in a song or type of music legitimises the music as children's music, leading to its validation as such by the adults nearby. Vestad describes how, in a joint interview, a five–year-old declares his younger sister's music to be 'a little girl's music', leaving his mother with a slightly embarrassed grin. Here, enhanced by the age difference and position in the line of siblings, the act of gendered classification conveys the impression that 'girl's music' is childish. The childity of girls' music and girls' voices is also discussed by Askerøi and Vestad (2021), leaning on Walkerdine (1998) and describing a girl's transgressive powers in terms of breaking the rules that her teacher establishes regarding how to use her voice when performing 'Jolene' by Dolly Parton: 'The teacher says I have to sing like a child'. Taking Askerøi and Vestad's case of 'Jolene' as an example of gendered musical childing, the girl, her vocality and the music itself undergo a procedure of genring which constitutes childity as well as femininity by expecting the girl to express a certain timbre of voice, naivety of interpretation and absence of sensuality. Meanwhile, the girl herself contributes to the childing of the music, musical body and musical situation by leaning on alternative quality measures of voice belonging to other genred practices than children's music as it is framed in her music classroom. She is a skilful player still in the game, albeit as a troublesome rule breaker, having her musical agency and individuality become visible in the school discourse and, in that sense, be paradoxically validated by the teacher.

The social, aesthetic and subjectifying childing of music may be even more readily validated when performed by players with legitimate voices in the prevailing discursive practice, especially voices that are taken for granted and thus appear to represent something neutral or even to non-represent. In school, teachers may be such influential, genring agents. As previously described, one of the ways in which musical gentrification in education happens is by a strategic or even unplanned re-genring of the music at hand to fit immediate pedagogical purposes and contexts. In some cases, this entails simplification rather than refinement and displays of pedagogical rather than musical connoisseurship on the part of the teacher. The result might be the alienation of pupils who, at the outset, identified themselves with and through the music. A telling example is the way that school music is genred as 'rap' and 'hip-hop' through procedures which adapt the music, lyrics and musicianship to the imagined concerns and capacities of primary and even lower secondary school children, and to their formative social education. Assignments that task pupils (often via group work) with 'writing their own rap' tend to generate texts about friendship, kindness, peace and care for the environment (Ellefsen, 2021). Rap music also presents a welcome case for morally educating children and youth about the demeaning sexualisation of the female body, masculine stereotyping and bad language (Skjelstad and Ellefsen, 2024). Furthermore, when genring rap and hip-hop as a historical trajectory and practice, teachers choose an American musical narrative, thus avoiding confronting Norwegian children with the potentially charged and complicated social issues latent in Norwegian music historicity (Ellefsen, 2021). All in all, when music is genred as rap or hip-hop for educational purposes, the musicological focus on musical and socio-historical protest is adapted and attenuated in favour of a more neutral craft and utility perspective. Moreover, the socio-aesthetic fabric is childed – that is, re-imagined and re-purposed as a vehicle for a child's self-expression and self-understanding – as conceived and allowed for within the school structures of power and knowledge.

Genring as play

If music education can be considered a game, genring is a key strategy of playing. Indeed, as we have argued in this chapter, the game can hardly be played without acts of genring. As genring is a performative procedure which produces the effects of truth, it maintains the apparent autonomy of the game as an aesthetic, non-profit, pure practice. It obscures the players' exchanging of symbolic and material capital and conflates the game's dual character in favour of purity.

That the games of music education are about power (in both the Foucauldian and Bourdieuian senses) as well as pleasure is not a radical stance among researchers, politicians, teachers and other invested players. The last decade in particular has shown an increased interest in the powers and politics of music and music education, with particular attention being directed towards inclusionary and exclusionary music educational practices and racialised and gendered discourses. However, in pursuing equity, the field at large still tends to act as if the game's dual character is a flaw to be fixed or, at least, as if the pure side is more proper, more ethical, than that of power. Therefore, music educational discourse includes the illusion of an end goal where negotiations of capital and positions are history, because the true, universally accessible aesthetic powers of music have overcome the need for human conflict and strife. This also has the unfortunate effect that, when recognising and acknowledging the double game of music education, one risks undermining the self-same 'true aesthetic powers'. When calling attention towards negotiations of capital and power, one risks devaluing music and music education.

Bull's (2019) ethnography of four youth classical music groups in England, for example, received harsh critique for reducing children's classical musicking to a social, strategic and middle-class power game (Whale, 2022). In our opinion, however, Bull provides good descriptions of the youth groups as ordinary, everyday, aesthetic practices. The participants play, enjoy, experience and are empowered in and through their music, not primarily to achieve status but because it feels meaningful and enjoyable. However, their musicking is also a game of social status, and their experience of aesthetic meaningfulness comes also from experiencing a feeling of rightness or properness and belonging to a certain socio-aesthetic regime. This is true for all musicking. Art and music, as Bourdieu has noted, represent an extremely effective arena for social negotiation and distinction (1984, 1992/1996). What Bull (2019) warns against is the hidden nature of the middle-classed game of classical music. She calls our attention to the institutionalised structure of the game, which creates and naturalises benefits for certain groups of people.

In this book, our agenda is to insist on the duality of all music educational activity and to acknowledge the relevance and productivity of the field of power. To deny the productivity of human negotiations of capital and power is to trivialise the ways in which music matters – indeed, to trivialise the potential of music education as social and individual, economic and aesthetic, pure and powerful, play. We will expand more on this main point in the concluding chapter. For now, and to return to the matter of genres and genring, the genrifying cultural work being performed by music educational players – individuals, groups and institutions – across the various games being played in the field shows how the duality of these games works productively, with inclusionary as well as exclusionary effects.

Of course, genring could be conceptualised as a music education game of its own. However, its analytical value, we find, is even higher when conceived of as a strategy of play which is learned and applied across a range of games. Genring, then, 'is not a "discursive practice" in itself; rather, it might be understood as one of the ways discourse practices (itself). In other words, genring can be comprehended as one of the ways by which discourse and discursive power/knowledge are exercised, sustained, challenged, and/or changed' (Ellefsen, 2022: 62). Genre concepts are widely used in the music field, primarily to describe the musical qualities of a piece. However, the significance of genre extends beyond its musical implications. Genre terminology plays a crucial role in the negotiations of social positions, relationships and power structures within the music industry as well as within games of music education, research, politics and everyday life. It provides a means of categorising people and musical expressions, placing them within knowledge and value hierarchies. This categorisation also influences the distribution of symbolic and economic capital in the field. Players in the double games of music and music education may claim to surpass genre boundaries, but they often do so by implicitly defining and delimiting themselves from existing genres. Therefore, genre is not only a tool for discussing music but is also a social practice that shapes the dynamics and hierarchies within the music fields. Indeed, the obviousness of a music field's use of genre terminology leads us to overlook the importance of genre and genring when playing with and within the social positions, relationships and power structures of the music field. Revisiting the point made by Bourdieu and Wacquant (1992) about players' creative power, play strategies, like genring, work by opening possibilities for subjects to play in multiple ways. No matter how they play, however, they subject themselves to the game, becoming players as they do. Genring is a subjectivising procedure where players establish meaningful 'relations of self-mastery or self-knowledge' (Foucault, 2000b: 87). In this capacity, genring, as an analytical concept, sheds light upon the processes that enforce and maintain contemporary socio-economic dynamics and classed subject positions. Thus, acknowledging genre as a social meaning-creating practice in general and as a strategy in the double game of music education specifically enables us to continuously consider which positions are given legitimacy and support and which ones are deprioritised and perhaps even denied.

Note

1 The activities of schools of music and arts are, in the advisory curriculum framework, divided into three programmes: breadth, core and depth. The depth programme should be offered to a limited selection of students with special qualifications and interest in the art discipline (Norwegian Council for Schools of Music and Performing Arts, 2016).

5

Musical parenting and the child as investment

Petter Dyndahl, Anne Jordhus-Lier, Ingeborg Lunde and Siw Graabræk Nielsen

The ambiguous game(s) of musical parenting in late modern society

As stated in the first chapter, there are two forms or levels of the term 'game at play' in this book. On the one hand, games are referred to in the plural, meaning the variety of particular practices of recognised social interactions being played according to specific, established rules. In this chapter, the interrelational social fields that encompass parenting and music (education and upbringing) constitute several variants of such social games, which will be described and discussed in detail. To do this, however, it is necessary to delve into the dual logic that is inherent in the book's concept of the double game (singular), which points towards an overriding structure that forms a social framework that works on its own terms independently of the rules and regulations of specific games. The following sections therefore have two functions. Firstly, they fulfil the need for a theoretical approach that takes into account the complex ambiguity of parenting in late modern society, precisely by seeing parenting as a game in general and of music education in particular. Secondly, by reviewing previous research, concrete aspects of the symbolic economy that apply to parenting as a game are made visible. These in turn form the basis for the empirically based analyses that follow.

Music and parenting in terms of theory and research studies

If one looks at the research literature on music and parenting, it may immediately seem as if several multifaceted dimensions are taken into account. Koops (2020), for example, makes a conceptual distinction between, on the one hand, *parenting musically*, or 'using music to accomplish non-musical goals, e.g., to support social, cognitive, or kinaesthetic development' (2020: 2), and, on the other hand, *musical parenting*, which she interprets as 'supporting children's musical development through activities at home, at school, and in the community' (2020: 2). The development of the two concepts is grounded in ethnographic case studies conducted over the course of one year in the metropolitan Cleveland area in Ohio, United States, and is discussed through aspects of music and parenting in relation to home life, media, community, schooling and more. Moreover, Koops is careful to emphasise that the 'relationship between parenting musically and musical parenting can be understood as a continuum or axis, with parenting goals on one end and musical goals on the other' (2020: 7), and she further complicates the picture by pointing out that, in a given context, parental couples or different parents might perceive the situation or the action as one or the other of the two taking place, respectively. In addition, she expands on Small's (1998) notion of *musicking* by differentiating between *practical musicking*, referring to musicking that has a goal, such as 'calming a child, passing the time while in a traffic jam, or acquiring skills on the piano sufficient to pass the percussion entry test in fifth grade' (Koops, 2020: 10), and *relational musicking*, meaning musicking that is characterised by creating or deepening relationships with family, peers or oneself – for example, by 'listening to music as a parent-child duo just for fun, going to concerts together, or a child composing a song on a keyboard to express frustration with school' (2020: 10). Again, Koops emphasises that musicking can be a combination of both its practical and the relational aspects.

Put together, the axes 'parenting musically~musical parenting' and 'practical~relational musicking' form an analytical framework or grid that Koops finds suitable for capturing a number of multidimensional possibilities regarding the relationships between parenting and musicking. However, although both conceptual distinctions may seem productive, and not least nuanced in Koops' emphasis that they represent subtle variations along a continuum, her model lacks sufficient grounding in social theory that may help to conceptualise the aforementioned double dimensions of the game metaphor more clearly, which is an ambition for this book. What is more, a continuum does not take sufficient account of the fact that things may happen at the same time – i.e., that the music often has several functions at the same time and within the same practice. Education in and through music takes place in such a simultaneity, with all that it entails, and this is important in connection with the double games that musical parenting represents. This does not mean that our chapter cannot benefit from Koops' conceptual development and distinction. In several ways, she also points beyond her self-imposed limitations – for example, when she indicates how relational musicking is a significant factor in the work that people do with their own and with their children's social and cultural identity (not to mention *habitus*) by quoting the following excerpt from Small:

> How we relate is who we are. If that is so, then those taking part in this [a symphony concert] or any other musical event are, at some level of awareness, saying, to themselves, to one another and to anyone who may be taking notice, *This is who we are*. (Small, 1998: 43)

Also, when referring to how Ilari and Young (2016) describe musical parenting as the 'beliefs, values, attitudes, and behaviors of parents toward their children's musical experiences' (2016: 4), Koops (2020: 4) indicates that there might be something else behind the more or less aware or intentional approach to parenting that she otherwise seems to imply – at least when it comes to how society's long-established beliefs, values, attitudes and acknowledged parental behaviours (i.e., the rules of play) get through to the players of the game.

Although we acknowledge Koops' conceptual nuances as significant, it is nevertheless the latter, border-crossing mindset she hints at that becomes most important in this context. In order to maintain our focus on exactly that, we have chosen to use *musical parenting* as an overarching term that covers the content that Koops defines as belonging to both 'parenting musically~musical parenting' and 'practical~relational musicking', not least because both of these might represent ways of seeing the child as a matter of investment with different social and/or cultural yields. If it may become necessary to clarify distinctions according to Koops' terminology, we can still do so.

For her part, Ilari (2018) brings to the fore a broader social and historical contextual framework for the comprehension of musical parenting and music education. She relies on Bronfenbrenner's (2001) bioecological theory of human development when she describes parenting as a central mechanism in the transfer of cultural values between generations, and as a 'complex interplay between sources of support and stress in a child's life, as well as the interactions between them' (Ilari, 2018: 46). Bronfenbrenner's theory is built around the four aspects of *Process*, *Person*, *Context* and *Time*, which form the so-called PPCT model (Bronfenbrenner, 2001). Ilari then uses the bioecological theory of human development and the PPCT model as a lens through which to situate, interpret and discuss what she summarises as musical parenting studies, which are taken from the disciplines of music psychology, sociology and music education. The survey of these studies is divided into the themes 'Musical parenting in a developmental perspective', 'Musical parenting of young performers' and 'Musical parenting in Western contemporary societies'. To a certain extent, one can say that the first two themes correspond to Koops' divisions of parenting musically and musical parenting as well as to practical and relational musicking, respectively. However, contrary to Koops' strong interest in and justification of parenting musically, there is a tendency in Ilari's authorship to see musical parenting in the light of a formal, institutionalised conception of music education, in which the music teacher represents a key player. For example, she ends a section on musical parenting with a developmental perspective applied to early childhood with the following summary: 'By attending to parental cognitions, music teachers may be better equipped to work with young children' (Ilari, 2018: 48). In a similar way, this time emphasising what is instrumental for musical outcomes, at the expense of relational musicking, Ilari sums up the section in which she examines studies of the musical parenting of young performers by focusing on the importance of parental music engagement and values as the strongest preconditions for music achievement (2018: 49).

It is obvious that such a focus would be limiting for the purpose of this chapter, which goes far beyond considerations of musical parenting in relation to school-like music education aims and practices. However, notwithstanding these facts, Ilari also criticises some of the research studies she has reviewed for having 'left out vital influences at the macrosystem and chronosystem levels. These influences include parental conceptions of childhood and their associations to specific social and cultural groups in specific historical periods' (2018: 49). Under the previously mentioned heading 'Musical parenting in Western contemporary societies' in the survey, she therefore highlights some late modern tendencies towards what she, using Bronfenbrenner's terminology, describes as 'macro-time issues' (2018: 49). According to Ilari, the issues that emerge most clearly relate to redefinitions of the conceptions of childhood, as well as the intensification of parenting. This corresponds to a large extent with how current issues regarding childhood and parenting have been described and discussed in the general research literature on these topics during recent decades. We will therefore pursue the same course.

However, we find that the systems theory-inspired understanding of individual and environment as being mutually dependent on each other and acting in an interplay, in which a time dimension has also been added, as insufficient to capture the dual nature of the game of musical parenting in late modern society. The main reason for this is that systems theory fails to analyse and conceptualise the culturally established rules according to which the particular practices of social interactions are being played, and also does not bring out the overriding structures that form a social framework that works on its own terms, independently of the rules and regulations of specific sociological games. Instead, when Bronfenbrenner (2001) describes the system levels and various factors that influence how individuals are socialised into a culture in terms of micro (e.g., parent–child musical interaction), meso (e.g., triadic interplay between child–parent–teacher), exo (e.g., music media experiences) and macro (e.g., ideologies and values surrounding music and parenting) levels of interaction, respectively, he simultaneously wants to distance himself from a more conflict-orientated sociological approach to how social structures affect the individual, and vice versa. This chapter has a different level of ambition in terms of examining how musical parenting is inextricably woven into a double game that both regulates and is regulated by social constructions of parenthood as well as childhood, which represents a coherent dynamic approach compared to the rather static division ranging from closer (micro) to more distant (macro) levels of interaction, as seen from the individual centre. Although the distance between the micro and macro levels should also be considered here as a continuum, the same problem arises as with Koops (2020) in that the model does not sufficiently convey the complex simultaneity within which the two levels of games are played out.

Conceptions of childhood

When speaking of conceptions of childhood, it still makes sense to refer to Ariès' (1962) historical study *Centuries of Childhood*, which was published in French in 1960 and in the English translation two years later. By claiming that there was no childhood in the modern sense in the Middle Ages, but that it was 'invented' in the fourteenth and fifteenth centuries (among other things, due to the new emphasis on education), Ariès laid the foundation for understanding childhood as a historical and social construction. This was followed up by next-generation childhood sociologists James and Prout (1990) and historians such as Hendrick (1997), where the former made the following statement in their seminal book *Constructing and Reconstructing Childhood*, in which childhood was:

> to be understood as a social construction. That is, the institution of childhood provides an interpretive frame for understanding the early years of human life. In these terms it is biological immaturity rather than childhood which is a universal and natural feature of human groups, for ways of understanding this period of human life – the institution of childhood – vary cross-culturally. (Prout and James, 1990: 3)

The conceptions of childhood therefore vary in time and space. Accordingly, at the turn of the millennium, current childhood trends were described from a Scandinavian perspective by Rasmussen (2001) using the following six categories.

The institutionalisation of childhood

This tendency is two-sided, as it accommodates both the fact that children live and spend much of their time in institutions, such as preschool, school and leisure activities, and that children's lives are largely organised, managed and formed according to institutionalised goals. In retrospect, it can be argued that the increased influence of neoliberalism in pedagogy and education has further strengthened this tendency.

The technologisation of childhood

The historical development of childhood is largely linked to the development of technology and the media, whether this is seen as positive or negative, and at the turn of the millennium the presence and use of technology was a matter of course for children. Later, the development of online and social media (among others) has brought children's interaction with technology to an even more pervasive level.

The commercialisation of childhood

Childhood and children's lives have become a well-established area of economic investment. Rasmussen particularly highlights the children's culture industry, which he believes is one of the most important regulators of childhood. This happens not least because children in prosperous societies increasingly have their own money at their disposal. Later, children's opportunities for economic action are further enhanced by online shopping and digital money transfers.

The detraditionalisation of childhood

Traditional culture and parental relationships have suffered a loss of naturalness, which means that what becomes natural instead is that everything can be negotiated. Flexibility and change have become a condition for more and more people, including children. One consequence is that the distinction between childhood, youth and adulthood becomes less obvious.

The differentiation of childhood

Children live their lives in a number of separate and independent, yet connected, everyday arenas, such as home and family (which itself may be differentiated into several homes and families), pre-school or school, friends (perhaps in different places), media, leisure activities, local environment (perhaps several environments), consumption, work and duties. This means that, from a very young age, children have to live relatively independent lives that require a set of different social and cultural skills. What is especially new in the twenty-first century (not least reinforced by the COVID-19 pandemic) is that many of these arenas are now digital.

The politicisation of childhood

This is also a two-sided tendency. On the one hand, childhood is made the subject of overarching political measures – for example, with regard to laws, regulation and institutionalisation. This is how childhood is controlled from above. On the other hand, there is increased attention to children's rights, which means that children are treated as human beings in their own right.

Rasmussen's childhood categories form mutually constitutive premises for the total setting that we understand as the double game of musical parenting in – in this case, Nordic – late modern society. In this context, it is important to emphasise that, even though the category relating to commercialisation is the only one that explicitly points out economic investments in childhood, all other categories also open the way to thinking concretely about the child as an investment in relation to the symbolic economy, with possible social and cultural returns for the child itself, the parents and the family. In Rasmussen's interpretation from 2001, these tendencies were seen as an indication of children's culture adopting new assumptions and forms of expression. They balance a typical Scandinavian criticism of societal trends with considerable faith in the child as a competent participant in their own life.

Childhood as being and becoming

This line of thinking also includes the conceptions of the *child as being* and the *child as becoming* (James and Prout, 1990), which means that investments in children and childhood in the present involve future prospects. This is a profoundly constituted idea that regulates ideas, actions and structures regarding children and childhood; contemporary settings and investments not only have an impact on contemporary children's lives, but also on how these children are able to care for themselves and handle their lives once they have become adults. Moreover, it involves the idea that today's children are the next generation's politicians and parents.

However, by using James and Prout's general considerations about the child as both being and becoming to shift attention away from the Nordic context to a more international one, we can see that, from one point in time, especially in the English-speaking world, a notion had taken hold that children's culture as well as childhood as such were under severe threat, as postulated by Postman's (1982) civilisation- and media-critical book *The Disappearance of Childhood*. In the wake of the widespread, but controversial, prophecy that childhood was disappearing in the modern Western world due to the interplay of childhood juvenilisation and the infantilisation of adulthood, in the sense that children cross into the adult world and adults cross into the world of the child, Prout (2000) nonetheless interpreted, from a British perspective, the paradoxes of childhood in a slightly more balanced way: 'On the one hand, there is an increasing tendency to see children as individuals with a capacity for self-realisation and, within the limits of social interdependency, autonomous action; on the other, there are practices directed at a greater surveillance, control and regulation of children' (Prout, 2000: 304). Cunningham (2006) elaborates on this by observing that adults are now more concerned about children and their safety than ever before. He claims that children are monitored more closely today because they are seen as being endangered by their engagement with the adult world. According to Cunningham's analysis, today's children are characterised by being innocent but corruptible, which makes them vulnerable and at risk. Stearns (2009) draws centuries-old lines back to Freud, Erikson and Piaget as the basis for the development of the so-called 'attachment theory', which emphasises the absolute need for parental (typically maternal) loving nurturing as a prerequisite for lifelong mental health. Faircloth (2014: 44) argues that 'the underlying paradigm developed by parenting experts – that experience in early infancy has lifelong implications and that this period of life is one entailing enormous risk – is now so taken for granted as to be unremarkable in contemporary parenting culture'. There is therefore a presumption of children, she continues, 'as, *de facto*, vulnerable, and at risk, which is the most distinct and important aspect of the social construction of childhood today. This has profound implications for the definition of the mothering and fathering roles' (Faircloth, 2014: 44). Likewise, it constitutes an important prerequisite for the intensification of parenting that Ilari (2018) described as also being a characteristic of musical parenting in Western contemporary societies.

In the wake of this brief historical, spatial and systematic summary of childhood conceptions, it seems reasonable to recognise several perspectives as valid, whether they focus on children's own cultural expressiveness in a given historical, socio-cultural and technological context or on childhood vulnerability and dependence on parents and guardians in an increasingly threatening world. What appears to be particularly interesting in this context, however, is that the respective perspectives can be seen as being part of the same game. Whether children's culture is interpreted as an arena for the exploration of new borders and forms of expression, or as an area of responsibility that calls for particular readiness and vigilance, both offer opportunities to play the double game of musical parenting in ways that are, however, only hinted at in some of the referenced childhood research. The ability to interpret what are the historically and culturally legitimate forms of (musical) parenting, obviously related to normative validity criteria for what and how children and childhood should be, is a prerequisite for parental manoeuvring in ways that, in the symbolic sense, are to be considered as investments, which in turn may provide profitable social and cultural returns. This of course leads to the recognition that parenting is also historically and socially constructed, in all the compound complexity this entails. Here, however, it is necessary to provide a reminder of the obvious fact that parenting also relates to inequalities, not least in terms of globalisation and social class. In fact, when it comes to musical childhoods, Young, supported by Prout (2004), points out that 'there may be more similarities across children of the middle classes internationally than between middle and lower classes within the same nation' (Young, 2009a: 695).

In the next section, research on (Western) parenting trends is reviewed, with particular emphasis on the form of (middle- to upper-class) parenting that is characterised as intensive parenting.

Parenting as a social construct

As with childhood, a foundation has been laid for considering parenting as being socially constructed – for example, in the intensive version indicated previously. In his book *Paranoid Parenting*, Furedi (2002) begins the 'Parent Identity' section by stating that parenting is not the same as child rearing. He links the latter to societies where 'children are expected to participate in the work and routine of the community and are not regarded as requiring special parenting attention or care' (Furedi, 2002: 106), and where it was assumed that the children would mature naturally. Instead, he connects the concept of parenting to modern society, in which:

> [t]he belief that children require special care and attention evolved alongside the conviction that what adults did mattered to their development. These sentiments gained strength and began to influence public opinion in the nineteenth century. The work of mothering and fathering was now endowed with profound importance. It became defined as a distinct skill that could assure the development of character traits necessary for a successful life. Alternatively, the absence of this skill – poor nurturing – could deprive a child of a positive future. This view of parenting is closely linked to the decline of large households and the rise of more individualized nuclear family arrangements. Once children are seen as the responsibility of a mother and father rather than of a larger community the modern view of parenting acquires salience. (Furedi, 2002: 106)

The term 'intensive parenting' originates from Hays' (1996) description of an approach she termed *intensive mothering*. Hays associates this ideal of motherhood with female professionals in the US in the 1990s:

> Why do so many professional class employed women find it necessary to take the kids to swimming and judo and dancing and tumbling classes, not to mention orthodontists and psychiatrists and attention-deficit specialists? Why is the human bonding that accompanies breast-feeding considered so important that elaborate contraptions are now manufactured to allow children to suckle on mothers who cannot produce milk? Why are there copious courses for babies, training sessions in infant massage, sibling-preparedness workshops,

and designer fashions for two-year olds? Why must a 'good' mother be careful to 'negotiate' with her child, refraining from the demands for obedience to an absolute set of rules? (Hays, 1996: 6)

Faircloth paraphrases Hays' definition of intensive mothering when she explains intensive parenting as 'child-centred, expert-guided, emotionally absorbing, labour intensive, and financially expensive' (Faircloth, 2014: 48). Although not all parents exercise intensive parenting, just as not all working mothers practice intensive mothering, she claims that it has become a kind of ideal, a social or 'cultural script' (2014: 31) or a benchmark against which parents negotiate what can pass as successful parenting in Western, late modern societies. However, there are differences regarding the performance of the cultural script when it comes to, for example, class, gender and ethnicity.

A pattern of intensive parenting that handles these cultural parameters is Lareau's (2011) concept of *concerted cultivation*, which is a middle- to upper-class strategy with the intention of designing children's extracurricular lives and social development to maximise outcome in terms of, ultimately, academic and economic success. A number of music education programmes, such as talent development programmes, schools of music and arts as well as private tuition, can be linked to concerted cultivation and will be discussed in detail later in the chapter and in the book. However, Conkling (2019) has challenged Lareau's findings through her own study of an after-school music programme – as with Lareau's study, also situated in the US – in which children from a wide range of socio-economic backgrounds participated. Conkling found that practices and discourses with regard to parenting and community music did not operate at the level of race, ethnicity or social class, as Lareau had suggested, but instead operated at a local network level. This implies that strong local attachment (in this case) created a sense of community that overcame the dividing lines between class, ethnicity and race that Lareau found in her material. Lee's (2021) study of social class, intensive parenting norms and parental values for children in Hong Kong, however, shows that there were still subtle differences in parental values tied to class position, which contributed to maintaining class inequality and social reproduction, although there was – according to the author – a global increasing trend among both middle and working-class families to raise their children more intensively, and that social class differences in parenting beliefs and choices for their children had accordingly become more understated.

As indicated so far, parenting is at least both gendered and classed. In order to go into the broader intersectionality that obviously permeates parenting, it is necessary to also look at issues relating to ethnicity and race. In this regard, a few British studies have employed concerted cultivation as a theoretical lens when addressing race, ethnicity and gender as parts of an intersectional perspective on parenting (Mukherjee and Barn, 2021; Rollock, 2007; Vincent, 2017; Vincent and Martin, 2002; Vincent *et al.*, 2012). They argue for colouring concerted cultivation as they especially seek to understand 'the ways in which race and class (and gender) intersect in particular contexts in particular times' (Vincent *et al.*, 2012: 434), rather than seeing classed and racialised parenting as separate phenomena. More specifically, Vincent and colleagues (2012) find that Black Caribbean-heritage middle-class parents, through emphasising extracurricular activities such as music and sports, uphold a liminal position in seeking 'to raise and develop their children as both middle class and Black' in the UK (428). However, these parents' investments in concerted cultivation do not only serve to maintain their classed positions and their Black identity, but also to act as a 'potential defence' against racism in the form of 'still-pervasive low teacher expectations of Black children, especially boys' (Vincent, 2017: 548). This 'colouring' of concerted cultivation is also prominent in Mukherjee and Barn's (2021) study of middle-class British Indian parents' educational strategies. They identify two interlinked processes between concerted cultivation and race and ethnicity: 'cultural (re)production through organised leisure' and '(anti)racism and leisure' (532) which combine the parents' racial parenting strategies with those of concerted cultivation. For example, by investing in ethnic leisure activities (e.g., Punjabi lessons, cricket, Bollywood dancing) in order to gain 'ethnic cultural capital', the parents emphasise how these activities also 'were intended to unlock the child for new avenues for future transnational mobility' (532) to China or India. Another example shows how the parents also have to take racism into account as part of their child's future life in the UK, and act accordingly, by choosing

leisure activities that foster physical skills that may be used to protect the child from violence (e.g., Taekwondo classes).

Regardless of the intersectional contents, form and degree of
concerted cultivation, this approach to parenting should generally
be described as a future-orientated project. As such, intensive parenting is related to the investment of cultural capital in its embodied
and objectified forms (Bourdieu, 1986), and Skeggs (2004) pin-
points how the concept of investment signals an exchange value in
the child's and parents' future. Investments in cultural properties in
order to accrue value are therefore only made 'when we can conceive of a future in which the value can have a use', Skeggs claims
(2004: 146).

However, with regard to class differences in parenting style in the
US, Lareau (2011) pointed out that, in contrast to concerted cultivation, working-class parents were more likely to see the children as
complete in themselves rather than as the adults they would become
– a type of parenting she termed as the accomplishment of natural
growth parenting. But of course, this is just as much socio-econom-
ically determined as a 'natural' way of growing up. Reay (2017) has
shown the extent to which working-class parenting in the UK fails
to achieve social mobility for children in neoliberal societies' educational institutions. Since the mid-1980s there has been a growing
outsourcing of education and learning to the home, and she claims
that: 'As a consequence, parents, and especially mothers, are now
expected to become home-based teachers for their children' (Reay,
2017: 67). However, for the many who do not have the time, there
has been a huge growth in the offer of extracurricular activities and
private tuition for children. This favours those who already have the
money and resources, and helps to reinforce the class inequalities in
parental involvement: 'Material resources, educational knowledge,
parents' own educational experiences and the amount of domestic
and educational support parents, and in particular mothers, had
access to, add up to an important class difference that impacted on
their relationship to their children's education and the texture of
their involvement in schooling' (Reay, 2017: 72).

What is more, Faircloth (2014: 44ff) argues that today's intensification of parenting has gone so far that one can speak of an inflation of the parenting role. The view of the child as being particularly
vulnerable means that parents assume the role of 'risk-managers',

unless they are considered to pose a risk themselves. This does not necessarily only apply to 'bad' parents, such as the abusive father or the mother who smokes and drinks during pregnancy, but may eventually apply to all parents:

> It has also been noted that the risk parents present to children is not only considered significant when parents are considered to be 'bad'. Parenting is also problematized where parents are construed to be 'unaware' or 'out of touch'. This happens for example in discussions about the alleged threat represented to children by technologies parents do not understand (such as the Internet), or in the debate about parental 'lack of awareness' of how much exercise their children take or of the calorie content of the food they feed their children. (Lee *et al.*, 2010: 295)

The inflation of the role of the parent entails that parenting is perceived as increasingly essential for the child, but consequently also for the adult's identity as a parent. Faircloth (2013) investigated this in connection with her research concerning mothers who breastfeed their children 'to full term' (i.e., until the child is between one and eight years old) – a practice she has characterised as 'militant lactivism'. In that regard, she also refers more generally to Furedi's rather sardonic, but nonetheless apt, description of how intensive parenting is probably as much about constructing the adults' own parental, as well as social and cultural, identities as it is about caring for the child:

> So parenting is not simply child rearing. It is also how adults construct their lives through and in interaction with their children. Adults do not simply live their lives through children but, in part, develop their identity through them. When expectant fathers and mothers debate what name to give to a child, it is often obvious that they are using the occasion to express themselves. A 'cool' name for a newborn invites the conclusion that the parents are also 'cool'. An unusual name provides a hint that the parents are exceptionally clever. Parents who play classical music to their baby may do so because it reflects their agenda and not necessarily that of the child. Parents who pierce their infant's ears, dress them like little adults, or insist that they become vegetarians are in part making statements about themselves. Through raising children, parents are also inventing themselves. (Furedi, 2002: 107)

Of course, it is easy to make sarcastic comments about parents who apparently do not see how obviously they sometimes mark their own (desired) economic, social and/or cultural position through investment in or with the help of their children. However, this is an obvious part of the game: *illusio* must be sustained. Perhaps it is more interesting to ask why they are playing this kind of double game. Does it come from a fear of not following the specified cultural script one is expected to follow? Or, from the opposite perspective, what is the gain that can be achieved by participating in the game? But how conscious are the choices parents make about this in reality? Faircloth suggests that intensive parenting 'has not emerged "from below" or spontaneously from parents themselves, but rather as a product of cultural developments and influences at the levels of expertise, policy, and intergenerational transmission' (2014: 48). In addition, it is crucial to consider as cultural development and influence what has already been referred to in various ways as identity, especially that which originates from underlying levels that include class, gender, ethnicity and, not least, the ubiquitous economy, in both its material and symbolic forms.

Against this background, and as already mentioned several times in this chapter, parenting can be regarded as a form of investment, in both a concrete and a metaphorical sense. On the one hand, parents obviously invest in their children's future well-being and success in many areas – not least because many parents want the next generation to maintain their social position or to increase it by facilitating upward social mobility. On the other hand, they also invest in their own and their family's social position and status here and now – for example, by consolidating their social class affiliation or aspiring to rise up in the class hierarchy. Concerted cultivation would be a blatant middle-class example of the latter. However, this should not necessarily be seen as cynical, calculated positioning. We therefore support Faircloth's opinion that it does not arise spontaneously from parents themselves, but that it is part of their socialisation into or cultural interpretation of how the double game works. That which we, in this chapter, have allowed several scholars, directly or indirectly, to characterise as parental identity work can therefore be considered as cultural practices and influences at the basic societal level, which constitute a substantial part of Bourdieu's (1977) notion of *habitus* as was explained in Chapter 1.

In his own words, *habitus* refers to 'a subjective but not individual system of internalised structures, schemes of perception, conception, and action common to all members of the same group or class' (1977: 86). For Bourdieu, it was important to emphasise that the *habitus* is embodied and exists as dispositions or patterns of action that the individual applies in practical situations and contexts. This must also apply to musical parenting in late modern societies.

Double games of musical parenting

In order to get closer to musical parenting as a double game – or more precisely, as a set of games that can be characterised by various forms of ambiguity, that also accommodates the understanding of the child as an investment – we find it useful to recall the concepts of capital (Bourdieu, 1986), in addition to *habitus*. It makes sense to use both forms of what Bourdieu calls symbolic capital (i.e., cultural and social capital) in connection with musical parenting, and also to explore the various forms of cultural capital in particular, whether they are embodied, objectified or institutionalised, simply because there are so many ways, in so many different contexts, in which the double game unfolds. The use of these concepts makes it possible to apply to musical parenting the fact that (parental) *habitus* enables the individual (the player) to understand society (the rules of the game), while society (the game) also resides in the body (of the player).

Before we discuss this in more detail, using a couple of empirical examples, the mentioned point about parents investing in their children's future opportunities, while at the same time investing in their own and their family's social position and status, can be effectively illustrated with the help of Trulsson's (2015) examination of the narratives of parents in Sweden with an immigrant background regarding the significance of music education in their family lives. These were families who had experienced a drop in status as newcomers to their new country, where their previous education may not have been approved or where they experienced other barriers to entering working life at the same level as before in terms of income and prestige. A specific concern of the study was to examine the importance and functions of music education for their children. It emerged that music education in music schools or private lessons, preferably for what have traditionally been considered prestigious classical instruments, such as the violin and piano, was deemed to be a potential means of social progress and integration for the second generation of immigrants. The hope was that this would function as a tool for 'social reconstruction' and, ultimately, as 'class remobility' for the family, who, with the help of intergenerational investment in cultural capital by means of music education, would thereby be raised from what could conceivably have been a temporary decline in class.

In the example given by Trulsson, it was probably no coincidence as to which music genre and instruments should contribute to raising social status. In the international research literature on classical music education, Hall (2018), for example, in her study of choir boys in Australia, describes how musicality is attributed to them by their parents, who thereby make financial, social and emotional investments over time, which are, however, explained as the middle-class parents' desire to see their children's inherent talent redeemed rather than as a story about especially the mothers' intensive involvement in their music education. In line with this, Bull (2019) shows through her study *Class, Control, and Classical Music* that 'classical music's mode of pedagogy shares a logic with middle class styles of parenting, and underpinning both is a shared form of selfhood' (2019: 7). Bull especially links the classical instrumental education and its traditional one-to-one pedagogy to 'the intensively shaped, individualized middle class self described in sociological studies of classed parenting' (2019: 7).

Although we also find many examples of this in the Norwegian context, we will describe and discuss some empirical examples from our own research concerning intensive musical parenting that include several music genres, as well as different ways of organising and practising music education and parenting. The cases therefore include both school-like and family-like situations, which occur in both institutional and home settings and are often characterised as teaching and upbringing, respectively, but which in this context are connected by the fact that it is musical parenting and the child as investment that are emphasised in the selected situations.

The first case builds on research in a contemporary Norwegian context concerning musical parenting in extracurricular municipal schools of music and arts (see Nielsen *et al.*, 2023a). The schools of music and arts are publicly financed and offer extracurricular activities in music and other art forms, where each municipality is required by current legislation to provide arts education for all children and adolescents (Norwegian Education Act, 1998, § 13–6). However, although there are no auditions, grades or final exams, only a limited group attends these schools, and the schools show indications of social and cultural exclusion (Berge *et al.*, 2019). In both the Norwegian and Swedish schools of this kind, children with an immigrant background and/or from families with low incomes and little education are more likely to be excluded, with the typical student in the Swedish schools of music and arts being a Swedish-born girl with well-educated parents (Berge *et al.*, 2019; Jeppsson and Lindgren, 2018). Earlier research has shown a strong connection between middle-class *habitus* and a 'school of music and arts-appropriate habitus', where the middle-class students and parents are more likely to fit in with the practices and cultures within the schools (Jeppsson and Lindgren, 2018).

In general, one can argue that, according to the parents in this study, the children's participation in extracurricular music activities such as the schools of music and arts is seen as important for the children's own sake, but also for the parents themselves and their family. By enrolling and supporting their children in these kinds of music activities, they perform musical parenting competently, but differently, and make investments of time, energy and money, albeit to different degrees. Some parents also emphasise that they make sacrifices on behalf of the family by doing this. Through interviews with parents of music students, we have explored differences in musical parenting as well as classed distinctions (Nielsen *et al.*, 2023b). Musical parenting among middle- and upper-class parents is therefore exercised as intensive musical parenting, albeit with different levels of intensity.

A few of the parents were particularly intensive in their musical parenting and investment in the children. For those, belonging to the upper class, it was a matter of going 'all in' in their parental involvement in the children's musical activities at the schools of music and arts. The musical parenting involved challenging and criticising the school's offering of music activities for not taking good enough care of their own child's talent, and, in that respect, they worried that what the school could provide was not enough to cater for their child's musical progression and future. They would therefore capitalise on their economic and cultural resources in order to provide extra teachers and musicians for music education activities at home. Alternatively, they considered moving to places where they could get better access to musical expertise. In this case, musical parenting involved being totally immersed in and centring their family life around the children's musical activities to such a degree that it becomes an all–consuming activity – spending not only a great amount of their economic resources but also benefits, such as holidays and leisure–time, to develop their child's talent, fully acknowledging that this comes at the expense of socialising with family and friends. However, it must be said that this degree of intensive musical parenting represented an exception and is more widespread in connection with organised talent development pro-grammes run by conservatories and music academies.

Although we have documented that the aforementioned level can be found in the schools of music and arts, we found moderately high levels of intensive musical parenting to be the norm here. This form of musical parenting implies that the parents, mainly belong-ing to the middle classes, primarily engaged in resolving all the practical issues that surfaced in relation to the child's music activi-ties. They did not necessarily become greatly involved in the child's practising at home or in ensemble activities, but they made sure that instruments were available and easily accessible at home. They particularly took pride in attending all concerts and treated these as important events also for the wider family.

The intensive parenting common to late modern society described previously by Furedi (2002), Faircloth (2014) and others, obviously matches how musical parenting is performed by the parents who were included in the study of the Norwegian schools of music and arts. In addition, we find Lareau's (2011) concept of concerted cul-tivation to be highly relevant when describing the parental prac-tices. The available ways of performing musical parenting and concerted cultivation related to extracurricular music activities are constructed through social and cultural practices, both historically and as an ongoing process. The notion of intensive parenting is not only negotiated by the parents, but also by the music teachers and headteachers through their practices and expectations concerning the parents. For them, musical parenting at relatively high levels of engagement and commitment is required, and they emphasise that *not* being involved or being disengaged as parents is problematic. In their experience, low-intensity parenting has led to some talented students falling behind and, in the worst case, dropping out of school.

This indicates that the schools of music and arts enable some forms of musical parenting – those that require a relatively high level of engagement and commitment – but not others, which might be understood in relation to the growing outsourcing of education and learning to the home, as described by Reay (2017), which entails reinforcing class inequalities in parenting. For example, as the performed cultural scripts of musical parenting in schools of music and arts involve expectations of outsourcing guidance of the child's practising between lessons to the parents, the exercising of less intensive or non-intensive levels of parenting may become invalid scripts to follow.

The cultural script of successful parenting differs only to a limited degree with regard to the musical genres and instruments taught. However, the exceptional intensive musical parenting described above was performed in the context of violin teaching within the classical music genre, which is in line with the findings of Hall (2018) and Bull (2019). The highest levels of intensity in parenting were also found to tie in with the upper-middle class and the upper class's sense of developing entitlement in their children, where developing the child by orchestrating 'organized leisure activities, [is seen as] an essential aspect of good parenting' (Lareau, 2011: 3).

The parents invest time, energy and money in their children's musical participation and future. These investments mostly concern individuals, but some also invest in the community around the child. This is, however, not only for the community's sake but also for the sake of the child, the parents and the family. By performing intensive musical parenting, therefore, the parents not only invest in their child's (musical) future but also in maintaining or increasing their own social status and identity (Faircloth, 2014; Lee *et al.*, 2010). The latter involves the idea that social success is connected to having children that participate and develop in musical activities, but also to being the parent that 'handles all aspects of life' – both their work and their leisure activities – in addition to following up on the children's activities. In that sense, investments made in the children's musical activities may also be understood as a way to accrue value in the future, not only for the child's sake but also for the sake of the family and the parents (Skeggs, 2004). As such, musical parenting is related to the investment of cultural capital (as music education) in its embodied and objectified forms (Bourdieu, 1986). Time-consuming involvement by both the child and the parents is required in order to produce the anticipated profits in the future through the child's music activities in the schools of music and arts.

Regarding the relationships between the school of music and arts and the broader conceptualisation of childhood, it is interesting to see that the perceptions of the child within this kind of music education could be understood according to at least two of Rasmussen's (2001) aforementioned categories – namely, the *institutionalisation of childhood*, as the children are organised, managed and formed according to institutionalised goals, and the *politicisation of childhood*, as the children's music making is regulated and institutionalised at the same time as the school is focusing on children's rights to express themselves and participate in making musical decisions (Jordhus-Lier *et al.*, 2023; Nielsen *et al.*, 2023a). The latter is also described by Heimonen (2003) in her study on extracurricular music education in Finland, Sweden, Germany and England. She found tensions between the general (i.e., law and legislation), where the state has a duty to secure conditions for music education, referred to as the 'right to an education', and the particular (i.e., the individual needs of each student), which points to individual needs regarding content connected to the child's-best-interest principle, referred to as the 'right to freedom in education' (Heimonen, 2003). Within the Norwegian context, Jordhus-Lier (2018) found tension in how 'everyone' (as in the aim of the school of music and arts to be for everyone) should be interpreted, either according to a breadth discourse, where social inclusion and the collective are important values, or a contrasting depth discourse, in which specialisation and individualism are central.

The institutionalisation and politicisation of childhood (Rasmussen, 2001) could also be seen in relation to children as beings and becomings (James and Prout, 1990), where the need for institutionalising is, in many ways, connected to the idea of children as becomings. With regard to the schools of music and arts, this is particularly present in the tension between the discourses of the institution as a school or as a leisure activity, as described by Jordhus-Lier (2018). Within the school discourse, children are mostly seen as becomings because of the focus on what they can become and what they can master, where progression, continuation and career pathways are central. The leisure activity discourse, however, is connected to children as beings because of the focus on children as what they are and not what they can become, whereby having fun and good experiences are central. The school discourse, and therefore the concept of children as becomings, is the most central in the school of music and arts field (Jordhus-Lier, 2018). This concept holds hegemonic status in the mentioned talent development programmes, such as junior conservatories (Stabell, 2018). The different ways of understanding the concept of childhood link directly to ways of performing (musical) parenting: do we as parents need to cater for our children? Is it our responsibility? How much effort do we need, or is expected of us, to put in? And which level of intensity in parenting is required for my child to achieve a good life in the future?

Bearing these questions in mind, we move on to the next case, which is based on a series of interviews with parents focusing on how the children used music in their everyday family life (see Vestad and Dyndahl, 2021) and displays a range of what parents consider to be risks for their children, and how they subtly try to minimise them. The example is thus played out at the intersection between forms of intensive parenting, which involve elements from what Koops (2020) designated as 'parenting musically~musical parenting' as well as 'practical~relational musicking', and late modern conceptions of childhood (Rasmussen, 2001), especially those characterised as the 'technologisation', the 'commercialisation' and the 'detraditionalisation' of childhood, respectively. However, the 'differentiation' of childhood is also affected indirectly, as there is a focus on one particular arena (namely, family life), but this is necessarily connected to a number of others, such as school, friends, media, leisure activities, local environment and consumption.

The research design was based on the fact that the informant families were lent a video recorder and asked to record any instance involving music that occurred in their home over the course of one week. The interviews started with the researchers watching the recordings together with each family and obtaining further details from them about what was going on in the various recorded events. The interview of particular interest here was conducted with the parents of five and seven–year-old daughters living in a wealthy suburb on the outskirts of a Norwegian city. The family was distinguished by the parents' broad musical taste, nuanced consideration of the music in their family life and articulate verbal dealings with music. Music was not their profession nor was it the subject of their academic degrees, but it was described as being an indispensable ingredient in their lives, filling their days from morning until night as they listened to music, sang children's songs together, watched music on television and went to concerts. In accordance with this, one of the parents' most pointed opinions was that:

> they would like to offer their children the real stuff: emotionally, cognitively, musically/aesthetically and, with regards to themes, including intelligent humour. The mother, though, also makes a point to not be a strict gatekeeper and exercise censorship. The parents would like the children to become conscious individuals with a critical sense and ability to make their own choices. 'But if they do not become conscious music listeners, that's all right, too', the mother sums up. (Vestad and Dyndahl, 2021: 71)

The parents obviously follow a cultural script that prescribes intensive parenting, but in a Scandinavian upper-middle-class way that apparently recognises the children as human beings in their own right (one dimension of the aforementioned 'politicisation' of childhood) and they therefore negotiate rather than command. The corresponding parenting style appears to be authoritative rather than authoritarian. During the interview, however, an issue that came up was which kinds of music the parents did not consider appropriate for their children. The parents mentioned hip-hop, music by child stars, commercial children's music and Scandinavian dance band music, in particular. Hip-hop, music by child stars and commercial children's music tend to bring teenage life and adulthood into children's lives too soon by introducing artists with sexualised appearances and songs with explicit lyrics, according to the parents. These kinds of reservations are consistent with a well-known set of attitudes towards the mentioned topic regarding vulnerable children and parents as risk-managers.

However, protecting children from Scandinavian dance band music seems to be something quite different when it comes to risk management. This music culture is widespread in the Nordic countries and has a strong intergenerational appeal in the communities in which it is valued. However, in parts of public discourse, it is predominantly considered to be unambiguously 'low-brow' and associated with working-class and/or rural culture (see Dyndahl, 2016). What was probably happening here was that the parents were attempting to safeguard the children from what they perceived as an indisputably 'poor taste in music' that could devalue their potential cultural capital.

In a more or less similar way, we can interpret the parents' opposition to commercialism as a distinguishing practice. The father in particular seems to rely on a discourse about commercial children's music that considers it to be simple-minded and unchallenging compared to 'the real stuff', which both parents think of as pop and rock music, such as the Beatles, the Rolling Stones, Michael Jackson and ABBA. With regard to choosing music that is produced for and intended for children, they also want to justify it in relation to corresponding quality criteria. In that respect, they consider the term 'intelligent humour' to be a sign of good quality that may equip children for life by developing their cognitive and emotional capacities, which stand out as crucial assets of social and developmental benefits in the parents' discussion of the family's shared musical repertoire.

So, although these parents provide a broad range of music genres to their children and introduce them to a variety of musical practices, negotiated boundaries exist. The proclaimed broad taste in music therefore has socially and culturally defined limitations, even if they have long since transcended the traditional distinctions of 'high' and 'low' culture within which Bourdieu (1984) operated. Nonetheless, the anatomy of musical taste is still sociological as well as aesthetic. Therefore, the distinctions the parents make on behalf of the family's interaction with music determine the children's status as individuals and their own social status as parents, and contribute to the social constitution of the family culture in ways that might be seen as a sophisticated form of concerted cultivation, or as the double game of musical parenting.

To summarise, in this section we have presented and discussed two empirical cases of musical parenting – one from schools of music and arts and one from a family home. They both manifest the double game of music and parenting, where social positioning is at stake, and reveal that it covers several considerations at the same time. Moreover, these parents' games of musical upbringing are not only about the present – that is, the ongoing musical practice and structures here and now – but are also about the parents' eye to the future on behalf of their children. Their children's futures are at stake, as well as their identities and status as parents (Furedi, 2002; Trulsson, 2015).

We have argued that previous research concerning musical parenting (a conception that we use to encompass all forms of parenting involving music) fails to address the child as a matter of investment, and that by these investments parents aim to achieve various social and/or cultural yields. We also stress that musical parenting is perhaps just as much about becoming a parent as about raising a child. Despite this, we argue that the double game of musical parenting does not imply emotionally detached parents or that these parents have false pretences. Rather, we argue that investing in one's children is highly legitimised and has become the doxa of Western, middle-class contemporary parenting, steeped in contemporary theories and conceptions of children and childhood. Parenting is a social construct, and there are numerous ways of bringing up a child. Intensive parenting, for example, which is a pivotal point of this chapter's discussion, is described as 'child-centred, expert-guided, emotionally absorbing, labour intensive, and financially expensive' (Faircloth, 2014: 48). Nevertheless, we argue that the subtle games that parents play are not always conscious and deliberate, as culturally well-established rules may be either explicitly or implicitly available to parents' choice making. A crucial question is *how* the investments in children are undertaken, *what they are*, more specifically, and *what they achieve* in specific cultural settings, as far as social positioning goes.

We see both empirical cases as examples of intensive parenting. The first is from a setting similar to those described as concerted cultivation (cf. Lareau, 2011), involving a more formal yet leisure-based music educational activity. It shows that this particular game of music education demands a lot from all participants, including the parents. Their performance is one of resourceful caretakers, who can scaffold and pave the way for their child by drawing on their *habitus* – socially, culturally and economically. Their efforts aim to serve their child's best interest in the here and now, aiming to reach the optimal realisation of a future mature artistic talent and the social position this offers. Their way of parenting also works to position themselves as 'good' parents of the (upper) middle class. Their efforts are highly visible to others and not only meet the standards of other parents, but also push them forward, making them stand out and appear very intensive (Faircloth, 2014: 48), almost to the extreme.

The second empirical case deals with a domestic kind of family, home-based musical parenting. The parents' cultivation of musical taste and the capacity to relate to music, and thereby ensuring their social positioning as reflexive middle-class parents, has a more subtle quality, in the sense that they appear to be searching, free and open to new ideas. The example shows a more ambiguous and covert game of musical parenting. The game is not guided by the rules of an institution, such as the school of music and arts or the path towards higher music education, but by broader and seemingly more diffuse and private taste hierarchies, a love for music and reflections on conceptions of childhood that involve less pressure and less specific career hopes on the children's behalf, and focus on emotional knowledge and competence together with building relations through music and musical practices. However, although genuine, regarding the best interest of their child, their seemingly innocent ways of acting as providers and gatekeepers of their daughters' music are part of their *habitus* and are nowhere near being innocent as far as social positioning goes. The demonstrated reflexivity on their children's behalf, their eloquent verbalisations of their likings and their intentions to make the children acquainted with a broad range of music, their own broad musical preferences and quite firm boundaries regarding what they do not like and what they do not find suitable for children – at least not for their children – reveals a kind of social position and positioning that sets the course for their daughters' musical endeavours as agentic, knowing and competent music lovers, and for themselves as parents as authoritative connoisseurs of music, which can again be considered intensive parenting, according to Faircloth's (2014) description, quoted previously. Also, the subtleness of their game of musical parenting stands out. They make the intense seem natural and relaxed, as if nothing is going on, while they fill the loss of self-evidence in child rearing (Rasmussen, 2001) firmly with (upper) middle-class values.

The subtleties of the game

It is easy to get caught up in the differences between the two examples from the previous section. However, they both include using music to achieve non-musical goals and supporting children's musical development (i.e., *parenting musically* and *musical parenting*, cf. Koops, 2020). Therefore, the investments these parents make in their children are not only about child rearing but are also investments in parenthood and in developing their identities as parents (cf. Furedi, 2002). These parents' parenting is both strategic and loving, and the social positioning of themselves as parents is both the outcome of and the prerequisite for caring for their children. The investments they make are a form of currency that is valuable in specific social and cultural settings – it may work in some settings, it may have a different meaning in others, and there may be settings in which it has no relevance or value. What is more, the investments can be made both on the basis of conscious strategic considerations and on the basis of the embodied dispositions that are intersectionally embedded in the parental *habitus*. Musical parenting is therefore a subtle game of music and social positioning that requires simultaneous and skilful handling of a number of possibilities and constraints, value and taste hierarchies, conceptions of children and childhood and more. In light of the aforementioned considerations, it is evident that the concept of musical parenting and the child as an investment warrants further investigation, as discussed in several chapters of the book.

6

Children's games of music: play as investment

Ingeborg Lunde and Live Weider Ellefsen

Children's play and the social expectations of childhood innocence

In his famous allegorical novel *Lord of the Flies*, Golding (1954) describes how the childhood innocence of a group of boys stranded on a remote island is shattered. As the days on the island pass without the arrival of help, the lost children are torn between order and chaos. Their gradual transition from good behaviour to savagery is rooted in their subconscious desire for power, and their innate evil hinders them from building a civilisation. The boys' loss of innocence is thus described not as something done to them but as the result of their natural openness to savagery and evil. The lesson to be learned is that evil can be mitigated but never eradicated. Furthermore, because the characters are all children, a cultural category whose members tend to be shrouded in a veil of innocence, this lesson is a particularly harsh one. In terms of societal expectations, it seems, children do and are good and will do no harm unless they are corrupted. Indeed, children are our future and, if they turn out to be innately evil, this undermines hope for the future. Imagining children as naturally open to cruelty and even evil, then, can create an uncomfortable cognitive dissonance.

A similar cognitive dissonance may arise from pieces of contemporary popular culture, such as Collins' (2008) novel *The Hunger Games*. Inspired by the Greek myth of Theseus and the Minotaur, the story is set in a post-apocalyptic world where the people are forced to play a cruel game in which two teenagers must be selected from each of the twelve districts to take part in a televised fight to the death in which only one can survive. In this dystopia, the protagonist, Katniss Everdeen, represents Theseus, who offers to slay the beast. Again, the experience of the game's brutality is heightened by the fact that the participants are teenagers, and the readers are especially challenged at the point in the story when it looks like Katniss's little sister will have to take part. Certainly, the idea of killing the innocent and forcing innocent children to become killers may thoroughly confuse and compromise readers' beliefs and ethics.

Society's belief in and assumption of children's inherent innocence, utilised so successfully by Golding and Collins to explore human nature and the playing of social games, is also prevalent in the field of childhood studies and early childhood research, in particular, when the topic concerns children's games and play. Children's play, as a topic of both scholarly and educational interest, tends to be studied for its presumed support of positive traits in children, such as imagination, development and progress (see Sutton-Smith, 1997). When German educator Friedrich Froebel invented kindergarten in the early nineteenth century, he modelled his pedagogy on children's play as he perceived it. It is through play that children construct their understanding of the world, Froebel argued, believing play to be 'the highest expression of human development in childhood, for it alone is the free expression of what is in the child's soul' (Early Education – The British Association for Early Childhood Education, 2021). In play, children's souls are, potentially at least, freely expressed, unhindered, unaltered, untamed and uncorrupted.

Froebel's ideas have spread across the world and continue to influence contemporary early childhood education and care. The preoccupation with children's games and play in the educational field finds its parallel in the effort in the corresponding research field to construct game typologies, for example, aiming to outline the diversity within play's positive potential. Categories of play appear in clusters that are dependent on the perspectives and research interests of their creators. One example of such a cluster, underscoring the power of play for children's development and progress, comprises physical play, language play, exploratory play, constructive play, fantasy play and social play (Gray, 2015). Alternative but overlapping typologies are attunement play, body and movement play, object play, imaginative play, social play, rough and tumble play, celebratory and ritual play and storytelling and narrative play (National Institute for Play, 2024). Generally, endeavours to classify children's play tend to be descriptive rather than analytically orientated. Furthermore, despite acknowledging the obvious social and socialising functions of play, they tend to regard the typology produced as an almost self-sufficient structure, descriptive of children's interaction with their immediate surroundings but negligent of the macro discourses governing all social game-playing and positioning all social players. The same applies to efforts to convey the 'darker sides' of play (Schechner, 1993) to counter social, educational and academic biases which block aggressive, destructive, rough, rude and obscene play from the common gaze. Dark play, a term coined by Schechner (1993), director and scholar in performance studies, is a type of performance or playfulness that explores intense and provocative behaviours, taboos and violence, and allows the expression and experience of desires, fears and anxieties (Chang-Kredl *et al.*, 2023). Surely, in their play, children might exhibit grotesque, illicit, disorderly, subversive and 'intentionally contrary' behaviours (Sutton-Smith 2008: 93), and in Sutton-Smith's (1997) work, he compares dark play to his own term 'cruel play' (see also Chang-Kredl *et al.*, 2023). However, even these efforts follow a logic which, as we see it, identifies children's play as a pure practice, in the sense that it is unfiltered and unconditioned, coming from a place within the individual child that is true, natural and unavoidable, whether dark or light, evil or innocent. This logic becomes even more evident when children's games and play are set within the domain of music and music education.

Music educational play

Research in early childhood music education is, understandably, preoccupied with children's everyday life cultures, where musical play takes on many forms, from singing and clapping games (Marsh, 2008) to role-playing in groups of peers using music from the soundtracks of television series (Vestad, 2010). With the rise and impact of social media applications, like TikTok, in children's lives, their everyday musical playgrounds have expanded into the digital world, which is still essentially uncharted by scholars

despite the undisputed significance of these new arenas for (musical) upbringing and socialisation. Undoubtedly, the structures and
algorithms of TikTok and similar applications – operating by and
from child-initiated activities on their devices and screens – frame
and govern children's experiences of themselves as musical individuals. However, similar to how early childhood education research
operates through and by an innocence/evil dichotomy, the field of
music education research in early childhood tends to rely on an
assumed dichotomy between child-initiated and adult-structured
play, implicitly and explicitly preferring and arguing for the value
of the former. Marsh and Young (2006), for example, define children's musical play as follows:

> the activities that children initiate of their own accord and in which
> they may choose to participate with others voluntarily. Like other
> modes of play, these activities are enjoyable, intrinsically motivated,
> and controlled by the players. They are free of externally imposed
> rules but may involve rules developed by the children who are play-
> ing (Rogers and Sawyers, 1988; Isenberg and Jalongo, 1993). They
> are 'everyday' forms of musical activity, happening in places children
> inhabit when not engaged in organized educational, recreational, or
> economic activity. (289)

Child-initiated play is to be protected, Marsh and Young argue,
because it facilitates their experience of flow-like modes of being,
enhances their vitality and possibility to become immersed in the
activity and takes them close to liminal experiences. Based on this
line of thinking, Marsh (2008) further notes that children's self-initi-
ated hand-clapping games played in the schoolyard provide greater
learning challenges than those offered by teachers in the classroom,
resulting in children performing far more complex rhythmic patterns in the schoolyard than in the classroom.

Meanwhile, in formal and institutionalised musical educational
settings, musical play often takes place as a form of guided play
combining free play and instructions (Weisberg *et al.*, 2013) or as
games led by a teacher, in contrast to play-centred approaches where
the children themselves initiate music activities during their play
(Young, 2009b). Thus, Marsh (2008: 318) argues for a 'playful'
(child-initiated) rather than a 'play-like' (adult-initiated) pedagogy,

with their main criticism of play-like pedagogy being that it may miss the inherent 'drive' of the child voluntarily involved in playing. Marsh and Young's criticism is echoed in contemporary argumentation for 'setting children free' in playful pedagogy in terms of what they learn, implying that the teacher adopts a broad approach based on curiosity, directed at the child's exploration and creative engagement and allowing the child to lead the way.

As illustrated by the TikTok example, however, what is perceived, celebrated and idealised as children's own, intrinsically motivated, innocent, uncorrupted, pure and enjoyable play does not escape the kind of social and discursive structuring characterising all game-playing. Furthermore, children's games are double games played in parallel in the general field of social power and the specific, game-related field of pure play.

Investing in play

Play has long been a multifaceted concept in various disciplines. There have been discussions about play in the contexts of children, animals, the arts, education, music and sport. Regarding music, and especially music education, the multifaceted and ambiguous nature of play becomes obvious. What might be the most intriguing aspect of play is that it offers a realm of its own – a space outside of normal life where we can try out various actions or identities – deeply connected to the aesthetic power of music. Huizinga's (1944/1949) definition of play, found in his book *Homo ludens*, has long been an important point of reference for scholars of children and childhood. He describes play as follows:

> a free activity standing quite consciously outside 'ordinary' life as being 'not serious', but at the same time absorbing the player intensely and utterly. It is an activity connected with no material interest, and no profit can be gained by it. It proceeds within its own proper boundaries of time and space according to fixed rules and in an orderly manner. It guides the formation of social groupings which tend to surround themselves with secrecy and to stress their difference from the common world by disguise or other means. (Huizinga, 1944/1949: 13)

While aligning with educational and scholarly assumptions about the purpose-free, disinterested interaction of children's play, characterised by flow experiences and enjoyment and confined to its own 'magic circle' (Huizinga, 1944/1949), there is also a doubleness to Huizinga's conceptualisation of play. Play is pleasurable pretence but absorbs the players utterly and intensely. There is no purpose to play, but it guides the formation of social groupings while disguising that it does so by stressing play's difference from the common world. Huizinga's definition of social play, then, includes an understanding of the players' sincere commitment to and investment in their games, which Bourdieu later came to refer to as *illusio*: the players' *belief* in the pure play of their game, understood as their adherence to the implicit values of its stakes (Bourdieu, 1990; see also Bourdieu, 1992/1996). For both Huizinga and Bourdieu, play unfolds as a double game where social structures and negotiations over power, positions and resources in general are invisibly intertwined with the game-specific actions and rules belonging to the temporary and seemingly autonomous magic circle.

The same applies to children's play. The celebrated free and playful spaces children seek and roam in, commended and prized by educators and researchers, are also always arenas where double games are played. There is no such thing as free space. Indeed, most categories and typologies of play fail to capture the cultural meanings of forms of musical play, the players' social positioning, the social statuses and hierarchies of the play practices, their ambiguities, the 'darker' sides (Schechner, 1993; Sutton-Smith, 1997) and the social and cultural connotations they carry. Children are brought up as players, and their play is taken for granted, deliberately or unconsciously, in a way that is invisible in the moment. The child player's *habitus* (Bourdieu, 1990) enables them to understand society in the specific context of the game played, and, in the form of the child's *habitus*, society simultaneously resides in the body of the child player. Possessing adequate and legitimate competence and skills, knowing the rules of the double game, and being able to perform and participate in the cultural endeavours of peers function as symbolic capital (Bourdieu, 1986). The ability to learn what counts as symbolic capital quickly is also a form of symbolic capital. Moreover, children's investments in play are linked with their parents' investments in them as their children.

Thus, whereas in Chapter 5 we discussed parents' investments in their children's musical upbringing, here we explore children's own investments in musical play and games. That children's ways of experiencing and engaging with music influence their musical tastes and attitudes has long been established (see, e.g., Barrett, 2006, 2009). For children, like adults, music might unfold according to a specific contract of aesthetic rules and regulations that are valid – indeed, meaningful – only within the circumscribed limits of the music game, as noted in Chapter 1, with reference to Huizinga (1944/1949). In the present chapter, we take the exploration of children's games of music even further by considering children's play also in terms of social structures and positioning, arguing that the children's play may be less innocent – on the contrary, more profoundly serious and multifaceted, as far as reconstituting social structures and positions goes – than is usually brought to our awareness. We examine four cases of children's musical play. The children involved are between four and nine years old, and their play involves recorded music and/or popular culture. In three of the events, the children play by themselves, while one game is partially guided by a teacher who is present in the room. Three of the cases are situated in day care settings, and one is from a child's home environment (examples one, two and four are discussed in Vestad, 2014a, 2014b, and Askerøi and Vestad, 2021, respectively).

Children's double games of music

It is well documented that schooling reinforces social differences, but that the free play of day care, where children can come as they are and play together on equal terms, might be a romanticised assumption that is harder to accept. For very good reasons, parents, educators, researchers, politicians and others who speak on behalf of children, with the children's best interests in mind, want them to be free to play, to release and realise their innate capacities, to flourish and to experience flow, joy and self-worth. What tends to be misrecognised is the doubleness of children's games. While the experience of being intensely and completely absorbed in the game in the here and now may be the meaning of it, there are social mechanisms in play that paradoxically regulate the disinterestedness of the experience, even in children's play, not least in relation to what it means to be a child of a particular (or not) gender and ethnicity and from a family with more or less accumulated resources and agency with regard to both material and symbolic capital (Bourdieu, 1986). Moreover, while the fields of education and upbringing finally show a greater awareness of the regulating functions of gender and race, as discourses, on education and upbringing, the circulation of capital in all its forms in children's play may be less visible. The examples of play that we share in this chapter show in different ways how musical agency and competence constitute symbolic capital for children in day care when they play (Bourdieu, 1986). That is, their knowledge and ability to play games in certain ways, musically, constitute a form of currency that they use to occupy legitimate and high-status positions in the play groups, to interact with each other, and that can be invested to gain future benefits. Indeed, it provides a way of making important social distinctions between and within friend groups.

Game-specific musical currency

Four girls are listening to a song from the Junior Eurovision Song Contest (JESC), playing it repeatedly, gradually learning the lyrics and the melody. The atmosphere is intense, and a competitive spirit is evident when they alternate between criticising and confirming each other's moves in their game. The girl leading the game already knows parts of the song quite well, having learnt them from her older sister. At home, she is described as the 'not so musical' little sister. Here, however, she plays the game as the expert, setting the agenda and showing the others how to perform, in song and movement, like the original JESC artist. One of the others, who also knows many songs from home, initially resists, but ultimately, they all accept her as the leader.

Later, together with a third child, the two girls who competed for leadership in the JESC game create a musical role-playing game with a soundtrack from a children's TV series. The point of their game is to 'live' the events and emotional content of the series, illustrated and supported by the music tracks. When the roles are divided between them, the same two girls want to be the main character. The girl who managed to take the lead before succeeds again, simply by stepping into the role she wants without hesitation. Her playmate tries to argue her way into the role, waiting for the others' approval, which never comes.

While these girls might initially appear to possess a similar *habitus* (Bourdieu, 1990) – given their shared age, middle- to upper-middle-class family background and outgoing dispositions – their differing capacities for social positioning and navigating the field of day care musical play suggest a variance in their embodied cultural capital. As players, they are all in the game together, co-constructing a specific doxa (Bourdieu, 1990), or shared understanding, which again comes to constitute their unique cultural subfield: their own rules of the music game. However, there are nuances to the four girls' individual senses of the game – that is, to their disposition to play the game in ways that take them successfully and with legitimacy across the game's field of possibility as this field appears to them. In both the play events outlined above, the same girl takes on the role of leader. Although she occupies a rather subordinate role in her family as far as music is concerned, playing the entrepreneurial expert in the day care setting is obviously a strategy available to her. The larger field of power within which the day care musical games are played is governed by implicit rules and norms that she actively uses and relates to, by performing distinctions musically, bodily and verbally that position her favourably in the games, also according to her own expectations and past strategies of investment and the ongoing strategies of investment in her, as a child, by her family and teachers (see also Chapter 5).

The ongoing interactions and negotiations of the girls' game serve as mechanisms of symbolic differentiation where the children, through their embodied practices, delineate what and who is musically and socially valuable or significant within their group. Consequently, they collectively accumulate and transmit symbolic capital (Bourdieu, 1986), refining their musical taste and competence over time, which may also contribute to the reproduction of social hierarchies within their peer group, based on nuances in their sense of the game.

Dancing on the margins: 'othered' capital

A group of girls has just left the room where they were playing with a CD player. Amanda enters alone, goes to the CD player and jumps around to find the track she wants. From a wooden chest, she pulls out two skirts in transparent fabrics with 'diamonds' and ribbons and puts them around her head and waist. Amanda dances to the music, moving her body sideways with her arms raised in the air on either side of her head in a soft, gliding way that evokes associations with Arabic dance. Amanda's dancing goes unnoticed by everyone except one of the girls who stops in the doorway, looks at her for a few seconds and then walks away. In a later observation, a group of girls discuss who they should invite to take part in a role-play to the soundtrack of a particular children's television series. One of the girls suggests that they invite Amanda, but another girl replies that this is not a good idea because Amanda doesn't know the show and therefore wouldn't know what to do with the different tracks.

Amanda's dancing occurs outside of the collective play, in a moment when those with dominant positions – the expert players – have abandoned the game. The play event represents a rare happening in a research study where day care facilities have been selected for their diversity in children's cultural and socio-economic backgrounds, yet the musical play events themselves fail to display such diversity in participation (Vestad, 2013, 2014b). Amanda's situation exemplifies the earlier argument that children collectively and over time accumulate and exchange symbolic capital (Bourdieu, 1986) through their musical games, a practice that solidifies a specific game-related currency, reinforcing social hierarchies within the game. Her (presumed) lack of familiarity with children's television music equals a lack of game-related symbolic capital which could have been traded for a position in the collective musical play. Amanda thus occupies the role of the excluded, thereby reinforcing the inclusion and dominance of the others. Nevertheless, Amanda possesses a parallel musical repertoire that her dancing demonstrates proficiency in, indicating that her cultural capital, while remaining unrecognised by the other players in their day care games of music, could grant her a legitimate position in another social game where her knowledge and skills would be valued as interchangeable currency. However, if the same logics of symbolic capital and social distinction apply across the other games of society, Amanda would likely remain on the margins, continually serving to validate the dominance of hegemonic insiders.

'The best of boys': masculinities in musical play

Four boys of the same age, but from different ethnic and socio-cultural backgrounds, share a common interest in music. Their favourite artist is Captain Sabertooth, a popular children's character portrayed by Norwegian actor Terje Formoe. Inspired by the music from the films and shows, the boys enthusiastically embody the pirate persona, imitating Sabertooth's fierce expressions, brandishing imaginary swords and jumping around the playroom to the rhythm of the music. Described by day care teachers as 'the best of boys', the children nevertheless have a complex relationship dynamic, marked by frequent conflicts during play. Their rough-and-tumble style, while energetic and engaging, often escalates into loud arguments and tears, making it difficult for them to play without tension. The teacher, who is present throughout, actively supports their musical pirate play by providing verbal validation and introducing common vocabulary, laughing and encouraging the boys, perhaps to maintain a positive atmosphere despite the chaotic and noisy nature of the game interactions.

Butler (1990/2007) argues that no subjectivity or identification process avoids the gendered, normative 'matrix' that drives Western societies – 'that grid of cultural intelligibility through which bodies, genders, and desires are naturalized' (194). The Bourdieuian perspective we take in this book similarly highlights the gendered *habitus* and symbolic capital associated with being male or female in Western society (Bourdieu, 2001). Therefore, supported by the field of power, children benefit, game-wise, from investing proper gender-specific capital in their play. This also applies to those with subjectivities that reject the gender binary but who still need to play their games in subtle, gendered ways to be seen, heard and accepted.

This raises questions about how children, in the subject positions of 'boys' and 'girls', are objects of investment for society and how they themselves are investing in societal games. In the above play event, the boys' engagement with Captain Sabertooth, a character embodying both villainy and kindness, allows them to explore masculine identities through musical doings and (gendered) ways of being and acting. Although displaying an awareness of the fact that there is a multitude of ways of being and acting male and doing masculinity, the day care teachers of the 'best boys' in this case seem to focus on two specific forms of masculine play: 'rough villainy' and 'empathy'. The boys' empathy is seen as challenging traditional masculinity, thus acknowledging and reinforcing the boundaries of masculine play. The teachers' efforts to combine roughness and empathy (through the use of pirate music) are aimed at crafting a form of masculinity that conforms to societal ideals, transforming villainy into socially acceptable, forward-looking and outgoing child masculinities, for the benefit of the child himself, the social life of the day care facility and perhaps society as a whole.

Conversely, the girls in the first example receive less investment from the teachers, who celebrate their conformity to norms, like quiet and cooperative play. However, within their own social interactions, particularly in musical play, the girls engage in complex negotiations for social positions, a dynamic overlooked by the teachers. The teachers focus more on fostering community among the diverse and less independent boys, reinforcing the existing social order and potentially perpetuating gendered hierarchies of capital within the day care and beyond (Bourdieu, 2001).

Singing like a child: the symbolic value of subversive behaviour

A girl is singing 'Jolene' (Parton, 1973) to herself in her family's living room in a way that shows every sign of being satisfying to her. She accompanies herself on the piano, listening to and apparently enjoying the sound and timbre of her own voice. She places the voice deep in her body and tries it out by imitating ideals from the popular music scene. Later, when talking about her singing, the girl reveals that she only sings like this at home. At school, she explains, the teacher tells her to sing 'like a child'.

In Bourdieuian terms, the girl's musical play can be seen as a site of negotiation between her individual (but socially constituted) *habitus* (Bourdieu, 1990) and the expectations imposed on her by the double game she participates in. On one hand, she engages in playful improvisation, seeking to experience and produce a certain musical quality that resonates with her personal aesthetic. On the other hand, she is navigating the social field by investing in music as a form of self-expression, where her vocal performance is both emotionally charged and aligned with social expectations.

Her singing is 'childed' when she participates in classroom play (see also Chapters 4 and 7), conforming to the stereotypical vocality expected of schoolchildren. While this conformity allows her, strategically, to gain symbolic capital within the classroom, where singing like a child is rewarded, she finds this vocality aesthetically unsatisfactory. This tension mirrors the dilemma faced by many performers who must balance their own aesthetic preferences with the demands of the ensemble or social group they belong to.

Unlike Amanda in the previous example, this girl benefits from her alternative play strategy being recognised as valuable cultural capital among her peers at school, and potentially being traded to take up a high-status position in her social group. Her vocality, which entails a provocative performance of difference within the music classroom, is confirmed in her broader social environment as a positive performance of distinction, granting her a higher status among her friends, while she simultaneously is able to adjust to her teacher's demands and receive credit.

Indeed, the girl's privileged ability to navigate different musical and social contexts reflects her nuanced strategies in the field, where her accumulated cultural capital and habitual disposition enable her to oppose the hegemony of the classroom while being endorsed in her home environment. Her experience constitutes an alternative way of being in music, shaped by the differences in how the game is played across contexts.

Concluding remarks

To previous research arguing that children's play is regulated by structures created by adults and that discourses about children and childhood regulate how spaces for children's play are planned and executed (Clark, 2010; de Jong, 2005; Kragh-Müller, 2020; Nordin-Hultman, 2004; Vestad, 2013), this chapter has added the perspective of social positioning and an approach that includes how children themselves make investments and position themselves socially as they play. In conclusion, and in line with the overall approach of the book, we propose that children's musical play constitutes a double game in which the participants (whether children or adults) live the *illusio* of playing (Bourdieu, 1990) in the here and

now of the magic circle (Huizinga, 1944/1949), while simultaneously playing a second game of social positioning. This second way
of addressing the game is opaque to many of the players. However,
it might be unravelled and strategically played by other players,
who occupy relevant, more privileged positions. It could also be
played unknowingly and inadvertently as the power structures and
hierarchies that are working in society are both utilised and re-con-
stituted in the games and players involved, residing in the bodies of
the players as their *habitus* (Bourdieu, 1990).

Indeed, society's view of children's play as innocent, pure and
simply enjoyable, as reflected in art, popular culture, educational
discussions and even academic studies, often masks the social, strategic and intentional investments children make on the basis of their
interactions with power structures. Just as adult players are guided
by their *illusio* in a game, children's *habitus* shapes their inclination to play (Bourdieu, 1990), intertwining the rules of the broader
social power dynamics with those of the specific domain of play.
Investments have already been made in them, by parents, siblings,
teachers, the media and themselves, to prepare them for their future
lives and for the games they will enter and be drawn into. Children
are brought up to be equipped for life, and even when they use
music for play in their own networks and relations, they reinforce
the ways of knowing, being and acting that parents, siblings, teachers and broadcasters, for example, have made available to them as
possibilities and potentials that lie, as it were, in the atmosphere
of society, ready to be utilised by those who are equipped to do
so. The sense of being free, and of playing an innocent game, may
nevertheless be a fundamental drive in children's play and also in
games at other levels of society, but this chapter argues that strategic games of social positioning are not reserved for the adult population. In children's seemingly whimsical, playful engagement with
music, then, more is at stake than their immediate pleasure and next
move or action. Children's games are as socially powerful as adult
games, reflecting and reinforcing the classed, gendered and racialised discourses which influence broader educational and musical
games in early childhood education and care as well as the overall
educational games of the welfare state itself.

Following up on this, we are tempted to join the researchers of
children's play who claim that 'there's no such thing as free play'

(see Gems, 2007; Jonassen, 2015; Kragh-Müller, 2020). When children play with music, seemingly free in a space outside the real, they simultaneously participate in a game of social hierarchies and positioning. This is perhaps particularly challenging to accept since the discourses of children's play most often underscore innocence, inclusiveness and positive values. Thus, strategic play for social positions is rendered to be in conflict with the pureness of play.

7

Public broadcasting: investments in children and childed television music

Ingeborg Lunde, Odd Skårberg and Petter Dyndahl

Introduction

Syvertsen and colleagues (2014) state that the 'media and communication systems have been vital building blocks of the welfare state'
(3). They also posit that the media plays an indispensable role in
society as a 'social glue' forging and reinforcing imagined communities, such as the nation. The concept of the nation as an imagined
community is an abstract yet emotionally charged notion intended
to unite people across diverse geographical and cultural boundaries. Anderson (1983) emphasises the emergence of a synchronous
understanding of time as the basis for the nation as an imagined
community. The dissemination of synchronous messages over large
distances via the media (e.g., newspapers, telegraph, radio, television, Internet) is therefore of great importance.

Moreover, media content has played a pivotal role in the formation of Scandinavian childhoods. It has served to promote the ideals of equality and personal autonomy and disseminate the values
of the welfare state to subsequent generations. This has included
the transmission of what can be regarded a 'value curriculum' that
fosters solidarity, a sense of belonging, inclusion and opposition
to exclusion. The music featured on children's television plays a
role in shaping the narratives of the nation, the welfare state and
the related concept of childhood. Furthermore, children's television,
including televised music, anticipates, constructs and legitimates
ways of being a child. This is based on social and cultural expectations and beliefs, as well as adults' perceptions of children's needs.
The subject positions made available to children in the audio–visual

compound of children's television represent a value curriculum in themselves (see also Lunde, 2023; Vestad, 2022). However, it should be noted that the content of this value curriculum changes over time.

This chapter is based on the assumption that 'specific historical moments give rise to distinctive children's culture' (Mintz, 2012: 41). It proposes that the content and reception of television programmes for children can provide insights into the concept of the child audience at which a series is aimed as well as the childhood concept that is constructed through the mediated content. From a historical perspective, the Norwegian Broadcasting Corporation (NRK) occupies a distinctive position within the Norwegian media landscape. This position is inextricably linked to its relationship with the authorities of the society, situating the public service broadcasting corporation at the pinnacle of the power hierarchy. As a public broadcasting corporation, NRK is accountable to the Department of Culture, which serves as its General Assembly. It is bound by regulations mandating that the broadcaster must disseminate its content to all citizens with the objective of fulfilling democratic, social and cultural requirements within the society (Norsk Rikskringkasting, 1996/2022, art. 12). Additionally, it is obliged to 'promote children's rights to expression and to information and protect children from harmful content' (Norsk Rikskringkasting, 1996/2022, art. 22). One of the objectives is to disseminate the prevailing regulations and standards of behaviour within the society to the audience. This is intended to contribute to the education and upbringing of the nation's children, including the inculcation of the values and behaviours expected of a good citizen and, by extension, of a good child. It can thus be argued that the welfare state makes an investment in children.

However, the value curricula conveyed in broadcast narratives must appear to flow naturally, integrated into stories that feel authentic and resonate with the audience. One of the key challenges in children's broadcasting is to present stories that are relevant and engaging for young audiences while ensuring that the characters and narratives portrayed in these stories are perceived as credible and authentic by the intended audience, which may also include parents and grandparents. Music plays an integral role in the portrayal of characters and the narration of stories in children's broadcasting.

Based on the preceding paragraphs, it can be stated that a similar duality, or double game, is evident in public broadcasting as in
public education. This duality pertains to the *Bildung* or formation
of individuals as well as their adaptation to society.

A brief history of children's broadcasting in Norway

The first Norwegian radio broadcast for children was aired in
1929 (Dahl, 1999). During the late 1940s and 1950s, the national
broadcasting corporation assumed a position of *loco parentis*
– the nation's parent (Goldson, 2004) – facilitating upbringing
and cultivation. In particular, during the initial decades following World War II, NRK presented a form of national curriculum
for younger audiences, comprising stories and songs that gave
rise to a range of derivative products, including books, theatre
plays and recordings. These cultural artefacts fostered a sense of
national unity, both through the selection of cultural content and
the promotion of a shared understanding of the social framework
underpinning the nation. The initial children's programmes fostered this sense of national unity by bringing together Norwegians
through the medium of radio, creating shared experiences and references (Frønes, 1998). The upbringing of children was based on
the assumption that the children's best interests should be served
and that the children should be taken seriously. This approach
was reinforced by the involvement of Åsa Gruda Skard, one of
the country's leading child psychologists, in the development and
evaluation of children's programmes, particularly *Barnetimen
for de minste* (Children's Hour for the Youngest), which was
transmitted in the latter half of the 1940s. From the outset of
children's broadcasting in Norway, international influences were
pervasive, including those pertaining to beliefs about children's
needs, which were shaped by the diverse contexts of childhood
across the globe, particularly in Western societies. *Barnetimen for
de minste* was based on the Australian concept of *Nursery on
the Air*, a children's programme devised when Australian children were required to remain at home during wartime and were
deprived of the pedagogical input typically provided by day care
(Tønnessen, 2015).

Since the outset of broadcasting content for children, the relationship between education and entertainment has been a topic of debate (Dahl, 1999). In the late 1940s, NRK articulated a philosophy of children's broadcasting that encompassed three key elements: *Opplysning* (Enlightenment), *Opplevelse* (Experience) and *Oppdragelse* (Education; Vestad, 2022). The initial broadcasts of *Barnetimen for de minste* were predicated on the pedagogical approach espoused in early childhood education and care facilities, drawing from Froebel's legacy. This approach entailed incorporating songs with accompanying movements, songs pertaining to the body and the senses and songs about everyday life routines, weekdays, seasons, holidays and other elements, which collectively constituted the programme's core. A teacher and a pianist performed the songs, nursery rhymes and activities in the studio together with a group of children, thereby encouraging children at home to join in from their own living rooms. In the initial years, *Barnetimen for de minste* underwent further content development, and it achieved considerable popularity during the 1950s. The programme's objective was to familiarise children with a diverse range of stories, songs and nursery rhymes from across the country. These were presented by radio presenters, who adopted the roles of 'aunts' and 'uncles' and spoke in a variety of regional dialects. The programmes were designed to be authentic and diverse and to speak directly to children (Skard, 1953). The combination of aesthetic value and educational purposes was emphasised (Skard, 1954). The openings of the programmes, such as the well-known example of 'uncle' Alf Prøysen saying, 'Now, you put your hand on your radio, and I put my hand on my radio', established a relationship between the 'uncle' in the radio studio and the audience at home (see also Lunde, 2023). The conclusion of the programme addressed the concrete realities of the child audience, as exemplified by Prøysen's 'Now, I should go home, and you should go outside and play' (as cited in Tønnessen, 2015: 94). This contributed to the establishment of nearness, community and a sense of belonging. The programme played an integral role in uniting post-war Norway through the medium of radio, fostering a sense of community and belonging among children and families from diverse geographical locations (Frønes, 1998; Skard, 1954). The impact of the programme on the 1950s' reputation as the golden age of radio broadcasting for children was significant.

The programme enjoyed enduring popularity for decades, and its repertoire continues to serve as a repository of children's culture and a national treasure for those engaged in the musical upbringing of children, even extending into the new millennium (see Chapter 4 as well as Vestad, 2018; Vestad and Dyndahl, 2017, 2021).

Following years of testing, regular television broadcasting was introduced to Norwegian audiences in 1960. In the 1970s, the British Broadcasting Corporation's (BBC) *Play School*, an educational and entertaining television programme for young audiences, had a significant impact on Norwegian children's television programming, leading to the creation of the series *Lekestue* (Playroom; Høien, 1971–1980). This marked the advent of a new era in children's broadcasting in Norway. The introduction of audio-visual content, comprising both sound and moving images, represented a significant departure from the preceding radio broadcasts. Additionally, there was a notable shift in pedagogical content thinking. The programmes included repeated segments presenting learning content, such as the names and sounds of letters and numbers, as well as concepts, such as the clock and telling time. The musical vignettes, performed by musicians from NRK, introduced snippets which were distinct and highly recognisable. The importance of songs and stories was maintained. Although it was based on a British concept, *Lekestue* maintained the fundamental idea of the early children's radio broadcasting of presenting children with the Norwegian tradition of children's songs and stories, conveying a cultural repertoire and cultural values. Children's public broadcasts were and continue to be firmly embedded in a *Bildung* tradition, which encompasses the development of a knowledgeable, reflective and independent human being capable of engaging in ethical, critical thinking and assuming responsibility for themselves, others and the wider world, including the democratic process and the welfare state. *Lekestue* was aligned with global trends in children's broadcasting, reflecting international perceptions of children's needs. Concurrently, it aimed to facilitate the formation of distinct Norwegian identities and foster a unified national community through the promotion of shared cultural traditions and values.

Another notable development in children's broadcasting in Norway occurred in the 1990s, when NRK, in collaboration with its Nordic counterparts, invited American puppeteer, animator and filmmaker Jim Henson to contribute his expertise to the Nordic broadcasting community. NRK also collaborated with the American Children's Television Workshop (CTW) to create a Norwegian co-production of the popular series *Sesame Street*; *Sesam stasjon* (Sesame Station), during the 1990s (Gran and Høien, 1991–1999). At this juncture, NRK was no longer the sole broadcaster in Norway. The advent of competition necessitated a shift in strategy to capture the attention of young audiences and their parents in a novel way. While NRK's reputation for reliability in the upbringing of the nation's children remained a valuable asset, it was no longer a sufficient differentiating factor in the context of the heightened demands for entertainment and engagement among children.

The dual approach of entertainment and education remained a fundamental element, but compared to earlier Norwegian television programmes, the production of CTW was more explicitly anchored in rigorous psychological frameworks for learning skills (Hake, 2006; Tønnessen, 2000). A significant endeavour was undertaken to establish the series as an educational and entertaining programme concept for children in Norway (Tønnessen, 2000; Vestad, 2016). The translation entailed a shift from a programme with a strong American focus on skills to one that combined skills with the continued promotion of upbringing and *Bildung* through techniques such as storytelling and music. As an illustration of the significant role of music in children's television programmes and the importance of considering children as a key audience, Norwegian composer Sigvald Tveit and lyricist Eivind Skeie were commissioned to create new songs and music for more than 200 episodes of *Sesam stasjon*. Their contributions not only maintained the tradition of children's television music but also enhanced it.

This kind of content indicates a social positioning of children as human beings/becomings in need of adequate programmes for their age group. It implies that the programmes are designed to provide a safe space for children where they can have fun and be educated without the parents needing to worry (for further information, see Chapter 5 in this book and Tønnessen, 2000). Furthermore, educational television programmes, such as *Sesam stasjon*, explicitly sought to obscure the differences between children from working and middle-class backgrounds (Tønnessen, 2000) by promoting the potential for social mobility through education. In terms of musical content, *Sesam stasjon* demonstrated a remarkable diversity of genres, thereby expanding the musical repertoire available to children. Furthermore, at the turn of the millennium, NRK began to address cultural diversity in children's programming (Hake, 2006; Lunde, 2023; Vestad, 2022). The series *AF1*, launched in 2008, thus exemplifies a way of making children's television that conveys issues of diversity through an engaging narrative, based on a long tradition of storytelling in children's broadcasting in Norway, and where the earlier tradition of diversity in music in children's programmes culminated in a way of making diversity, inclusion, musical genres, practices and cultures part of the narrative.

This concise account of children's broadcasting in Norway reflects a societal perception of children as the future of the nation. Without a stable and prosperous future for the children, the country's future is uncertain, making it crucial to foster a supportive environment for them to grow into responsible and well-adjusted adults. Children are positioned as active participants in the sociocultural milieu as well as agents of change. The objective is to instil in them a sense of responsibility and ethical conduct, which is essential for the functioning of the welfare state. Additionally, they are encouraged to develop a comprehensive set of knowledge, skills and values, along with a repertoire of ways of being and playing.

Children's music – childity – childed music

The genre of children's music, seen as music for, by and with children (Lunde, 2023; Mouritsen, 2002; Vestad, 2010), may be understood in a similar manner to children's musical cultures in terms of the content and process (see also Chapter 4). Furthermore, the genre of children's music is understood as a continuous performative act involving processes of canonisation (Vestad and Dyndahl, 2017, 2021). The most salient features of children's media music even today are derived from a long-standing tradition of kindergarten songs and pedagogy. This tradition was initiated by pioneers such as Pestalozzi and Froebel, who offered and promoted songs for children to support their growth. This included engaging in singing to establish a bond between mother and child and teaching children about the world, the senses and emotions, as well as the body and limbs. This involved aesthetic and kinaesthetic approaches. Furthermore, a historical investigation of Norwegian children's phonograms (Dyndahl and Vestad, 2017) demonstrates that from 1945 to 1959, traditional children's songs, created by authors and songwriters such as Margrethe Munthe, Torbjørn Egner and Alf Prøysen, constituted a prevalent repertoire. During the 1950s, jazz also emerged as a significant genre in Norwegian music, including the first child star in Norway, Lille Grethe. Her musical style may have been influenced more by the popular music of her parents' generation than by the emerging genres of pop and rock music. Nevertheless, this resulted in the introduction of a new sonic vocabulary within the context of Norwegian children's music (Dyndahl and Vestad, 2017). From 1960 to 1985, a new generation of popular music emerged, accompanied by the rise of teen idols. Artists such as Wenche Myhre and Anita Hegerland epitomised a kind of Scandinavian middle-of-the-road pop for children and young teenagers, encapsulating a range of emotional experiences and sentiments, including 'the sounds of pain, lust, ecstasy, fear, what one might call inarticulate articulacy: the sounds, for example, of tears and laughter' (Frith, 1996a: 192; see also Dyndahl and Vestad, 2017). By the conclusion of this period, pop-rock had become the dominant genre of children's phonograms. However, the period also witnessed the emergence of notable artists, such as the highly popular acoustic folk duo Knutsen and Ludvigsen. Additionally, the traditional children's song continued to assert a significant presence. The final period under examination, spanning from 1986 to 2016, was distinguished by the proliferation of musical styles within the domain of popular music. This period witnessed the repurposing of traditional children's songs through a process of musical reinterpretation, infusing them with the characteristics of diverse popular musical forms. Dyndahl and Vestad (2017) posit that 'pop-rock constitutes the warp of today's intergenerational fabric – or, rather, that it forms the current cosmopolitan *lingua franca*' (4).

It is evident that the genres constituting the foundation of children's music have undergone a significant evolution over time. Additionally, genres that were previously regarded as exclusively for an adult audience have been incorporated into the musical landscape for children. The delineation of what constitutes children's music and what does not is a contentious and nebulous issue.

Nevertheless, it can be reasonably deduced that the genre of children's music (if it can be defined as such) is a complex entity comprising a multitude of styles and genres. The unifying factor that distinguishes it from other genres is the 'childed-ness' of its aural, visual, material, social and cultural features and aspects.

To examine the childed-ness of the cases to be presented in this chapter, we have introduced the concept of childed music (see Chapter 4). The concept of childed music extends beyond merely noting that some music is designed to appeal to children. It also encompasses the idea that music is adapted to suit children and, at the same time, is shaped by and reinforces social and cultural expectations associated with the concept of the child. In other words, childed music both responds to and contributes to the construction of the subject position of the child. In this work, musical signposts and cultural connotations of the aural and visual are employed to indicate that the programme, series and/or music is intended for children. In approaching these signposts, we are inspired by Sjöberg's (2013) work involving the concept of 'childity'. In her research on commercials with and for children, Sjöberg develops the concept of childity as a parallel to masculinity and femininity, with the aim of providing a tool for discussing the visual construction of someone as a child. Sjöberg posits that childity is a pivotal concept in the analysis of age-related social and cultural practices. This concept enables a discussion of the ways in which children are constructed, including the entities that facilitate an interpretation of what is perceived as a child. Sjöberg's argument is based on Craig's (1992) approach to masculinity and femininity. Craig argues that gender is a concept that is culturally constructed, and that masculinity and femininity can be examined as sets of social expectations (as cited in Sjöberg, 2013). Sjöberg highlights the absence of concepts equivalent to masculinity and femininity when considering age. Childity, therefore, serves as a valuable tool for examining the social expectations associated with age. It is crucial to distinguish between childity and the concept of 'childish-ness', which is often used pejoratively to describe irresponsibility, naivety and infantility (Sjöberg, 2013: 54).

In our examination of children's music, we are interested in the concept of childity as a means of exploring and describing not only the visual signposts but also the aural ones. In particular, we aim to analyse how age is indicated aurally, as well as in other modes, to ascertain that the music in question is intended for children. In the following section, we acknowledge the fact that when discussing the category of the child, other cultural categories intersect, including ethnicity, gender and social class. Furthermore, the difficulties encountered in classifying children's music pertain to the act of differentiating between pieces of music. These distinctions may be found in the manner in which the music is perceived as childish, as discussed in Chapter 4. From an intersectional perspective, a pivotal inquiry is how music shapes the representations of class, gender, ethnicity and race, as well as the intersections between these categories. This, in turn, illuminates the ways in which social positions for child audiences are constructed and made available through music on screen. In this chapter, we are particularly interested in examining these categories in relation to the central values of the Nordic welfare state – namely, equality, inclusion and a sense of belonging.

Traces of childity and childed music in children's television: sounding images of social expectations

The following sections present a discussion of the ways in which the music of particular instances of children's television programming is perceived as childed. Overall, the notion of childity can be identified as a fundamental aspect of children's programming, as evidenced by its classification as a discrete category. This implies an assumption that children are a distinct and separate audience with their own specific needs and preferences. It also suggests that the concept of children as a discrete category is widely accepted within the broader discourse. Music contributes to the representation of children on screen and also shapes how social expectations shape the perception of children.

In this context, expectations regarding childity would include a kind of childed vocality that functions as a sonic–aesthetic symbol and as a signpost indicating that the music in question is intended for children. There is a range of sonic expressive parameters actualising bodily representations, including those associated with age. The singing voice is the most significant of these (see Askerøi and

Vestad, 2021). In Hawkins' (2016) words, 'The microgestures of an individual's musical makeup in a pop recording convey the vicissitudes of vocality, inherent in inflections, tones, and nuances, all of which establish a sonic image; it is this that actually individualizes the body' (171).

When adults perform for children, the singing style is frequently characterised by a communicative approach, a sense of proximity and the formation of relationships between the performer and the audience. In the context of 1950s radio, the voice of, for instance, Alf Prøysen was positioned within a narrow register and range. His voice conveyed groundedness and calmness, and he adapted the tone of his voice to align with the various characters in the stories and songs, thereby enhancing their dramatic qualities (Tønnessen, 2015).

Additionally, in the aforementioned *Sesam stasjon*, it is possible to discern distinctive differences between the characters' singing voices, yet they share a common trait: they sing in a high-pitched and 'thin' timbre, which lends the voice a quality akin to that of a child. Fabbri (1982) makes a comparable observation regarding the characteristics of songs for children: 'children's songs are sung by children, or by singers of various genres who imitate the voice most adults consider should be used when speaking to children' (67). It appears that the instinct to communicate in a higher-pitched voice than is typical in adult conversation when interacting with infants (see Malloch and Trevarthen, 2010) persists in children's music, becoming an aesthetic ideal of consciously downplaying a serious, adult vocal style, regardless of whether the performer is depicted as an adult or a child.

However, the thin timbre of the female characters' voices serves to undermine their authority. A comparable argument has been put forth in the context of girlhood and the sonic character of young female voices in popular culture (Warwick and Adrian, 2016). However, the exaggerated timbre in the case of *Sesam stasjon* represents a further threat to the authority of the female characters. It may also threaten the authenticity of the portrayal, leaving the female characters as sonic clichés, as Warwick and Adrian (2016) describe it from the perspective of mainstream popular culture: 'girls are frequently depicted as frivolous, silly, and deserving of contempt' (2). Consequently, the female characters appear to be a far cry from the grounded composure that Prøysen's voice is said to embody, as outlined by Tønnessen (2015).

In contrast, the male station master at *Sesam stasjon* employs a vocal style that is not aligned with a childed vocal quality in the same manner. The voice displays a quality of nearness and kindness, yet it remains deep and conveys a sense of calm and inclusivity. Therefore, the childed female and male vocalities appear to contribute to the portrayal of female voices as more childish and naive (see Warwick and Adrian, 2016), while the male voices remain deeper and calmer. It can be seen that the innocence associated with a childed vocal quality is not entirely innocent when it manifests in this way. It represents ideals and modes of being that render female and child characters with thin, high-pitched voices, which results in a lack of authority and authenticity, and thus perceived weakness. In many ways, this goes beyond the performers' intention; sonic meaning is complex and multi-dimensional (van Leeuwen, 1999), and the discourses that regulate meaning-making are deeply embodied in our habitual ways of thinking and being, functioning as sonic taken-for-granted doxas that subjects will habitually adjust to. However, this indicates that the double game suggested at the beginning of the chapter is played in more complex and power-laden ways than the more obvious opposition between formation and adaptation, and that it implicates intersectional layers.

To gain deeper insight into the social positioning of children in music, several examples of children's television music representing different ways of performing childity have been selected for analysis. These examples have been drawn from *Sesam stasjon* and the more recent series *AF1*.

Sonic images of conformity and diversity

In terms of the suitability of the series for children, an important consideration is the use of puppets in conjunction with human characters. Puppets and dolls have a long tradition in children's television, and this was also presented as a key selling point of *Sesame Street*. The use of puppets with bright colours rather than skin colours facilitates the crossing of diversities and provides objects of identification, including for a number of cultural categories.

However, the collection used in *Sesam stasjon* was unique to the Norwegian co-production.

One of the central roles is performed by the puppet character Max Mekker, a large, blue, furry, animal-like character referred to as 'he'. He is described as benevolent, affable and obliging and he has a resonant male voice. In some instances, he behaves in a manner consistent with that of an adult; at other times, his actions and speech patterns align with those of a child. He is the series' handyman, utilising his tools to rectify various issues, with the majority of the outcomes being beneficial.

The song 'Max Mekker mekker maks' (Høien *et al.*, 1996) was featured in a week-long sequence dealing with the senses in 1991 (Tønnessen, 2000: 127). It is performed as a tribute to Max, who has just repaired the train station's microphone for announcing train arrivals and departures. The lyrics portray Max as a straightforward, helpful and friendly individual, consistently available and willing to address and rectify any issues that may arise. In this way, the song conveys an ideal of society and social expectations that are stereotypically associated with a male handyman. The song is characterised by an upbeat, cheerful and generally easy-going quality, which presents no significant challenges to the child audience or the segment of parents. The rhythmic pattern, which can be described as a variant of polka using alternating bass, and the overall tempo and the cheerful voices of the characters singing produce a joyous atmosphere that emphasises the apparent harmony that follows from playing well-known games with taken-for-granted rules.

The transition from conformity to diversity can be conceptualised as a journey by train. The image of *Sesam stasjon* depicts a relatively modest railway station, rather than a street (the setting of the original *Sesame Street*), with railways extending to the farthest reaches of Europe. This symbolism represents the global reach of children's television and children's music. Furthermore, the protagonist Leonora, an opera singer played by a human actor, arrives at *Sesam stasjon* by train, having recently performed in Italy. She finds the ambience of the convivial station and its inhabitants so agreeable that she decides to prolong her stay. In a single act, the locale is simultaneously identified as pertinent and worthwhile, as well as appealing to a cosmopolitan individual with global connections and providing an inclusive atmosphere that welcomes her with open arms.

The presentation of a diversity of cultural expressions in the form of songs and music has a long tradition in children's broadcasting in Norway. However, the concept of diversity itself has evolved over time, from its initial definition in the 1950s to its contemporary interpretation (Dyndahl and Vestad, 2017; Lunde, 2023; Vestad, 2022). The sonic image of diversity presented in *Sesam stasjon* encompasses an expansive range of musical genres, including those representative of popular music scenes. Similar to the American *Sesame Street*, the Norwegian co-production is structured as a magazine programme comprising studio segments and inserts. It is noteworthy that the Norwegian version incorporates original music from the original American production in its use of such inserts. These inserts paved the way for new genres to be presented to children in Norway, thus enabling Norwegian children to become part of *Sesame Street*'s long-term engagement in introducing children to music by artists from a multitude of ethnic backgrounds. This broadened the child audience's musical and cultural horizons in terms of sonic references long before diversity and inclusion became a crucial topic on the agenda for children's television (Ryzik, 2019).

One of the most prevalent of these inserts is the so-called 'Number Song' – 'Pinball Number Count' – a brief animated sequence that was repeatedly employed in the 1991 season of the Norwegian co-production and subsequently throughout the Norwegian series. 'Pinball Number Count' was first released in 1977 by the African American musical group the Pointer Sisters. In the Norwegian co-production, the original vocals are replaced by those of ethnic Norwegian vocalists Håkon Iversen and Elin Rosseland. The song is in the form of the blues, with jazz improvisations provided on a variety of instruments, including steel drums, guitar and saxophone. Consequently, the song may be defined as a sonic melting pot, incorporating elements of American jazz, funk, Latin and jazz rock from the 1970s. It is noteworthy that the musicians perform with a high level of skill and exhibit a mature approach to improvisation. In other words, there is no evidence that the musical language has been adapted to appeal to a younger audience. The theme and content of counting and numbers are, in a sense, wrapped in music that could just as well be targeting adults. In addition to the visuals, it is the lyrics that provide the key to identifying this piece as children's music. In the context of children's television in

Norway, the song is a notable exception to the prevailing norms of the era. Nevertheless, the song was received as an effective and engaging musical tool for developing children's visual numeracy. Additionally, the music indicates that broadcasting for children during the last decade before the turn of the millennium needed to become catchy and appealing, and that NRK sought to achieve this by introducing popular international music genres while fulfilling its obligation to educate.

'You can be whatever you want': a game of social mobility

The series *AF1*, produced by NRK and launched in 2008, takes a different approach to children's music. As described by NRK, the series is a furious mix of hip-hop, breaking and ballet, with topics like falling in love, friendship and jealousy (Halvorsen, 2008–2011). The characters in the series reflect the demographic composition of the suburban area in which the narrative is set. The main character, Lisa, is a twelve–year-old blonde girl from a middle-class background who dances ballet. She is caught between the competing expectations of her parents and her ballet coach, who want her to pursue a career in ballet, and her own desire to become a hip-hop dancer. The characters Faiza and Mira are both female and of immigrant families from the Middle East. Faiza aspires to become a prima ballerina, while Mira is a breakdancer with a strong personality, who oversees the activities of her crew and is a prominent figure in the breakdancing and hip-hop communities. Tariq is a hip-hopper who plays a significant role in the narrative. Mira offers a critical assessment of Lisa's demeanour, asserting that it is too conventional to align with the characteristics typically associated with both breakdancing and hip-hop culture. Conversely, Faiza's father imposes restrictions on her participation in ballet. Lisa endeavours to bestow upon Faiza the principal role in Tchaikovsky's *Swan Lake*, a role for which Lisa herself has been cast.

The series addresses and challenges the notion of a correlation between ethnic background and destiny in terms of one's potential for achievement in life. Music serves as an illustrative example of the processes of identity formation and negotiation. The series explores the process of transcending social expectations and locating one's sense of identity and purpose. Consequently, the series communicates profound values pertaining to the welfare state and democracy. The series also addresses the formation of friendships and participation in music and dance. However, it also touches upon the aspect of personal development, particularly the beliefs in one's own capabilities and that one can make a difference. It also addresses the formation of a sense of belonging, the concepts of inclusion and exclusion, and the importance of equal opportunities. Additionally, it highlights the value of role models who exemplify the virtues of citizenship, supporting both oneself and others. Tariq, in one of the final scenes of the season, offers a commentary on these values particularly in relation to the way they conduct themselves. The concept of unity is paramount. In this way, the media serves as an agent of cohesion and social bonding (cf. Syvertsen *et al.*, 2014: 13) across diversities. Rather than discussing these elements or presenting them as isolated educational units, they are integrated into a coherent narrative. The values are embodied and enacted by the characters in the television series, and the challenges and potential pitfalls are revealed and subsequently challenged as they impede the characters' progress and efforts to overcome them. This is likely to evoke emotional responses in the audience. Furthermore, the audience is invited to engage with the narrative from a position of empathy. The musical genres in question, with their connotations of high culture and countercultures, respectively, help to narrate the story. The defeat of homologies regarding the children's participation in musical genre-related practices and cultures represents the freedom of choice (cf. Jensen, 2017), which can be understood as the ability to become whoever one wants to be.

The methodology of childing the music in *AF1* differs from that used for *Sesam stasjon*. The most evident alteration is the replacement of puppets with child actors, which reflects a shift in the targeted age group of children. The music from *Swan Lake* is the original orchestral composition, but the audio-visual sequences in which this music is featured have been adapted for a television script that does not allow for extended segments. Furthermore, it is presented in a manner that aligns with the social expectations associated with childhood. Lisa and subsequently Faiza participate in the ballet performance as dancers, socialised into its rules and demands, which they aspire to meet. With regard to music-related education and upbringing, it is evident from the narrative that their achievements necessitate dedication and investment on their part, in terms of investing in a cultural expression by acquiring knowledge and skills through a considerable amount of practice.

The hip-hop sequences of *AF1* are designed to facilitate the expressions of children's voices in a different manner. The practice of hip-hop encompasses a range of elements, including rap, dance and graffiti. The latter is the most problematic in relation to legislation and is treated with care in the series to avoid inspiring unlawful behaviour. NRK continues to operate within a secure environment for its young audience, thereby alleviating parental concerns (Tønnessen, 2000; see also Chapter 5 in this book). The genre of rap music is frequently represented in musical competitions, which are also a prominent feature of *AF1*. The characters participate in these battles, which frequently include roasting their opponents. The content of the battles and their outcomes form an integral part of the narrative. In general, the hip-hop lyrics are aligned with the experiences of the child characters in the series, yet they are also 'clean', free from profanity or other problematic and/or derogatory content. Furthermore, the lyrics are in Norwegian, a convention that has been established in the context of Norwegian hip-hop since the turn of the millennium. The rap songs elucidate and/or augment the characters' perspectives on the circumstances depicted in the series. As such, these are voices articulating children's points of view. The performances are noteworthy for several reasons. They may form part of the narrative, as in the case of battles or when the characters practise rapping, singing and dancing as part of the narrative. Alternatively, they may halt the narrative and provide an opportunity to appreciate the music and gain insight into how the child characters think and feel. By the end of the series, hip-hop and especially rap serve as a shared musical genre, a genre of inclusion.

Regarding the duality of power and empowerment as depicted in *AF1*, the characters within the series exhibit a dichotomy in their perception of the rules of the game, oscillating between belief and disbelief. As previously stated, they represent opposing homologies and the social expectations derived from them. The characters are positioned as potential agents of change, exemplifying the potential of the welfare state to foster a diverse and inclusive society. This is, at least, as depicted by the narrative presented by the welfare state's own broadcaster. If the audience accepts the narrative and the rules and norms of the characters and the social expectations they convey, it may be assumed that they will also accept the rules of the social expectations at a more general societal level. It could be hypothesised that such television series may help to consolidate the welfare state by enhancing beliefs in equal opportunities, freedom of choice and inclusion in societies where virtually everyone takes part. However, this chapter does not answer these questions; it can only conclude that the identity material presented may convey these messages.

Conclusion and epilogue

This chapter has presented a historical analysis of the welfare state's investments in children's upbringing, education and entertainment. The analysis has been conducted through the lens of children's television music and the concepts of childity and childed music. We have examined a selection of programme series that, in their own ways, represent particularly illustrative cases of music in broadcasting for children. The concepts of childity and childed music have enabled us to identify how the musics in question are recognised as children's music, and thus to gain insight into the role of NRK in enhancing personal *Bildung* as well as social and cultural competencies. It can therefore be stated that NRK fulfils the mandate given by the welfare state – namely, that the state channel should target children especially and that it should offer children's programmes of high quality. In that respect, internationally, NRK's children's productions are highly ranked, and Norwegian producers have received various prizes in international competitions, such as the prestigious *Prix Jeunesse* and *Prix Japan*.

By entertaining, informing and educating children in accordance with the democratic, social and cultural norms and values of a Nordic welfare society, NRK has contributed both to the upbringing of its youngest citizens and to socialising them for qualified participation in and reproduction of the welfare state. This is the overarching double game, played simultaneously at various intersectional levels, charged with aesthetic, cultural and social values, political interests and power. It can thus be concluded that the game of public service broadcasting is worthwhile for most players. It is, however, essential to highlight that while a conclusion is reached within the framework of the narrative, an epilogue subsequently occurs and provides insights into future prospects. Arguably, NRK's position in the Norwegian public sphere is attributable, at least in part, to the fact that, following the example of the BBC, the corporation was granted exclusive broadcasting rights upon its establishment in 1933 and maintained this right until 1981. The advent of neoliberalism at this time, however, resulted in a shift towards a market-based approach to the organisation of society and public enterprises. This has resulted in a reduction in the overall capacity to operate public broadcasting services that take account of the needs of specific groups and the broader societal context. For example, Norway's only commercial public broadcaster, TV 2, has no children's programming in its regular schedule. Moreover, the liberalisation of media policy has fostered a competitive environment where public and private broadcasters, as well as local, national and global media entities, compete for audiences and content on a multitude of platforms beyond those addressed in this chapter.[1] Nevertheless, it is clear that the double game of music, which also involves children, power and intersectional dimensions, is occurring and will continue to occur in new media and technological contexts. However, the role of the welfare state and public services in this future context remains unclear.

Note

1 The ways in which children engage in the double game of music on social media platforms, such as TikTok and YouTube, are discussed in Chapters 6 and 8, respectively.

8

Talent and talentification

*Petter Dyndahl, Anne Jordhus-Lier
and Friederike Merkelbach*

Introduction

Perceptions of talent seem ubiquitous in today's public discourse. Perhaps the most eye-catching examples are the countless game and reality shows which, in various ways, revolve around discovering, nurturing or celebrating musical talent of many shades. As radio, television or Internet programming genres, these include global media hits that are licensed to public or private media corporations worldwide (e.g., *Idol*, *The X Factor*, *The Voice*), international media events (e.g., the Eurovision Song Contest) and regional or national talent competitions (e.g., *Sámi Grand Prix*, *Britain's Got Talent*). The motivation may be linked to the media and music industries' need to discover new talent, to promote national artists internationally or to make established or former stars compete against each other in musical reality shows, such as the Norwegian TV show *Stjernekamp* [Battle of the Stars]. Although popular music genres dominate, as in the music market in general, there are various examples of media-transmitted talent competitions in classical music as well (e.g., the Queen Sonja Singing Competition), and there are also both international (e.g., the Annual Grammy Awards) and national music awards covering a multitude of music genres (e.g., the Norwegian *Spellemann* [Fiddler] and *P3 Gull* [P3 Gold]). With the rise of social media in the 2000s, such competitions were obviously no longer just about discovering, nurturing or celebrating talent but just as much about the communication, self-presentation and staging of talent, which we will examine more closely using a netnographic case study about YouTube, on which fans and critics alike share their musical experience and perceptions of talent, related to the performances of a selection of Norwegian child stars.

While Butler (2019) has shown that there is a clear music education dimension to music talent reality TV in describing such shows as events 'where experts and audiences make educative judgements about performers who are then mentored or excluded depending in large part on their social and cultural capital' (400), the mediated representation of musical talent has been largely copied and reproduced in schools and even in kindergartens, where they often create their own versions of singing (or miming) competitions. The music subject in Norwegian primary schools has quite routinely been given the character of a local Melodi Grand Prix (the national version of the Eurovision Song Contest), where the concept is that each class comes together to create a song or choreography to a song which they perform in front of the whole school and/or the parents. A winner is often chosen, but in keeping with Nordic educational culture, one avoids naming someone a loser. In line with this, the Norwegian municipal schools of music and arts, which are supposed to be a statutory offer for everyone, do not describe their activities as talent development. Instead, an in-depth programme is offered for those who are particularly interested or qualified. However, individual teachers or schools of music and arts can recommend selected students between the ages of thirteen and nineteen to regional talent development programmes in classical music, folk music, jazz and improvisational or rhythmic music at music academies and conservatories, aimed at facilitating recruitment to higher music education. Some private colleges and some of the typical folk high schools found in the Nordic countries also focus on talent development, application preparation for higher music education or qualification for work duties in the media and music industries.

The perceptions of talent that exist in the complex field of media, the music industry and music education, and how actors and institutions perform their respective roles and functions as players in the double game of talentification will be discussed in detail in this chapter. As an extension of this, towards the end of the chapter, we go into more detail about how artistic talent relates in various ways to indigeneity, ethnicity and race in today's Norwegian society.

Concepts of talent and talentification

The concept and discourses of talent can be found across ages at all levels, from local amateur communities to global media events. They exist in all musical forms and genres, and they function as assessment and quality distinctions in everyday, commercial, educational and academic settings. The academic approach to talent and talent development has been largely influenced by quantitative studies on children who play classical music or children with particularly good mathematical skills within developmental psychology and neurology (e.g., Gagné, 1998, 2004; Gagné and McPherson, 2016; Ruthsatz *et al.*, 2014; Shavinina, 1999). In addition, some ethnographic studies have explored children's talent from a more culturally orientated perspective (e.g., Bickford, 2016, 2020; de Mink and McPherson, 2016; Freeman, 2005; Stabell, 2018; Vestad, 2014a). In her research on the learning cultures of classical talent development programmes and junior conservatories in Norway and England, Stabell (2018) identifies four different assumptions about musical talent among students and teachers in her material: that talent is innate and unteachable, that it can be graded, that musicality is something other than technique and that talent must be nurtured.

If talent is perceived as innate, as something one has in oneself, then it becomes something that not everyone has, or as Stabell's informant claims, talent is something 'most people don't have' (110). Such an absolute concept of artistic talent can be thought of as being fairly widespread in the population. This probably also applies to the somewhat more relativistic assumption that talent can still be graded, from fairly talented to exceptional or super talented (112). In Stabell's context of aspiring performers, musical talent appears to be more or less synonymous with musicality, which can probably be more nuanced in a broader context. Here, however, its inherent, absolute nature is specified among the interviewed students: 'Technique is something you can learn, but with musicality, you either have it or you don't' (113). However, the students in this study were aware that having talent is not enough to become a musician; it must be nurtured as well. In addition to emphasising the importance of discipline and a work ethic for aspiring classical musicians, such a view obviously also legitimises music education as significant practices. Whether it helps to demystify the concept of talent is another question.

Although we recognise Stabell's categories as widespread and common descriptions of both music education and general discursive assumptions of musical talent, it is imperative for our project to emphasise that from a critical, theoretically informed point of view, the concept of talent does not by definition represent any fixed value or refer to the inherent characteristics of music, genres, styles of expression and the like. Instead, we will attempt to discern the common usages of the term talent from a corresponding perspective as given in Moore's (2002) critical approach to notions of authenticity as essentialist properties of something or someone. Contrary to this perception of authenticity, Moore investigates how or by what processes such characteristics have become firmly associated with what appears to be authentic. This analysis involves a de-essentialisation of the seemingly intrinsic qualities of authenticity or, for that matter, of talent, instead acknowledging that these features are attributed by historical, social and cultural processes, which can be described as authentication, or, for our part, as talentification. Moore (2002: 220) further argues, 'So, in acknowledging that authenticity is ascribed to, rather than inscribed in, a performance, it is beneficial to ask who, rather than what, is being authenticated by that performance'. The corresponding questions to be asked concerning talent are as follows: who exercises or what causes the talentification of whom and whose characteristics in which contexts and with which intentions and/or interests? This obviously brings power to the table, but in Foucault's (1980) sense, it is more important to understand the significance of the *who*, *what* and *which* for the production of meaning and truth than to detect guilt and culprits. What is apparently inscribed in the talent is discursively ascribed or attributed to the assumption of it, whereas its symbolic power lies precisely in the notion of *illusio* (Bourdieu, 1992/1996) as a principle of assumption, emotional investment and belief in the game to which the players actively commit themselves. These matters open the way to an exploration and scrutiny of musical talent and talentification considering the double logic that otherwise pervades this book.

Talentification therefore constitutes an open research approach aimed at identifying and investigating the conceptual and practical representation of activities and processes that contribute to the construction, negotiation and assessment of talent from a critical, multidimensional perspective. Much like the way 'musicking' (Small, 1998) has instituted a widened perspective to understand musicianship in terms of the verb 'to music', musical talentification opens ways to relate to and understand what and who builds musical talent, and how and why it is built. Musical talentification as a social construct captures all that is going on, not only in the artists-to-be but in the processes and players surrounding them and is intended to shed light on the social positioning of all parts involved. Portraying talentification as a double game, where the co-creating aspect inherent in the concept – the one never being without the other – plays a key role in making sense of the economic, symbolic and socio-cultural power structures that underlie all processes of talentification.

In the following sections, the concepts of talent and musical talentification will be discussed within the framework of music education in classical and folk music as well as in relation to social media and indigeneity, ethnicity and race. Thus, a range of conceptual adaptations, further developments and clarifications will also be carried out.

Assumptions of talent in music education

One of these paths concerns music educational understanding and cultivation of talent. The public school system in Norway, which accommodates most children, is municipal and does not generally focus on special education or benefits for those who stand out in any way. It is free of charge and is 'based on the principle of equal and adapted education for all in an inclusive comprehensive school system' where the children are 'to be included in a common knowledge, culture and value base, and experience mastery and challenges at school' (Nokut, n.d.). The music subject is based on these principles, where the curriculum (Utdanningsdirektoratet, 2020) states that music is a central subject for creativity, cultural understanding and identity development, and it should prepare the students for participation in a social and working life that requires practical and aesthetic skills, creativity and social interaction. The music subject in Norwegian schools is thus not only a performing subject but a general music subject influenced by the *Bildung* tradition and the development of the welfare state (see Chapter 2).

Within this school system, there are possibilities to apply to special music programmes in upper secondary school (ages sixteen to nineteen). These are free of charge and admission is based on the combination of grades and an audition. There is, however, an emphasis on a broad education including both the music subjects and other subjects, such as languages, mathematics and social sciences. This has led to criticism from the fields of musical expertise and higher music education, connected to the view of the music programme in upper secondary school obstructing 'talented' students in their progression towards expert musicianship (Ellefsen, 2014). Arguments connected to this include that the students are not getting enough time to practise their instruments; consequently, some students who are viewed as talented by their teachers, parents or others are advised not to attend these programmes. To cope with this, Young Talents Barratt Due – a talent development programme within the classical music genre for students under the age of 19 (see Barratt Due Institute of Music, n.d.) – has proposed that testing the concept of what they call '"toppidrettsgymnas" for musicians' begin in the 2025–2026 school year. Toppidrettsgymnas are private upper secondary schools which aim at preparing their students to become top athletes, while they do the minimum number of subjects required to receive a diploma (Senter for talentutvikling Barratt Due, 2024).

The music programme in upper secondary school is in many ways torn between mandates. On one hand, the music programme is expected to constitute a good basis for further training as a musician or music teacher (Vilbli.no, n.d.) and thus prepare students for auditioning into higher music education with a focus on addressing individual talent. On the other hand, it is supposed to be a part of the general comprehensive schooling rooted in welfare state ideas. This tension is at the core of the music programme's relevance. Ellefsen (2014) has studied the constitution of student subjectivities within the discursive practices of the music programme, and she asserts that the programme's relevance is 'constituted in a careful, institutional balancing act between expectations and demands that are all solidly and legitimately anchored in other educational, professional or everyday (musical) practices' (307). She finds dedication, entrepreneurship, competence, specialisation and connoisseurship to be prominent discourses at play in the music programme practices of musicianship. Talent and musicality are concepts that are seldom applied in the students' language, however, similar connotations are used when addressing and constituting the 'ability' of the proper student, where 'the apt and the able have a superior inherent capacity of understanding and doing music, theoretically and practically' (Ellefsen, 2014: 296). There is thus a doubleness in building institutions for being democratic and not addressing talent and expertise but still using the concepts and ideas of talent, authenticity, expertise and related connotations as building blocks.

This is related to what Stabell (2023) addresses as a social democratic discourse to which the talent development field connects through the emphasis on social democratic ideas, such as access, equal possibilities and adapted training. In her analysis of reports and other documents concerning specialised musical training for young people under the age of nineteen, Stabell identifies three discourses that contribute to the construction of 'talent development' – namely, a social democratic discourse, a professionalism discourse and a *Bildung* discourse. She asserts that drawing on social democratic ideas could be useful for achieving a political impact and receiving economic support. However, neither the talent development programmes being free of charge nor being geographically distributed outside the largest cities solves the problem that to be accepted into these programmes, the children are required to hold a high level of expertise in playing their instruments – which is not possible without years of training and effort (Stabell, 2023). Moreover, we know this favours children from families with economic means and cultural capital (Berge *et al.*, 2019; Nielsen *et al.*, 2023b).

The Norwegian municipal schools of music and arts are, like the compulsory school system, rooted in social democratic ideas that developed alongside the growth of the welfare state from the 1950s onwards. Their main vision is to be 'for everyone' (Norsk kulturskoleråd, n.d.), focusing on accessibility and economy. The schools are extracurricular and not part of the regular school system, and, although they are publicly financed, it costs money to attend them. In line with their vision, the term 'talent' is commonly avoided in the schools' policy documents. However, research shows that a specialisation discourse is strongly present (Jordhus-Lier, 2018), that a strong classical music hegemony is visible within the schools' curriculum framework (Karlsen and Nielsen, 2021) and that the teaching practices are largely connected to established musical goals (Jordhus-Lier *et al.*, 2023). Thus, although the schools aim to be 'for everyone', attendance is, to a certain degree, stratified by class, gender and ethnicity (Berge *et al.*, 2019). Within such an open (but not fully open) school, where the term 'talent' is generally avoided, the discourse of an educational pathway is central in the idea of preparing students for entrance into higher music education, for the music and musical traditions they will encounter in upper secondary school (which is seen as a preparation for higher music education) and for a professional life as a musician (Jordhus-Lier and Nielsen, 2025). The curriculum framework actually declares that the school's training should create a foundation for the students to be able to qualify for the music programme in upper secondary school, talent programmes and higher music education (Norwegian Council for the Schools of Music and Performing Arts, 2016).

Within this school system itself, there is also a pathway organised as a pyramid from the breadth programme at the bottom, focusing on broad participation and outreach activities; advancing to the school's main activity, the core programme, which is based on progression, systematic training and development in different stages; and reaching the in-depth programme at the top, which is an offer for a limited selection of students with 'special qualifications and interest in the art discipline' (Norwegian Councils for the Schools of Music and Performing Arts, 2016). The curriculum framework further states that access to the in-depth programme should be regulated through auditions, which is an open selection mechanism in theory. However, the criteria for selection are often unclear, resulting in the 'best' students winning the audition without transparency regarding the rationale behind the selection process. The pyramid implies a decrease in students from the breadth programme to the in-depth programme at the top. Therefore, due to both the 'pyramid way' of seeing the pathway and economic reasons, a selection of students must be made. From auditions for admission to national talent development programmes, we know that the 'identification of talent' is important, where talent is described by teachers as having a natural expression, intuition and personal sound (Stabell, 2018; Stabell and Jordhus-Lier, 2017). In addition to open and hidden selection mechanisms regulating access to the in-depth programme, the learning culture within the school will enable what is considered 'the valued currency' in that respect (Stabell and Jordhus-Lier, 2017).

The idea of the in-depth programme being open to all is central within the schools of music and arts field. Thus, the Norwegian Council for the Schools of Music and Performing Arts (2021) has made a strategy plan called 'in-depth learning with diversity'. However, diversity is only expressed as geographical diversity, focusing on collaboration with other institutions to be able to offer in-depth/talent programmes independent of where the students live. This could be seen in relation to the social democratic discourse described by Stabell (2023), where underlying mechanisms of selection and viewing some students as more talented than others are not considered, and thus, a double game is played. Stabell and Jordhus-Lier (2017) argue in favour of an 'in-depth breadth programme' comprising a breadth of genres and art forms, which could increase the accessibility of specialisation and diversity in the school's activities, where everyone with an interest in going deeper into something is included. However, is this openness reachable or will there always be a double game of perceptions of talent within a music educational institution focusing on instrumental tuition, being part of an educational system which also aims at educating the next generation of musicians?

Talentification in classical music

Knowing well that 'classical music' is a reductionist, and in many cases also misleading, term, for the sake of simplicity, we choose to use the term to address Western art music (which is not an unproblematic term either) from approximately 1600 to today. This is in line with how Bull (2019) uses the term, as it resembles the way in which her informants denote this broad music tradition. In Norway, too, 'classical music' is routinely used by institutions, such as the Norwegian Academy of Music and the Norwegian Broadcasting Corporation.

The classical music tradition goes back a long time, and celebrating the 'best' musicians, the virtuosos, those who can play the fastest, with the most intensity or those who possess a special talent, especially at an early age, has a history within the classical music tradition with Mozart, perhaps the greatest child prodigy in history, as well as violin virtuosos, like Paganini and his Norwegian counterpart Ole Bull, as examples. We find such talent portrayed in today's music education in Norway, for instance, in *Salaby* (Salaby, n.d.).[1] Here, in order for the children to learn about classical music, they can either 'visit' the virtual rooms called 'superstars of the old days' or 'Mozart-town', which both focus especially on the individuals with an emphasis on the fact that they all started to play music early on and that there was something special about them. This illustrates how talent is viewed in an individualistic way in the Western world, which incidentally is the place of origin of the authors of this book as well. In addition, the examples of classic superstars in *Salaby* invariably showcase white, male bodies. Within the framework of the sociology of music education, one can place a few critical studies on race, class and classical music education (and talentification). While Bull (2019: 111) observes in her study 'that race is present in classical music not just through its representation and discourses, but that the very practices that are required to produce the aesthetic of classical music encode and reproduce whiteness through [. . .] historical continuities', Baker (2014) has, through his extensive critical examination of the Venezuelan, and eventually global, orchestral education programme *El Sistema*, argued that its conceptualisation of music education 'rests on a salvationist narrative – the idea of saving the poor through the transmission of high art' (Baker, 2016: 24). However, while we continue to touch upon the classed nature of classical music, for the moment, we will leave the discussions about interrelations between music and race, ethnicity and indigeneity to a later section of the chapter.

In the field of classical music education, it can often seem that one strives for a given or fixed form for the piece of music in question. Bull (2019), in her study on youth classical music groups, describes the idea of 'getting it right' as an important component of classical music education and aesthetics, where correction, musical standards and gendered disciplining is formative for the aesthetics of the 'rightness' of classical music. This is not merely connected to getting the notes right but also to the sound and expression of an established standard. When seeing this in relation to Stabell's (2018) finding of musical talent appearing as more or less synonymous with musicality (as compared to technique) within classical talent development programmes and junior conservatories, we can ask who sets the standards of the most valued musicality. The answer may be that all of us who are trained in classical music contribute to setting them, most often without being aware of it. As classical musicians, we play the double game of talentification, where the rules for and belief in what constitutes talent are embodied in our *habitus*, all while trying to unveil what is not recognised or is misrecognised (Bourdieu, 1977). Stabell (2018) finds talent to be a powerful criterion for positioning students, because talent 'pointed to an innate trait and thus appeared to be an important asset of a student's symbolic capital' (231). Most of the children playing classical music are from privileged middle-class homes, where the parents have invested in them to be musically talented, enabling them to develop a strong identity connected to their musicality (Bull, 2019). However, this identity, according to Bull (2019: 190), means that 'they uphold the boundaries of classical music and the rules that they have learnt about what is valued in this genre', which contrasts with narratives on opportunities for all. Bull (2019) uncovers connections between the tradition and practices of classical music and the middle class's boundary-drawing around their protected spaces. Exclusionary mechanisms connected to classical music practices operate in subtle ways, where the discourse of talent is used to give the impression that it is open to everyone (Bull, 2021).

There are several investors in the game of talentification in classical music, for instance, the parents, as mentioned previously. Bull (2019) shows the connection between classical music and middle-class forms of identity. The parents invest not only in their child but also in their family's position and identity to ensure success (see also Chapter 5). Stabell (2018) finds talent to be strongly connected to something perceived as natural, innate and unconscious. Also present is the recognition that hard work is needed, but it must be complemented by an innate talent. Bull (2019) describes students and parents putting in a lot of work to achieve excellence and be seen as talented, but at the same time, they want to conceal the labour to be seen as naturally talented. Thus, 'the "talent" becomes the property of the individual rather than the outcome of the labour of teachers, parents, conductors and others in investing in this body' (Bull, 2019: 80). Bull further claims that 'high levels of parental/ adult investment can masquerade as "talent" or excellence and in classical music education musical ability rests on long-term invest-ment, which is currently premised on being middle-class' (186).

Institutions also play a significant role in the game of talen-tification in classical music. Bull addresses what she names 'the "institutional ecology" of youth classical music', describing 'an institutional landscape that appears natural and eternal' (29). One of the five categories of this ecology is the 'talent scouts', which are both publicly and privately funded 'institutions or schemes that identify "exceptional" youth "talent"' (31). The most promi-nent of such institutions in Norway regarding classical music is Young Talents Barratt Due, which denotes itself as 'a greenhouse for the musicians of tomorrow' (Barratt Due Institute of Music, n.d.). Stabell (2023) claims that we see more and increasingly ear-lier specialisation due to, among other things, talent development more often being justified in the society's need for producing top musicians who are able to compete for positions in Norwegian orchestras. The talent to invest in, in that respect, includes those who are believed to able to win competitions and not necessarily those who, for instance, have a special interest in music or who experiment with new expressions. Higher music education insti-tutions are suppliers of premises for what is considered musical talent. Here, the concept of talent is, in many ways, inscribed in the practices and learning cultures, as well as being connected to specialisation, hierarchies and power relations. Perkins (2013) identifies four intertwined learning cultures within a UK conserva-tory, including 'performing specialism' in which '[l]earning to be a specialised and high-quality performer [. . .] is positioned as a key and dominant part of the conservatoire's practices' (204), and 'musical hierarchies' describing a field 'in which there is space for only a *limited* number of "stars"', and 'to achieve such a status one needs to be visibly "successful"' (206). The learning cultures are constructed differently depending on the student's position within them, which again depends on the student's *habitus* and cultural capital.

Within higher music education institutions and junior conservatoires, both teachers and students themselves could be viewed as players in the talentification games. Stabell (2018) addresses talent as capital, emphasising talent being used to position students by being 'attributed *to* a student by significant persons in the learning culture' (232). Significant persons could be both teachers and fellow students. Bull (2019: 55) describes how singers would pick up signals from their fellow singers and use them to, among other things, position others as 'talented'. Positioning oneself in relation to others is also common and serves to build hierarchies (Perkins, 2013; Stabell 2018).

Brief excursion into a traditional event of competition and talentification

Perhaps somewhat surprisingly, traditional folk music is the genre of Norwegian music most marked by competition. Since 1888, the so-called *Landskappleiken*, or the national championship in folk music and dance, has been held regularly. Furthermore, since 1923, it has been an annual event in which one can compete in Hardanger fiddle, fiddle, melodeon accordion and the sung-recited *kveding*, and usually also in Jew's harp, the zither-like *langeleik*, flute and other older folk music instruments as well as song dances, figure dances and couple dances (see Aksdal, 2022; Landskappleiken, 2024). There are no similar competitions in other Scandinavian countries, and thus *Landskappleiken* may be interpreted as an expression of a particular need for Norwegian nation-building, since the country was colonised or in union with Denmark and Sweden, respectively, for more than five hundred years. The competition is divided into several levels, from junior to elite, and the participants are assessed according to explicit criteria bound by a strict tradition. The most important and prestigious instrument in the competition has consistently been the uniquely Norwegian Hardanger fiddle, which is played solo.

Landskappleiken is still considered the most important event in Norwegian traditional music, and although folk music has expanded its repertoires, forms of interaction, basis of recruitment, education and performance arenas in recent decades, its normative authority has left very deep marks on the genre. This implies that *Landskappleiken* has ensured the hegemonic status of certain instruments, styles and subgenres. Moreover, it has highlighted the music of particular regions and districts as more authentic, and thereby more valuable, than others. Furthermore, it leads to selected performers (often representing established family dynasties within Norwegian folk music) being acknowledged as master fiddlers with enormous status and power of definition, meaning that the apprenticeship mode of learning is probably stronger here than in the classical tradition. There is an obvious gender dimension to this as well. Of all the winners of the Hardanger fiddle class from 1896 to 2023, for example, 119 were male and 3 were female (FolkOrg, 2024). Finally, the format of *Landskappleiken* moulds a pattern for talentification and socialisation into Norwegian folk music, as so-called *Sjokoladekappleiker* are organised for children aged four to twelve years in folk music communities around the country, where the young participants get chocolate, instead of points, from the jury (Møre og Romsdal Folkemusikklag, 2012). Anchoring in tradition and certain perceptions of authenticity means that there are also strong expectations that children who participate in folk music education in schools of music and arts, which are located within one of the 'core areas' of Norwegian folk music, should be dressed in the traditional *bunad* when performing. The *bunad* is a very elaborate folk costume, which is 'often made of high-quality fabric with lots of embroidery, and silver jewellery to go with it' (Karlsen *et al.*, 2023: 280). As these are very expensive items of clothing, it is no exaggeration that it involves a significant investment for a family to participate in the traditional folk music culture in a proper way. While *Landskappleiken* has undoubtedly been very stimulating for the maintenance and esteem of Norwegian folk music, the talentification exercised has also fulfilled a distinct gatekeeper function based on the iteration of the power of tradition.

Media talentification and cyborg talentification

Another significant path of talentification concerns the media's interest in constantly discovering new talent and the media and music industries' investment in talent development, including how talent is interpreted, talked over and valued in and with the help of social media. Research studies on televised talent shows include that of Keinonen and colleagues (2018), who analyse audience engagement with these talent shows as 'sets of experiences' (59), uncovering a rather subjective nature of talent judgements. Butler (2019), conversely, emphasises the authoritative evaluation in music talent reality television as 'experts and audiences make educative judgements' (400) based on their *habitus*, creating class divisions within musical talent. Moreover, the ongoing negotiation and evaluation of musical talent on social media are described as fluid, shapeable and yet distinct processes of talentification in Merkelbach's (2022) case study on how YouTube's countless users actively reproduce, share and comment on videos of child pop stars.

The cultural, historical, and not least social and technological processes on social media platforms provide a magnifying glass for tracing and analysing multiple de-essentialisations of talent perceptions. Social media platforms are, much like talent reality television described by Butler (2019: 400), cultural spaces 'where processes of judgement and distinction are more easily identified than in many other music education sites'. Furthermore, YouTube has, since the platform's launch in 2005, incessantly extended its reach, absorbing the main media, and many popular TV programmes are – almost simultaneously to their broadcasting – available as video footage on YouTube. This is especially true for all types of talent shows involving children, which are popular video material with high numbers of views and shares.

Considering YouTube beyond particular subject-related content, it appears primarily as a complex communicative environment. Its participating functions, audio and video enhancements and algorithmic filtering together stimulate, and in turn are stimulated by, the activities of its online users. As human and technological impulses interconnect increasingly closely on social media platforms, human autocracy is challenged, pushing forth the question of 'how to conceive of humans and their augmentations' (Wells, 2014: 16).

To problematise these processes and the consequential dissolution of boundaries, such as the one between human and machine in the online environment of YouTube, Merkelbach (2022) uses different aspects of cyborg theory based on Haraway (1991) who, with her *Cyborg Manifesto*, inspired an academic cyborg revolution.

Importantly, a cyborg in this context is identified as being at the core of augmented human communication and not as a science fiction creature with superpowers. In the context of music, the conceptualisation of the cyborg may serve as a theoretical framework to analyse how the online environment affects modes of music listening and appreciation and, consequently, the talentification of musical artists on social media. By incorporating the cyborg, online talentification can thus be conceptualised as *cyborg talentification* (Merkelbach, 2022). In this cyborg talentification, players are shaped by and communicated with and by means of technology, and the signs and functions on YouTube – such as likes, shares and comments – work as cyborg tools that organise all talenting impulses.

Each case of cyborg talentification is closely connected to the artistic persona and narrative of the artist. At the same time, the inductive mechanisms behind all talenting impulses show some common traits that overrule their case specificity. First, the empirical data from different YouTube comment sections can be found to each develop a recognisable discursive space. In these spaces, fans cultivate specific perceptions and descriptions of child star talent, manners of speech, choices of concepts and particular ways of relating to 'their' star. Second, overruling case specificity, all comment materials can be analysed as driven by either one or a combination of three main motives: the specific song and performance; the associations with other artists; and the culturally, historically and socially related norms of childhood and innocence. The latter motive seems particularly important in the negotiation of talentification, across online and offline environments, as the young and innocent child plays and is made to play a central role in the pursuit of pure talent and in (cyborg) talentification.

Pure, innate talent as a fixed size, received at birth and consequently innocent stubbornly holds on to its characteristic glow and links itself tightly to the artistic persona of the discussed case. Relating to child stars, this implies that the specific idea of talent within a particular group is synonymous with the child artist's voice and demeanour. Here, we touch on the core in the double game of (cyborg) talentification involving young children, dictating culturally defined qualities of innocence to create experiences of awe when extraordinary talent meets ordinary – adult – audiences. In the double game of talentification, much seems at stake to uphold the dichotomies of age versus innocence, normality versus extraordinariness. Marking a clear line between what can be expected from the young child and what cannot, in terms of both technical and emotional abilities and knowledge, is crucial.

As talent is paired with innocence, it receives a 'mission', which, as in the case of child pop star Angelina Jordan Astar, whom fans call 'their angel' (Merkelbach, 2022), might imply a superior and healing force reinstalling disillusioned adults' faith in wonders beyond their cognitive understanding (O'Connor, 2009). However, the gifted child may be accused of upsetting the balance of what Askerøi and Vestad (2021) describe as an *aesthetic vocality* when singing in an adult manner and thus retreating from their – expected – innocence. Here, multiple intentions and discourses are at play: the adult's impulse to protect the child from enacting grown-up sensuality and the child's 'vocality discourse [. . .] appropriated from listening to recordings' (52).

On YouTube, the negotiations of child stars' innocence and talent are well guarded within each comment section. The comment sections on YouTube are spaces which the content creator and administrator (the one responsible for sharing the video on YouTube) may control, assisted by algorithmic filtering. Anyone may post a comment in these spaces, and comments vary both in length and content. They may simply express feelings, often supported by emoticons, they may reflect reactions to details of the musical performance or simply be part of a conversation with other users. Comment sections can be turned off by the administrator for various reasons. Once they are posted, comments will move around and be sorted according to their popularity. In that sense, these spaces serve as gatekeepers of a specific aesthetic culture.

As of 2025, YouTube has performed this kind of aesthetic cultivation within the limited spaces of its comment sections for 20 years. At the same time, YouTube has, since its launch, vastly expanded the platform's reach across the globe. Due to this geographic expansion, the platform's aesthetic cultures are in a constant flow, blending, communicating or just existing tangentially to each other. Burgess and Green (2018) describe this negotiation of cultures as a platform-particular type of *cultural cosmopolitanism*, rendering YouTube 'a place in which individuals can represent their identities and perspectives, engage in self-representations of others, and encounter cultural differences' (129).

Burgess and Green's somewhat ideal representation of an almost automatic cultural exchange on YouTube has been criticised as naive and superficial. Hull and colleagues (2010) argue that cosmopolitan activities must balance free and guided parts for young people to be able to take 'steps forward in cosmopolitan understandings' (361). Even more critical voices have countered the idea of an all-embracing cosmopolitanism on social media as practically impossible as YouTube's echo chambers and algorithm-sorted spaces make its users cluster in homogeneous places and oppress rather than further cultural understanding and exchange (Zuckerman, 2015). Other voices report the opposite and accuse critics of cultural and aesthetic cosmopolitanism on social media of exhibiting a 'narrow conception of the virtual as an imitation of the real' (Hall, 2018: 4). Considering the cases of child pop stars on YouTube, Merkelbach (2022) identifies distinctive aesthetic cosmopolitan agency in each artistic narrative, such as The BlackSheeps' style of ethno-cultural uniqueness within the universal punk rock genre (249). As a Norwegian–Sámi band, they also add a dimension of indigeneity to the various dimensions of cosmopolitanism, which are addressed in the next section.

Indigeneity, ethnicity and race

In the Nordic context, there has been a clear tendency for Sámi culture and music to increasingly become part of the public and the media, not least in connection with talent shows and competitions. In Norway, it is especially interesting that Indigenous music, such as the Sámi joik, has gone from being represented in the ethnically genred Sámi Grand Prix song contest, from the 1990s onwards, to being included as a regular genre in the primetime television success *Stjernekamp* [Battle of the Stars] in the 2010s, a trend that peaked in 2018, when the winner of *Stjernekamp* was Sámi artist and activist Ella Marie Hætta Isaksen. Sámi elements in music competitions have, however, been present in three Norwegian entries in the Eurovision Song Contest over the decades, but in quite different ways. Already in 1960, Norway's first contribution to the international competition,

'Voi-voi' (Elgaaen, 1960), had some vague reminiscences of Sámi language and culture. The song was performed by Norwegian singer Nora Brockstedt, dressed in a Sámi-inspired outfit. In retrospect, it appears as an instance of cultural appropriation. In 1980, however, the Norwegian entry, 'Sámiid ædnan' (Kjelsberg *et al.*, 1980), included an authentic joik performed by Sámi joiker Mattis Hætta, and in 2019, the group KEiiNO, including Sámi rapper Fred Buljo, represented Norway with the song 'Spirit in the Sky' (Hermansen *et al.*, 2018). Notwithstanding these contributions, an even more important turning point came in 2008, when the rock band The BlackSheeps won both the Norwegian and Nordic finals in the song writing and performing contest Melodi Grand Prix Junior (MGPjr) for children and young people aged eight to fifteen years with the Sámi-Norwegian song 'Oro jáska beana' (Johnsen *et al.*, 2008). As shown later in the chapter, this performance had unexpectedly great significance for the spread and recognition of Sámi culture in Norway and abroad. Thus, although renowned Sámi artist Mari Boine has been a significant voice within international Indigenous music since the 1980s, it can be argued that it is mostly in recent decades that Sámi music has started to become more mainstream in the Nordic countries. An indication of this is that Sámi music is the only genre, style or culture that is particularly highlighted in the music curriculum of the current Norwegian National Curriculum, *Kunnskapsløftet 2020* (Utdanningsdirektoratet, 2020).

Today, the Sámi – being the only Indigenous people of Europe – have been recognised as such through the establishment of autonomous Sámi parliaments for matters affecting the Sámi minority in Norway, Sweden and Finland, whereas the cultural region historically inhabited by the Sámi people, *Sápmi*, extends over the northern parts of these countries as well as the Kola Peninsula in Russia. Estimates of how large the Sámi population is vary from seventy thousand to one hundred and ten thousand since there are few common criteria for what being Sámi actually entails. The most common estimates are that there are between forty thousand and sixty thousand Sámi in Norway, twenty thousand to forty thousand in Sweden, seven thousand to eight thousand in Finland and two thousand in Russia (Josefsen and Skogerbø, 2021). Sámi is not one language but a language group in which about ten different languages are counted, some of which are spoken by very few active language users. This is due to, among other things, long-term oppression and discrimination against Sámi language, religion and culture. From the 1850s to the 1960s, Norway had a targeted Norwegianisation policy directed at the Indigenous Sámi people and other national minorities. It was not until 2023 that this policy was subjected to earnest self-criticism and regret from the authorities. This happened when the Truth and Reconciliation Commission, appointed by the Norwegian Parliament, submitted its report on the Norwegianisation policy and injustice committed against these vulnerable groups (Sannhets- og forsoningskommisjonen, 2023).

Notwithstanding this fact, Sámi music's increasing presence in the Norwegian public has not happened without friction and conflicts. When 'Sámiid ædnan' [Sámi Land] was voted as the Norwegian entry in the Eurovision Song Contest in 1980, it was against the background of the so-called Alta case, which was a political conflict from around 1968 to 1982, where Sámi and environmental protection interests opposed a large-scale hydropower development in the Alta River in North Norway (Berg-Nordlie and Tvedt, 2024). The case had great significance for the development of later Norwegian Sámi discourse and policy. 'Sámiid ædnan', performed by Sverre Kjelsberg, included a joik by the young Sámi Mattis Hætta. This might be the only joik most Norwegians know, and in retrospect, it must be stated that it has probably been used just as much to bully and stigmatise the Sámi people as to pay tribute to them. Against this background, it is noteworthy that The BlackSheeps' 2008 hit song 'Oro jáska beana' gained unprecedented acknowledgement for the Sámi language in popular culture across Norway at the time, as shown in Merkelbach's (2022) aforementioned study on child star fandom and talentification on YouTube. Overnight, a language long banned in Norway was suddenly on the lips of young fans. As YouTube comment materials demonstrate, the unfamiliar sounds also intrigued listeners from all over the world and the few drops of the exotic, Indigenous language embedded in the spirited rhythm of the music, was received enthusiastically. Especially listeners without any knowledge of the Sámi language commented on its musical sound. The BlackSheeps combined the local with the global, creating *glocal* material in a probably quite unconscious but, when investigated retrospectively, very particular manner, and they went viral with a song that merely had a few selected and rather meaningless phrases in the Northern Sámi language.

Without much ado, The BlackSheeps had awakened consciousness around an Indigenous culture that for a long time had been suppressed by the Norwegian government, much like other Indigenous cultures in the world. In that sense, The BlackSheeps co-created 'a cosmopolitan worldview that is produced through aesthetics' (Papastergiadis, 2018: 200). The banal yet mysterious and poetic line, 'Oro jáska beana' [Shut up, Dog] succeeded in igniting a kind of communal feeling in fans, making them feel like a part of something independent of their own cultural heritage. Thus, the local, explicitly present in The BlackSheeps' musical project, interacts with the global, carrying the possibility of identification for individuals beyond Nordic borders. As Sámi-inspired punk rock child stars on the pop scene, they were, in many ways, social media pioneers (Merkelbach, 2022). The youth band from a tiny place with approximately 880 inhabitants represented a unique type of aesthetic cosmopolitanism (Regev, 2007), blending the ethnic-local with global punk rock. In disrupting the understanding of ethnic exclusiveness 'to which certain cultural products and art works inherently belong' (Regev, 2007: 125), The BlackSheeps opened a door to the Sámi heritage for a global public.

Later on, in 2018, by winning the popular talent show *Stjernekamp*, televised by the Norwegian Broadcasting Corporation, the young Sámi artist Ella Marie Hætta Isaksen was widely recognised both as a very versatile singing talent and as one of the most promising innovators of Sámi music since Mari Boine. However, her talent proved to be even more versatile when she debuted in 2023 with the lead role in the film *Ellos eatnu* [Let the River Live] (Giæver, 2023), which is about the aforementioned Alta conflict, seen from a Sámi perspective. Just as Mari Boine has been a spokesperson for Sámi music, language and culture for decades, Ella Mare Hætta Isaksen quickly stepped into the role of a leading Sámi activist, not only in a cultural but soon also in a political sense. Thus, the multi-talentification of her came to play an important part in the case, which, to the greatest extent after the Alta conflict, has accentuated contradictions between Sámi interests and the development of the Norwegian society at large.

Moreover, the Fosen conflict has revolved around a fight over the location of wind power plants and Sámi reindeer herders' rights within the same area. In 2010, the Norwegian Water Resources and Energy Directorate granted permission for two large wind power plants at Fosen in mid-Norway. The two plants are located in the winter grazing area of two groups of Sámi reindeer herders. The decisions concerning permits for the wind power plants were appealed by Sámi groups and the case ended up in the Norwegian Supreme Court. In 2021, the Supreme Court handed down a judgement stating that the decision regarding permission for wind power development at Fosen was invalid because the power plants infringe on the right of reindeer-herding Sámi people according to Article 27 of the United Nations International Covenant on the Civil and Political Rights of ethnic, religious or linguistic minorities to exercise their traditional culture (United Nations, 1966). However, the Supreme Court did not decide what should happen to the wind turbines, and they continued to operate. This caused great frustration among the affected Sámi and eventually also among others. In 2023, demonstrations were held in the Government Quarter in Oslo against the government's failure to follow up on the Supreme Court's judgement five hundred days after it became legally binding. Ella Marie Hætta Isaksen acted as a very media-savvy and visible spokesperson for the activists. The Sámi protesters occupied the reception of the Ministry of Oil and Energy and refused to leave until they were forcibly removed by the police three days later, which escalated the action and led to extensive demonstrations and civil disobedience in the form of blocking the entrances to various ministries, not unlike the actions in the Alta conflict. In the spring of 2023, mediation was initiated between the two Sámi groups and the respective wind power companies, and around the following turn of the year, the mediation resulted in an amicable agreement. When implemented, the agreement must compensate for the natural interventions that have led to the loss of winter grazing land for reindeer by providing financial compensation, replacement of grazing areas, which the state has undertaken to provide, and a right of veto for the Sámi in the matter of further licensed operations after the current license period of twenty-five years has ended (Skogvang, 2024).

Following these events, however, eighteen Sámi activists were fined for the occupation of the Ministry of Oil and Energy and the blockade of other ministries. Nevertheless, in April 2024, all activists were acquitted in the Oslo District Court, where the court placed particular emphasis on the fact that the demonstration was aimed at a state human rights violation that had been established in a Supreme Court judgement. However, the prosecution was not satisfied with the judgement and justification provided by the District Court and thus decided to appeal the verdict for the thirteen Sámi youths who demonstrated at the Ministry of Oil and Energy. At the time of writing in April 2025, the Supreme Court has decided to hear the appeal. Therefore, at the same time that the state and public media celebrate Indigenous music and talent, and young Sámi are gaining increased political respect – not least because of the leadership shown by the now Greta Thunberg-like role model Ella Marie Hætta Isaksen – the government is attempting to buy its way out of human rights violations against the same people and even prosecutes Sámi political activists to the very end. Therein lies a paradox which probably illuminates something crucial about the double game of musical talentification and about music's functions of potentially acting as both a sedative and an energiser in social conflicts and power struggles. At the same time, it highlights that conflicts between the interests and needs of vulnerable minority groups and the majority society are loaded with meaning and power as well as massive economic and cultural investments.

A parallel to the functions that Sámi musical talentification has taken on in contemporary Norway can be found in a multitude of examples of young musical talent often labelled in the Norwegian context as having 'a multicultural background' or simply 'multicultural' individuals being taken for granted as representatives of an ascribed culture of origin. Such more or less forced ethnic or racial discourses of authenticity are often given weight in the attribution or promotion of talent, especially in popular music contexts. The most widespread public reception of such practices is that they manifest a cultural, social and economic form of abolition of racism and ethnic oppression in a liberal society. A striking example is the arts (education) organisation or 'talentification factory' Fargespill (Kaleidoscope in English), which has been nominated for the Nobel Peace Prize by Norwegian politicians for its work in producing performances with immigrants and Norwegians between the ages of seven and twenty-five:

based on the cultural treasures the participants bring with them, such as traditional songs, dance moves and rhythms from their upbringing or heritage. The musical expressions are merged together in medleys, with Norwegian folk traditions or expressions from modern youth culture. The performances are elevated by professional musicians, choreographers, instructors, sound- and light designers. (Fargespill, n.d.)

The notion that music has the power to build bridges between cultures and that xenophobia and racism can be met with art projects that highlight the cultural resources in immigrant environments has been investigated by Kvaal (2018) through an ethnographic study on the case of Fargespill. On one hand, Fargespill obviously succeeds in exciting its audience, and the organisation is designated as a role model for successful integration in several political, educational and art- and culture-orientated contexts. In exploring how the music and dance work of those involved in Fargespill, and further to what extent the musical engagement that is made possible in this connection can be said to strengthen or weaken their agency, Kvaal, however, finds that, in reality, parts of the actual diversity are in danger of being sacrificed at the altar of recognition. Fargespill wants to present the audience with diversity, but this must, at the same time, be presented in ways that move them emotionally by playing on well-established means to achieve audience engagement and success. Thus, the underlying thinking about multiculturalism, representation and identity as well as considerations about music as universal and immediate communication are challenged.

However, an even sharper criticism of Fargespill has come from Solomon (2016), who argues as follows:

> At worst, Fargespill can be seen as a cynical manipulation that uses the voices and bodies of children to tell a story that, while reassuring for majority white Norwegians, grossly misrepresents the reality for, and experiences of, people of non-white, non-European immigrant background in Norway, sidestepping ongoing problems of racism and intolerance toward minorities and immigrants endemic in contemporary Norwegian society while providing a smoke screen that distracts from the Norwegian state's problematic treatment of child refugees and asylum seekers. (201)

Solomon paraphrases Spivak's (1988) question of whether it is really possible for the subaltern to speak, implying that the subaltern is situated within a discourse that only allows the superior to speak on behalf of the subordinate: '"Can the subaltern sing?" Fargespill may indeed be colorful, but its colors paint over issues that, frankly, have a lot to do with Norwegian ideologies regarding black and white' (Solomon, 2016: 201). Here, Solomon makes connections to international critical race theory and suspects that Fargespill, instead of helping to embrace diversity in Norway, is rather retelling a narrative Norwegians tell to reassure themselves that Norway is a multicultural society. This triggered a polarised debate in which Fargespill itself, journalists and scholars countered and defended Fargespill as an idealistic enterprise whose aim is to release the inherent resources of the participants.

This gives certain associations to mystified notions of the purity and innocence that surround the particularly gifted and talented child (in this case also of 'exotic' origin) as discussed in this chapter. In this connection, it is interesting that some of the research studies that have been conducted on Indigenous music in the Nordic countries also tend towards reproducing essentialist and exoticising notions of Sámi culture (e.g., Kallio and Länsman, 2018), whereas others have been able to approach the issues of authenticity, tradition, revival and modernisation with a respectful but still critical-analytical view of the politics of indigeneity and music, seen from a local as well as a global perspective (see Hilder, 2015). However, it may seem paradoxical that despite the increasingly large amount of critical research on the relationships that music (education) has with race, ethnicity and indigeneity, some mythical imaginations are still alive and well. However, and with reference to Baker's (2014, 2016) aforementioned studies on El Sistema, it is perhaps equally striking that certain music education programmes aimed at underprivileged groups are so well suited to reap recognition and support from the fields of politics as well as education, apparently unaffected by critical academic efforts. The 'salvationist narrative' (Baker, 2016: 24) must be assumed to be of greater importance. Therefore, a notion of musical talentification as the release and escape from racial and material conditions, for example, in terms of socio-cultural mobility or class remobility (Trulsson, 2015), is being encouraged. However, as we have pointed out in the above examples of the talentification of Indigenous and 'multicultural' musics, it could just as well be about the moral grandstanding (Tosi and Warmke, 2020) of the majority (or the political and/or cultural elite), which is probably as much about contributing to the public moral discourse in ways that should appear morally respectable as actually being so.

Conclusion

The various concepts of musical talent – from being born with it to having a strong dedication to hard work that results in excellence – cover the obvious need for distinction in both individuals and families who feel entitled to it. In some cases, attributing musical talent to someone can apparently result in them being saved from a life of misery and degradation – even from poverty, discrimination or racism. In addition, a number of different institutions – schools, talent programmes and higher education, as well as the art world, media and entertainment industry – are in constant need of new talent both as raw material for further processing and as a justification for their activities and entitlement in society. Eventually, the assumption of talent can act as a confirmation that cultivating something or someone gives results and a feeling of participating in something bigger than oneself – in many cases, helped by social media algorithms.

Seeing musical talent as talentification – that is, as a social construct in which talent is ascribed to, rather than inscribed in, those who are awarded such a distinction by those who are granted or assume, or are simply invited or enticed to, the authority, inclination or habit to perform and iterate such signifying practices – means that it appears to be a double game as far as several dimensions are concerned. Firstly, it implies that everyday perceptions of talent as something innate or inherent function as social, cultural and aesthetic realities. At the same time, they are discursive in the sense that they represent particular historical, social, cultural and aesthetic qualities that are attributed to particular objects in particular situations and contexts – in that way, attributing meaning to them as well as shaping the rules and the *illusio* of the game. Thus, in the Foucauldian sense (Foucault, 1980), the concept of talent represents a form of power/knowledge relationship, whereas, according to Bourdieu (1992/1996), talentification would represent symbolic power or something that is maintained by society because it is naturalised and not fundamentally questioned.

Against this background, talent becomes characteristics and qualities that appear authentic but may as well become an object of investment. In that way, investments can, on one hand, be considered as allocating power and, on the other hand, as gaining power. However, the duality entails that investments can be made both on the basis of conscious strategic considerations and based on embodied dispositions that are incorporated in the *habitus* – or perhaps a combination of both. A third option is that algorithms and artificial intelligence may also interact in cyborg relationships with regard to talent investment.

Eventually, musical talentification, in this specific context, represents an attempt to develop a critical, analytical concept with the intention of seeing behind or through the immediately apparent forms that are so strongly associated with the notion of talent and thereby help to de-essentialise them. Here, as mentioned at the beginning of the chapter, we have been inspired by Moore's (2002) similar efforts to conceptualise authenticity as authentication but also by the corresponding concepts of musical gentrification, genderfication, gendering, genring, parenting and childing that are used in this book to reveal the double logic of the game(s) being played.

Note

1 *Salaby* is a digital textbook produced by Gyldendal and developed with support from the Norwegian Directorate of Education and Training, building on the schools' curriculum framework LK20.

9

The double games of musical upbringing and schooling in the welfare state

Petter Dyndahl, Live Weider Ellefsen, Anne Jordhus-Lier and Siw Graabræk Nielsen

Introduction

The objective of this chapter is to synthesise and theorise the double games of musical upbringing and schooling in the welfare state, as presented in Chapters 2 to 8 of the book. In this chapter, we will examine the games related to music education and social class, gender, ethnicity, schooling, parenting, children's play and the media, respectively. We will discuss the peculiarities of these games and the similarities between them in relation to the theoretical points of departure put forward in the opening chapter. By framing such games through the lenses of theorists presented throughout the book, we also aim to foster heightened practical and theoretical understandings of the multifaceted and often double games of music in general. It is therefore pertinent to consider the following questions: what purposes do the double games of music fulfil? On what terms are they played? How are such games specifically connected (or not) to the characteristics of the welfare state? What do these games teach us about the potential of music in contemporary society, and what are their social, cultural and political meanings and significance?

The field of music education sociology is one in which small-scale, singular projects are of primary importance and practice and educational activism play significant roles (Karlsen, 2021). However, larger projects have also been undertaken, as evidenced by the chapters included in this book. These projects warrant broader and more scholarly generalisations, conclusions and theorisations. In this final chapter, we aim to demonstrate the potential of our approach and make contributions to music education sociology and neighbouring fields, such as music sociology and cultural sociology, and even to the broader field of general sociology. We begin at the theoretical meta-level by revisiting our core metaphor of the double game, assessing our various uses of the term in relation to the levels of human interaction to which we assign the metaphor and the various activities and social relationships we include in our analyses. In this context, we also consider the concept of field and discuss the sustainability of our premise and assumption that all games are played on a double playing field by following two similar but different and intertwined logics. In recapitulating the various uses and associations of the doubleness of music education as a game presented in the book, we attempt to provide the reader with a clearer analytical framework that will hopefully be beneficial for future sociologically orientated analyses in and beyond the field of Norwegian music education. Central to our discussion is the assumption of a cognitive split between belief in field purity and habitually present experiences of social power, somewhat analogous to Bourdieu's understanding of two economies: the material and symbolic economies.

Throughout this chapter, we will consider music and its inherent social dynamics as a unifying axis. Ultimately, our objective is to identify some of the epistemic unconscious (Bourdieu, 2000) associated with our culture's ideas about the potential and responsibilities of music in relation to individuals and society at large.

Doubleness and diversity

This book is based on three ideas about the social dynamics of a society which have been developed into a practical analytical framework using the metaphor of a double game. First, disciplinary fields, such as art and literature, music education, sociology and musicology, appear as autonomous practices that operate according to their own disciplinary, pure logic. However, the apparent autonomy of these fields depends on and is fuelled by a field of power that operates according to a logic linked to social status and hierarchies, material wealth and success, influence and prestige. Second, and in a corresponding perspective, human social relations and activities in disciplinary fields, such as art and literature and music education, take place through and by means of two distinct but closely related economic dimensions or logics: the material and the symbolic (cultural and social) economies (Bourdieu, 1984, 1986). The interconnectedness of these dimensions is known and experienced, but as with the apparent autonomy of a field, the apparent autonomy is assigned to social and cultural wealth and values, making it difficult to see how one economy is dependent on the other for support and how investments using one form of capital yield a surplus in another form. Third, people's actions can be discussed in terms of deliberate strategies on the one hand and habitual dispositions on the other hand. Again, however, there is an unrecognised dual dependence between what people consciously intend and intuitively initiate. People may have a deep belief that their actions are pure, in the sense of being deliberately professional and selflessly motivated, while neglecting to consider the social and material benefits conferred on them by their learned, embodied dispositions to speak, act and position themselves in deliberately professional and selflessly motivated ways.

In terms of the overall social dynamics of a society, then, the doubleness addressed in the various chapters of this book refers to the entanglement of the subject field of music education with the larger field of power and to the general symbiosis of material and symbolic currencies, as well as to people's habitual misrecognition of this entanglement, even when it comes to their own actions, motivations and privileges. Nevertheless, it is important to emphasise that the social dynamics of human interaction are complex, multifaceted and ambiguous with regard to the meanings they produce; the discourses that regulate them; the possible subject positions, subjectivities and agency they entail; and the powers that are enacted and negotiated. Furthermore, the choice to theoretically emphasise and analytically pursue the previously described and specified duality of human meaning-making is a choice made in accordance with the same dual logic: it results from the intertwining of disinterested (Bourdieu, 1998: 88), purely scientific and philosophical curiosity and dedication to insight and improvement with social, strategic self-interest, politically orientated advocacy and personal and professional motivations. Nevertheless, the approach has proved to be both open and specific enough to produce results that highlight the complexity and ambiguity of Norwegian music education in late modernity. Indeed, in emphasising the interdependence of purity discourses with power, interest with disinterest, play with strategy, symbolic with material economies and beliefs in inclusion with the realities of exclusion, the chapters of this book outline the diverse and multifarious manifestations of the doubleness of socio-musical game playing as it relates to different arenas, contexts and players.

For example, as a democratising double game (see Chapter 2), music education as part of Norwegian schooling is played for purely pedagogical purposes to educate competent, free, creative, self-confident, healthy individuals and citizens. However, Norwegian music education is democratising in another sense: it educates for a particular political and cultural system of values, distribution principles, power positions and social hierarchies. The case of musical gentrification presented in Chapter 3 shows how well-positioned players in the academic popular music game engage in the double practices of exclusion and inclusion. Despite the possible subversive intentions and beliefs of the gentrifiers, previous musical and social hierarchies and forms of establishment nevertheless survive and re-emerge in new, more subtle forms due to the doubleness and interconnectedness of the subject and power fields, symbolic and material capital and players' habitually constituted, field-specific *illusio*. The ambitions of Norwegian municipal music and art schools to be broadly inclusive – of repertoires, cultural practices and participants – have been described in several chapters of this book (see, e.g., Chapters 2, 3, 5 and 8). However, this ambition also unfolds as a double game through the intertwined social logics of field, forms of capital- and game-specific *illusio*: exclusion by and through inclusion; claims to playfully spent, disinterested leisure time by and through dispositions to invest in educational progress, success and social status; and perceptions of talent and specialisation by and through advocacy of diversity and breadth. There is certainly a double game going on; fun and leisure are hardly pure practices that escape the attraction and logic of capital accumulation and negotiation in all their social forms. Yet for the game to work, the players play 'as if' this were the case. Indeed, as shown in Chapter 8 on talentification, music education programmes, such as those hosted by the Norwegian

municipal schools of music and art, and even higher music education in Norway, might very well officially downplay their interest
in talent while simultaneously investing heavily in talentification.
The talent/talentification doubleness discussed in Chapter 8 finds
a similar form in our considerations of genre/genring in Chapter 4:
what appears to be given – talent, genre – is socially and discursively
constructed in procedures that identify its appearance. This double
practice tends to be hidden. Yet it plays a key role in perpetuating the
economic, symbolic and socio-cultural power structures that benefit
from the treatment of talent and genre as pure objects instead of
as procedures of distinction and investment. Genres, for example,
are acts of classification that involve so much more than the practical organisation and representation of the aesthetic world. Rather,
we see genring as a double game in which the apparent autonomy
of musical genres conceals their dependence on and contribution
to the social game of capital and power. Equally misrecognised is
the double game of children's musical play, addressed in Chapter
6. Society's belief in children's innocent, uncorrupted and enjoyable
play, evident in art and popular culture as well as in educational discourse and scholarly works, obscures the social, strategic, purpose-
ful investments children make on the basis of their experiences in
and with the field of power. In much the same way that adult players' *illusio* governs their performance in the game, children's *habitus*
gives them a disposition to play that weaves together the rules of
both the general field of social power and the specific, game-related
field of pure play. Another form of doubleness in children's musical
play, as well as in children's music, can be discerned in Norwegian
public broadcasting for children. Using the concept of childity
(Sjöberg, 2013), Chapter 7 clarifies how music is childed in television broadcasting to offer specific childed subject positions, narratives, interactions and objects for children and adults to relate to.
The doubleness of children's musical play as broadcast by the welfare state involves recognising and celebrating the educational and
aesthetic potential of music for children's development and general
well-being while simultaneously failing to fully recognise how music
conveys to children the social expectations of what they already are
and what they need to become and feel like citizens of the welfare
state (Chapter 7).

Game levels and domains of play

Reviewing how Bourdieu, Foucault, Gadamer, Geertz, Huizinga, Wittgenstein and others have used the concept of game to explore social, cultural and aesthetic dynamics, we begin this book by suggesting that the potential of the game metaphor for music education research might reside in the diverse and perhaps also dichotomous meanings that are teased out when game is used as a metaphor for musical interaction. Indeed, throughout the book, we apply the game metaphor to different aspects and levels of sociality. We use game to refer to specific, institutionalised social arenas or contexts for musical upbringing and socialisation, like those provided by formal schooling, the Norwegian schools of music and art, and musicology/music education as institutionalised academic practice (and the music and television industries). We also use game as an approach to understand the practices, procedures and strategies of meaning-making which operate across these and other sites and situations, like parenting, gentrification, talentification, genring, childing and genderfication. Assigning contexts and practices, the status of games is largely a methodological concern. In Chapter 2 on school(ed) music, for example, we take as our point of departure what we regard as democratic 'games of government', describing how the Norwegian welfare state, on one hand, performs as a conscientious, egalitarian society orientated towards social justice and, on the other hand, ultimately has self-preservation as its goal, like any other cultural game, and with that the preservation of the existing value hierarchies and power networks of the game. Considering how the micro–macro dynamics of social game playing at political levels work, we demonstrate how formalised music educational games are played in line with and in support of the same Norwegian welfare state game, aided by Norwegian and Nordic cultural and educational policy play. Furthermore, in Chapter 5 on musical parenting and the child as investment, we present and discuss two empirical cases of two particular, contextual, time-specific games. We use them to illustrate the subtlety of parents' expert sense of the set of games within the playing field of musical parenting in late modern Nordic society. The game metaphor, then, is applied to principles and practices, systems and single cases, and collectives' and individuals' interactions. Every game is a new game within a chain of games, some of them overlapping, that may challenge existing structures of power and knowledge and is also utterly dependent on socially and historically established power hierarchies to be played.

Nevertheless, a key analytical strategy is to keep two main levels of analysis operational at the same time: one referring to the general but also specific social dynamic represented by the doubleness of human social interaction and negotiation, as described earlier in this chapter, and the other constituted by the plurality of possible games facilitated by this social dynamic. This strategy is described in Chapter 1. Certainly, music education, broadly understood as a socio-musical upbringing across the whole spectrum of formalised and informal learning practices, is not one game but several, and some of them are quite subtle in the way they must be played, such as the games of gentrification, genderfication, talentification, childing and genring. Similar to terms and concepts such as social practice, field and discourse, game can refer to different aspects of the field of research and to both the micro and macro levels of interaction. Again, similar to the concept of discourse, even when adapted to a particular aspect or level of operation, the ambiguity of the term points to other aspects and levels that are operative, if not currently focused on. Our shifting focus is a strategy intended to capture some of the complexity of meaning-making, not by dividing a phenomenon into different parts and processes for closer scrutiny but by adjusting the focus so that some depths, details or relationships are highlighted while others are temporarily relegated to the background.

This approach to understanding music education, with its shifting emphasis on different aspects and levels of interaction, opens up a broader dialogue about the complex interplay of social forces shaping music educational games. In particular, the intersection of these forces becomes crucial when we examine how different social categories, including class, race and gender, converge and influence each other in educational contexts.

Intersectional games

As the subtitle of this book indicates, the text has a particular focus on paradoxes associated with class. Nevertheless, the class dimension is not a standalone phenomenon in sociological contexts. Indeed, since Crenshaw (1989) first introduced the concept of intersectionality, there has been a tradition of discussing how different social categories, such as class, race/ethnicity, gender, sexual orientation, age/generation and (dis)ability, can overlap and influence each other. Yet there has been a certain contradiction between theories that emphasise intersectionality and those that place a greater emphasis on socio-economic conditions. In that regard, traditional Marxist theory focuses on the working class's production of surplus value for capitalists as a relation of exploitation, while anti-racists and feminists interpret racism and sexism in terms of oppression.

Bohrer (2019) responds to this contradiction with the book *Marxism and Intersectionality: Race, Gender, Class and Sexuality under Contemporary Capitalism*, which aims to dispel the misconception that the traditions of Marxism and intersectionality are incompatible. In her theoretical approach, she examines the relationship between exploitation and oppression in greater depth. Bohrer argues that rather than reducing one to the other, as the intersectional and Marxist traditions have done in the past, one must conceive of the two as having an 'elective affinity' or a kind of consonance or amenability (200). She posits that the two must be considered 'equiprimordial', meaning that they are related to each other as 'equally fundamental, equally deep-rooted, and equally anchoring of the contemporary world' (199). To gain a comprehensive understanding of a phenomenon within the context of capitalism, it is essential to comprehend the intertwined nature of exploitation and oppression. These two phenomena 'feed off and play into one another as mutually reinforcing and co-constituting aspects of the organization of capitalist society' (201). Furthermore, Bohrer asserts that 'a full understanding of how class functions under capitalism requires understanding how exploitation and oppression function equiprimordially' (201). To achieve a nuanced understanding of capitalism, Bohrer argues, it is necessary to grasp the following four core concepts: '1) capitalism cannot be reduced to exploitation alone; 2) capitalism cannot be reduced to class alone; 3) class cannot be reduced to exploitation alone; 4) race, gender, sexuality cannot be reduced to oppression alone' (204).

Nevertheless, one might argue that, in contrast to Marx's somewhat monolithic economic definition of class, Bourdieu's concept of social class, encompassing cultural and social dimensions in addition to the economic, would prove more efficacious within the context of intersectional thinking. In general, although Bourdieu did not work directly with intersectionality, his focus on social structures and power relations provides a valuable framework for examining how different social categories overlap and influence each other. For example, his concept of social fields – networks or spaces of position and power – can be used to understand how different forms of discrimination and privilege (e.g., based on race, gender or class) interact and influence each other in different contexts. Similarly, his concept of *habitus* refers to the deeply ingrained habits, skills and dispositions one has due to their life history and social background, which can help us understand how oppression and privilege are internalised and reproduced.

Several scholars have demonstrated the applicability of Bourdieu's theories to the understanding of intersectionality. They have also highlighted some limitations of his work and proposed avenues for its expansion and improvement to more effectively address questions of intersectionality. For example, Collins (2000) builds upon Bourdieu's concepts of social fields and cultural capital to develop the 'matrix of domination'. This framework offers a comprehensive understanding of the complex interconnections between various forms of oppression, including racism, sexism, class oppression and heterosexism. It also elucidates the ways in which these power relations are perpetuated through social institutions and cultural practices. McCall (2005) develops a method for studying intersectionality that she calls 'intercategorical complexity'. This method takes into account both structural factors (e.g., Bourdieu's social fields) and individual agency. It recognises that social categories, such as race, class and gender, are not fixed or unchangeable but socially constructed and continuously reproduced through social practice, whereas Anthias (2008) offers a critique of Bourdieu's understanding of class and proposes an alternative approach that is more flexible and takes into account the interweaving of different social features. This approach is known as 'translocational positionality', which is structured by the interplay of locations relating to gender, ethnicity, race and class (amongst others) and their, at times, contradictory effects. While these intersectional concepts could be useful tools for analysing how music education practices can contribute to maintaining or challenging existing power structures and inequalities, for example, by identifying how certain pedagogical practices exclude or marginalise particular groups, and how these practices can be changed to promote a more inclusive and equitable music education, they have so far been applied to a negligible extent in music education research.

Conversely, Bull's (2019) *Class, Control, and Classical Music* represents a significant contribution to the sociology of music education, employing both intersectional and Bourdieuian approaches (see also Chapters 2 and 8). In her study, she examines the intersection of class, gender and race within the context of classical music in the UK, elucidating how classical music practices contribute to perpetuating inequality, particularly along class lines. Bull asserts that classical music in the UK has historically been associated with the upper classes. This association is not merely about who listens to or plays classical music but also concerns the values and behaviours associated with it, such as discipline, self-control and a specific kind of embodied 'classiness'. Bull also discusses the gendered aspects of classical music, noting that females are often expected to play certain instruments that are deemed 'feminine', such as the flute or violin, while males are encouraged to play 'masculine' instruments, like the trumpet or percussion. She also addresses the racialised dimensions of classical music, emphasising that it is frequently perceived as a domain reserved for white musicians and how musicians of colour may face marginalisation or exoticisation within the field. By examining the interconnections between class, gender and race, Bull's work illuminates the ways in which these identities intersect in the context of classical music. She demonstrates how these categories of identity not only determine who is permitted to engage with classical music but also how they are permitted to do so and the extent to which their participation is valued. Thus, Bull employs an intersectionality-based approach to critique the reproduction of social inequalities within the classical music field.

Furthermore, to gain a more comprehensive understanding of the complex interrelationships between parenting and other social factors, it is essential to examine a range of related issues. Thus, in Chapter 5, we discuss how parenting is classed, gendered and racial, referring to several studies aimed especially at expanding Lareau's (2011) concept of concerted cultivation, based on studies conducted among middle- to upper-class families in the US. A few UK studies have used the lens of concerted cultivation to explore race, ethnicity and gender in parenting from an intersectional perspective. Vincent and colleagues (2012) argue that class and racialised parenting intersect within specific contexts. Their study focuses on Caribbean and middle-class parents in the UK who prioritise leisure activities, like music and sport, in child-rearing. This strategy maintains class positions and Black identity and serves as a defence against racism. Mukherjee and Barn (2021) explore the parenting strategies of middle-class Indian parents in the UK who invest in ethnic leisure activities, such as language training and specific sports and arts. This 'ethnic cultural capital' is intended to enhance future transnational mobility. Parents also consider racism as a factor in their children's future and potentially mitigate its impact through leisure activities that physically strengthen their children, such as Asian martial arts.

Chapter 5 indicates that in the Scandinavian context, children from immigrant backgrounds and/or from low-income families with limited educational opportunities are more likely to be excluded from municipal schools of music and arts. The social class and ethnicity dimensions intersect with gender and generation, as evidenced by Jeppsson and Lindgren's (2018) assertion that the typical student in Swedish schools of this kind is a Swedish-born daughter of well-educated parents. Moreover, in Chapter 7, we address the question of how music on screen contributes to the construction of class, gender and ethnic/racial identity, as well as the intersections of these categories, in public broadcasting aimed at children. In other words, we examine the historical shaping and availability of social positions for child audiences in a media context typical of the Norwegian welfare state.

A subtle form of intersectionality is presented in Chapter 3, where the analysis of the empirical data shows that there are gendered differences in the rules of the game governing the opportunities for male and female academics to accumulate cultural capital through musical gentrification in Norwegian higher education and research. Gender and the power and status associated with social class intersect here in a way that allows male professors and students to assume the roles of pioneers or gentrifiers, which have become available owing to the inclusion of popular music in music academia. Female academics are instead given the opportunity to fill the space left vacant by male academics. Such shifts in patterns of gender dominance from male to female have also occurred in classical music and in academic interest in the educational or therapeutic forms and uses of music. In this way, there have also been shifts in the centre of gravity of status and cultural capital within the field of music scholarship. In her 2021 publication, Nielsen coins the term 'musical genderfication' to describe the intersection between gender and musical gentrification.

Regarding music education in schools (see Chapter 2), the Norwegian National Curriculum for Music (Years 1–10) requires teachers and students to address issues such as 'gender roles and sexuality' and 'cultural understanding' (Norwegian Directorate for Education and Training, 2020). Similarly, the curriculum framework for the municipal schools of music and arts outlines the school's role in contributing to inclusion, democratic participation and social mobility in Norwegian society and draws heavily on discourses of diversity to emphasise its importance for these purposes (Norwegian Council for Schools of Music and Performing Arts, 2016). In striving to be for all, terms such as inclusion and diversity are often used in curricula and strategic documents concerning both compulsory and extracurricular music education in Norway. However, what these terms actually mean, who is to be included and how are not necessarily specified. What is striking is that social class, either as a concept or as a phenomenon, seems to have no place in Norwegian music education. At least, it is not mentioned in the current curricula.

This is consistent with the observation made in Chapter 3 that, according to Bates (2019), who has examined a substantial number of international handbooks on music education and social justice, diversity and marginalisation, there is a dearth of contributions addressing social class issues in a specific and systematic manner. Conversely, there is a considerable focus on race, ethnicity, sexuality, gender and (dis)ability. Underscoring the timely interest in matters pertaining to ethnicity and race, it remains a paradox that an academic field defined by an overwhelming whiteness – namely, Western music education – has demonstrated a notable willingness to adopt anti-racist positions. Conversely, social class, even when considered in an intersectional manner, appears to be a factor of limited relevance to the same music educators and researchers. One possible explanation for their tendency to exclude social class from their analyses and praxes is that music education and social affiliation are inherently intertwined. This interdependence may contribute to the apparent lack of attention to class issues in music education, which is analogous to how the immediate aesthetic experience of music may obscure its social and cultural significance. In this context, we refer to the Piketty-inspired analyses of class interests and affiliations in late modern Western societies (Gethin *et al.*, 2021; Piketty, 2018) presented in Chapter 3 and to Reed Jr's (2018) suggestion that middle- to upper-class anti-racism might be viewed as a neoliberal substitute for a left-wing political stance.

Reed's argument is rooted in the critique of neoliberalism's emphasis on individualism and the market, which can co-opt social justice discourses, such as anti-racism, in ways that ultimately serve to uphold, rather than challenge, systemic inequalities. In this context, anti-racism becomes a form of identity politics focused on recognising and celebrating racial and ethnic diversity but does not necessarily engage with structural issues of economic inequality and class. This version of anti-racism can then become compatible with neoliberal ideals of market competition and individual success as it can promote a 'diversity' that is primarily about including different racial and ethnic identities within existing hierarchies of power, rather than challenging these hierarchies themselves.

However, compared to the American situation to which Reed primarily refers, there may be a reason to distinguish between racism and ethnocentrism in the Nordic and European contexts. According to Jugert and colleagues (2021), ethnicity, with its focus on shared ancestry, history, traditions and culture, has become more salient than race, which has traditionally been associated with physical characteristics. Notwithstanding, Bates (2022) argues that ethnocentrism in music education can be as manifest as racism in the exclusion of minority cultural practices and the assumption that students are deficient because of their cultural backgrounds.

Meanwhile, it does not have to be the case that only one game or one dimension of a game is played. In addition to the aforementioned curricular discourse on diversity, the examples of Sámi culture and the organisation Fargespill presented in Chapter 8 clearly show that when Indigenous and multicultural music is celebrated in selected contexts, it can, on one hand, serve as a vehicle for the moral grandstanding of the majority or the political and cultural elite, without necessarily addressing systemic and structural inequality and oppression. On the other hand, but often in a covert way, it can reflect several paradoxical games being played simultaneously without being mutually acknowledged.

According to Reed's critique, although the anti-racism movement is an integral part of the social justice paradigm, it must be coupled with a critique of the underlying economic and social structures (a stance more aligned with the tenets of the left-wing political tradition; cf. Bohrer, 2019) to effectively confront the systemic oppression and inequalities that persist. For music education approaches to intersectionality, such a dual perspective, seem to be a major challenge.

The sense of the game and the theory of practice: implications for the welfare state

According to Bourdieuian social theory, the differences between social classes are not only due to material inequalities but also due to the fact that each class has its own system of classification, embodied in *habitus*. Bourdieu has been criticised for being overly deterministic and for favouring structural dominance over individual agency. Nonetheless, he argues that *habitus*, being constituted by the sociological tension between structure and agency, provides a practical sense that enables actors to understand and navigate the configurations of symbolic power, thereby allowing individuals to position themselves strategically within the existing discourse and social field.

The concept of field, as elaborated by Bourdieu and Wacquant (1992), links structure and agency by emphasising how actors' positions within a field are shaped by the interplay of field-specific rules, their *habitus* and the capital they possess. The field can be understood as a system of social positions internalised with power relations. At a general level, this can be likened to what we refer to in the singular as the double game, which refers to an overarching social structure of interaction that we believe is effective regardless of the rules and regulations of the individual games of music.

According to this perspective, the different social classes are per-ceived as exercising their respective class-specific agency.

Against this background, in this book, we have arguably painted a picture of the cultural elite and the upper-middle class as if they were sanctimonious groups of people. We have shown, for exam-ple, how they try to appear as ordinary people – albeit particu-larly open-minded, tolerant and liberal – to hide their privilege. We have highlighted how the academic elite's adoption and inclusion of cultural expressions previously considered low status can func-tion as a social differentiator in terms of musical gentrification (see Chapter 3). We have also more than hinted that middle-class ideals of parenting have as much to do with social positioning as with the formation and upbringing of children (Chapter 5).

However, it is important to note that, as we have tried to remind both the reader and ourselves throughout the book, these examples should not necessarily be seen as deliberate and cynical acts. Rather, they should be seen as consistent with the logic of the double game of music to which individual players are subjected. This logic is embodied in *habitus* and the disposition to develop a practical sense of or a strategic capacity for action.

The concept of disposition is a fundamental tenet of Bourdieu's work. It may be defined as a sense of the game or, more precisely, as a skill that is partly conscious and rational yet also partly intuitive. In other words, disposition may be understood as a practical mas-tery of social fields and systems of classification, which appears to be spontaneously expressed. However, dispositions are conditioned responses to the social world formed over years, and it follows that the individual *habitus* is always a mix of multiple engagements in the social world throughout a person's life.

Furthermore, Bourdieu (1977) postulates that *habitus* is acquired unconsciously through social experience and embodied in the body rather than through conscious intellectual processes or verbalised forms of learning. He uses terms such as incorporation and embodi-ment to describe this acquisition, distancing himself from psycho-logical approaches that focus merely on individual and sociological approaches that solely investigate social structures. Consequently, Bourdieu emphasises the duality of the influence of culture on individuals and the agency of individuals in shaping and creat-ing culture. Thus, people are not passive participants in cultural dynamics but active players in a cultural-game context which is obviously played according to certain rules. This perspective allows for explaining and understanding the thinking and actions of social actors without relying solely on subjective life histories or structural determinants. Overall, Bourdieu's theory highlights the dynamic interplay between individuals and the cultural context in which they are situated. Since social fields are put into practice through individuals' agency, no social field or classification system can be completely stable; rather, it is possible to adapt or change them according to specific initiatives and interests. In other words, the theory of practice has the potential to bridge the gap between structure and agency.

To understand the defining features of contemporary social and cultural development, it is essential to consider the historical trajectories of social actors in the context of a system of social positions (Prieur and Savage, 2011). Sociologists have suggested that late modernity is a reflexive (Beck *et al.*, 1994) or fluid (Bauman, 2000) process of modernisation. This implies that the concept of late modernity, unlike the classical or high modernity concepts defined in opposition to traditionalism, is self-referential to varying degrees. One consequence of this is that both high and low cultural forms are now identifiable as providers of cultural capital at a sublevel or more specific level of social space. This contrasts with Bourdieu's (1984) view, based on multiple correspondence analyses of French society in the 1970s, that high and low cultures were an opposition denoting the consecrated classical versus the vulgar popular culture.

This offers a historically grounded explanation of why phenomena and concepts, such as Peterson's (1992) cultural omnivorousness, Piketty's (2018) Brahmin left and our own notions of musical gentrification, genring and so on, have been useful in refurbishing the cultural elite and (especially) the upper-middle class. It is evident that those occupying the cultural elite and middle class reacted to the changes that were occurring in Western society during the latter decades of the twentieth century. These changes manifested in a diversification of cultural tastes, the emergence of a new class rhetoric and self-understanding, as well as in political shifts and polarisation. One of the most challenging aspects of this phenomenon, at least empirically speaking, is determining the distinction between what is intuitively initiated or rooted in habitual dispositions and what is consciously intended or results from deliberate strategies. The exposition of the theory of practice and the sense of the game indicates that this process is probably played out simultaneously along the entire axis from unconscious to conscious, as well as along the spectrum of belief and conviction – that is, *illusio*, or the fact that the game is believed in, yet the players are unaware of their own interest in it.

However, in addition to *illusio* and its effect of drawing the players into the game and having them unconsciously accept the rules of the game, Bourdieu adds the concept of *libido* to the explanation of the social reproduction and existence of social fields. In summary, the concept of *libido* as a non-reflexive bodily drive can elucidate why 'people are motivated, driven by, torn from a state of indifference and moved by the stimuli sent by certain fields – and not others' (Bourdieu and Wacquant, 1992: 26). Bourdieu (2000) additionally identifies the *libido* as a desire for recognition:

> One may suppose that, to obtain the sacrifice of self-love in favor of a quite other object of investment and so to inculcate the durable disposition to invest in the social game which is one of the prerequisites of all learning, pedagogic work in its elementary form relies on one of the motors which will be at the origin of all subsequent investments: the *search for recognition*. (166)

An alternative, more economic–political model for explaining these tendencies is based on changes in the composition of capital. Bourdieu (1986) proposes that when the flow of economic capital is regulated or subject to other restrictions, which is the normal state of affairs under social democratic and related governance, as can be observed in the Nordic countries, cultural capital assumes heightened significance for the reproduction of the social structure. Both the school system and cultural life play pivotal roles in this regard. The changes in what is considered to provide cultural capital today, where the boundaries between traditional high and low statuses have become increasingly blurred, appear to affect the markers and boundaries between social classes. In societies that are relatively egalitarian, such as the Nordic societies, where this is a widely held ideal, social inequality is less perceptible and the idea of shared interests across social classes is promoted. Consequently, some individuals and groups – notably politicians – have postulated that class is an obsolete concept that should be consigned to history. Those who benefit most from such a depiction of the situation are precisely those who hold power and influence, since they cannot be challenged by those who lack power and status.

In this manner, the cultural elite and middle class are able to position themselves to target the working class, whose members appear to be most interested in advocating for their economic interests, seemingly without consideration for maintaining a sustainable economy or demonstrating responsibility for the environment and climate. Concurrently, this prompts a significant proportion of the working class to disengage from the traditional left-wing political parties that have historically advocated for their interests and instead gravitate towards populist right-wing parties. In contrast, contemporary left-wing politics, obviously inspired by Tony Blair's New Labour of the 1990s, have increasingly become responsible for the accountable management of late modern capitalism. This is evidenced by the espousal of values and premises that align more closely with and benefit other classes more effectively.

In addition to revealing a new twist in the cohabitation between consensual democracy (Lijphart, 2012) and political antagonism (Laclau and Mouffe, 2001), discussed in Chapter 2, this has implications for the relationship between the working and middle classes in the Nordic welfare state, which is a key point for Broström (2023). While Laclau and Mouffe (2001) see the danger of consensus having the effect of discursively appropriating and neutralising antagonistic social and political opposition, Broström sees the historical alliance between the working and middle classes, which leading Nordic social democrats advocated in the post-war period, as a prerequisite for the success and broad support of this welfare model.

Broström focuses particularly on Swedish political history, and it must be specified that, like Hansen and colleagues (2014), she divides the middle class into the upper and lower middle classes (see Chapter 3). Historically, the lower middle class in the Nordic countries has been recruited predominantly from the working class, which means that these two groups have common interests in many matters. This has been one of the reasons for creating universal rather than means-tested welfare systems. By making child benefits and retirement pensions available to everyone, for example, the middle classes have been drawn into the welfare project. This is also supported by the fact that in the Nordic countries, especially Norway, the distribution of income and wealth is more equal than in many other countries in the world. However, this in itself can become a motive for the upper, well-educated part of the middle class to distinguish itself with the help of cultural capital.

Broström's main point is precisely that the class coalition between the working and middle classes has been under threat for some time, which also implies a danger for the Nordic welfare model. If wage differentials increase and private welfare solutions are increasingly offered in the wake of New Public Management, the differences between the interests of the different classes and their respective practical sense of the game are likely to go in different directions. Broström believes that this is largely a matter of political rhetoric and that the increasing polarisation is taking place on proxy battlefields. In an interview with the Norwegian newspaper *Klassekampen*, she pointedly states her dismay at what she sees as a derailing of the debate on important political issues:

> It is so much easier to arouse commitment to issues of value. If I say homosexuality should be banned, people go absolutely mad. That is easy to discuss. But if I say we need to raise unemployment benefits by this or that percentage, who cares? If you do not get hung up on superficial differences in lifestyle, but emphasise the fundamental economic issues, there are good conditions for a new form of class solidarity between the working class and the middle class. But then we have to stop the culture wars and talk about the economy. I am incredibly tired of this leftist culture. It has been so dominant. Norms and constructions. It never ends and it leads nowhere. (Braanen, 2023, November 16, our translation)

Although Broström makes several important points regarding the necessity for the welfare state to enjoy broad, cross-political and inter-class support in order to survive in its current form, she appears to overlook the fact that there are always multiple competing games taking place, as is also the case within the welfare state game. Mouffe (2005, 2013) presents a more affirmative view of contradictions and conflict. She recognises conflict as a constructive part of politics when it takes place within a democratic framework and tries to find a way of dealing with it that allows for a productive outlet. Against an antagonistic mindset and its tendency to dehumanise opponents by attributing to them morally undesirable qualities and bad intentions, Mouffe advocates 'agonism' as a way of meeting opponents with recognition and respect. This involves accepting that conflicts are real but that they exist under conditions regulated by a set of democratic procedures accepted by both parties. In a democratic society, there are various interests and demands that should be regarded as legitimate, even when they are in conflict and no consensus can be reached.

Conclusion

In the context of the overarching concept of this book, it appears that an agonistic approach may prompt us to identify the existence of multiple games, each with its own set of rules. It is imperative that these differences are acknowledged and respected on their own terms, without the objective of allowing one particular game or way of playing to prevail. Conversely, the duality inherent in music arguably offers a twofold capacity for aesthetic and social interpretations, as an example of a variety of multidimensional games, thereby conferring a greater depth of meaning. A starting point may be to recognise that double games are actually going on, at the macro level, such as the welfare state, and in all the nooks and crannies of music life, including music education, and, not least, that these levels play together. Similarly, it is crucial to acknowledge that the double game of music is enacted simultaneously at additional levels: the conscious and deliberate, and the more implicit and bodily, comprising beliefs, drives and dispositions that are represented by the concepts of *illusio*, *libido* and *habitus*.

In line with this, the term epistemic unconscious was coined by Bourdieu (2000) to describe the deep, often unexamined, beliefs and biases that underpin our perception and understanding of the world. He further suggests that the epistemic unconscious is not limited to our everyday interactions but also greatly influences academic and scholarly knowledge production. It affects the questions we ask, the methods we use, the data we consider relevant and the interpretations we draw. Thus, Bourdieu and Wacquant (1992) contend that the objective must be to uncover and critically examine these assumptions through epistemic reflexivity. This is a crucial concept in Bourdieuian thinking. It refers to a process of critical self-examination in which we, as researchers, examine and challenge our own assumptions, presuppositions and biases that may influence our research. This includes being aware of how our own social, cultural and historical context, position and interests can shape our knowledge production. By undertaking epistemic reflexivity, we may avoid reproducing existing power structures and inequalities in our research practices and help to produce both reliable and critical knowledge. Nevertheless, it is our contention that this is primarily evidenced in the actual design and formulation of epistemic reflexivity and research publication and, to a lesser extent, by self-promotional discourse concerning one's own background.

Bibliography

Aksdal, B. (2022). 'Landskappleiken'. In *Store norske leksikon*. Retrieved 16 May 2024 from https://snl.no/Landskappleiken

Altman, R. (1999). *Film/genre* [Kindle edition]. Bloomsbury Publishing.

Andersen, P. L. and Ljunggren, J. (2014). 'Gylne ghettoer. Inntektselitens bostedssegrering i Oslo, 1980–2005' ['Golden ghettos. The residential segregation of the income elite in Oslo, 1980–2005']. In O. Korsnes, M. N. Hansen and J. Hjellbrekke (eds), *Elite og klasse i et egalitært samfunn* [Elite and class in an egalitarian society] (pp. 126–143). Universitetsforlaget.

Anderson, B. (1983). *Imagined communities: Reflections on the origin and spread of nationalism*. Verso.

Anthias, F. (2008). Thinking through the lens of translocational positionality: An intersectionality frame for understanding identity and belonging. *Translocations*, 4(1), 5–20.

Ariès, P. (1962). *Centuries of childhood: A social history of family life*. Alfred A. Knopf.

Askerøi, E. and Vestad L. I. (2021). 'Singing like a child'. In S. V. Onsrud, H. S. Blix and I. L. Vestad (eds), *Gender issues in Scandinavian music education: From stereotypes to multiple possibilities* (pp. 51–73). Routledge.

Baker, G. (2014). *El Sistema: Orchestrating Venezuela's youth*. Oxford University Press.

Baker, G. (2016). Editorial introduction: El Sistema in critical perspective. *Action, Criticism & Theory for Music Education*, 15(1), 10–32. Retrieved 13 April 2023 from https://act.maydaygroup.org/articles/Baker15_1.pdf

Barratt Due Institute of Music. (n.d.). *Young talents*. Retrieved 11 May 2024 from https://www.barrattdue.no/young-talents/

Barrett, M. S. (2006). 'Aesthetic response'. In G. E. McPherson (ed.), *The child as musician: A handbook of musical development* (pp. 173–191). Oxford University Press.

Barrett, M. S. (2009). Sounding lives in and through music: A narrative inquiry of the 'everyday' musical engagement of a young child. *Journal of Early Childhood Research*, 7(2), 115–134. https://doi.org/10.1177/1476718X09102645

Bates, V. C. (2019). Standing at the intersection of race and class in music education. *Action, Criticism, and Theory for Music Education*, 18(1), 117–160. https://doi.org/10.22176/act18.1.117

Bates, V. C. (2022). Intersectionality for social justice in music education. *Diskussion Musikpädagogik*, 94, 11–17.

Bauman, Z. (2000). *Liquid modernity*. Polity Press.

Beck, U., Giddens, A. and Lash, S. (1994). *Reflexive modernization: Politics, tradition and aesthetics in the modern social order*. Stanford University Press.

Benedict, C., Schmidt, P., Spruce, G. and Woodford, P. (eds). (2015). *The Oxford handbook of social justice in music education*. Oxford University Press.

Bennett, T., Savage, M., Silva, E. B., Warde, A., Gayo-Cal, M. and Wright, D. (2009). *Culture, class, distinction*. Routledge.

Berg, A. (2021). 'Klassetilpasset rådgivning i skolen' ['Class-adapted counselling in school']. In J. Ljunggren and M. N. Hansen (eds), *Arbeiderklassen* [The working class] (pp. 91–108). Cappelen Damm Akademisk.

Berg-Nordlie, M. and Tvedt, K. A. (2024). 'Alta-saken' ['The Alta conflict']. In *Store norske leksikon*. Retrieved 18 October 2024 from https://snl.no/Alta-saken

Berge, O. K., Angelo, E., Heian, M. T. and Emstad, A. B. (2019). *Kultur + skole = sant. Kunnskapsgrunnlag om den kommunale kulturskolen i Norge* [Knowledge base for the municipal schools of music and arts in Norway]. Retrieved 19 September 2024 from https://www.telemarksforsking.no/publikasjoner/kultur-skole-sant/3487/

Bickford, T. (2016). 'Justin Bieber, YouTube, new media and celebrity: The tween prodigy at home and online'. In G. McPherson (ed.), *Musical child prodigies: Interpretations from psychology, education, musicology, and ethnomusicology* (pp. 749–767). Oxford University Press.

Bickford, T. (2020). *Tween pop: Children's music and public culture*. Duke University Press.

Biesta, G. (2013). *The beautiful risk of education*. Paradigm Publisher.

Bjørklund, T. and Aksdal, E. (2012). 'Jazzlinja i fortid, nåtid og framtid' ['The jazz programme in the past, present and future']. In W. Waagen (ed.), *Musikkopplæring i 100! Hundre år med musikkundervisning i Trondheim* [Music education in 100! One hundred years of music education in Trondheim] (pp. 81–89). Schrøderforlaget.

Bjørnsen, E. (2012). *Inkluderende kulturskole. Utredning av kulturskoletilbudet i storbyene* [Inclusive music and art schools. Investigation of the music and art school programme in the big cities]. Agderforskning. Project report 5. Retrieved 3 November 2023 from http://www.kulturskoleradet.no

Blix, H. S. and Ellefsen, L. W. (2021). 'On breaking the "citational chains of gender normativity" in Norwegian art and music schools'. In S. V. Onsrud, H. Blix and I. L. Vestad (eds), *Gender issues in Scandinavian music education* (pp. 156–179). Routledge.

Bohrer, A. J. (2019). *Marxism and intersectionality: Race, gender, class and sexuality under contemporary capitalism.* Transcript Verlag.

Bourdieu, P. (1977). *Outline of a theory of practice.* Cambridge University Press.

Bourdieu, P. (1984). *Distinction: A social critique of the judgement of taste.* Harvard University Press.

Bourdieu, P. (1986). 'The forms of capital'. In J. Richardson (ed.), *Handbook of theory and research for the sociology of education* (pp. 241–258). Greenwood.

Bourdieu, P. (1988). *Homo academicus.* Stanford University Press.

Bourdieu, P. (1990). *The logic of practice.* Stanford University Press

Bourdieu, P. (1992/1996). *The rules of art: Genesis and structure of the literary field.* Stanford University Press.

Bourdieu, P. (1998). *Practical reason: On the theory of action.* Stanford University Press.

Bourdieu, P. (2000). *Pascalian meditations.* Polity Press.

Bourdieu, P. (2001). *Masculine domination.* Polity Press

Bourdieu, P. (2024). *The interest in disinterestedness: Lectures at the Collège de France (1987–1989).* Polity Press.

Bourdieu, P. and Champagne, P. (1992). Les exclus de l'intérieur [Excluded from the inside]. *Actes de la Recherche en Sciences Sociales Année, 91–92,* 71–75.

Bourdieu, P. and Wacquant, L. J. D. (1992). *An invitation to reflexive sociology.* Polity Press.

Braanen, B. (2023). *Forakten for middelklassen* [Contempt for the middle class]. Klassekampen.

Brackett, D. (2016). *Categorizing sound* [Kindle edition]. University of California Press.

Bronfenbrenner, U. (2001). 'The bioecological theory of human development'. In N. J. Smelser and P. B. Baltes (eds), *International encyclopedia of the social and behavioral sciences* (pp. 6963–6970). Elsevier.

Brook, O., O'Brien, D. and Taylor, M. (2020). *Culture is bad for you.* Manchester University Press.

Broström, L. (2023). *Medelklassen. 200 år i samhällets mitt* [The middle class. 200 years in the centre of society]. Verbal Förlag.

Bull, A. (2019). *Class, control, and classical music*. Oxford University Press.

Bull, A. (2021). La 'respectabilité' et la musique classique: Étudier les intersections de classe, de genre et de race pour comprendre les inégalités dans les formations musicales ['Respectability' and classical music: Studying the intersections of class, gender and race to understand inequalities in musical training]. *Agone, 65*, 45–63.

Burgess, J. and Green, J. (2018). *YouTube: Online and participatory culture* (2nd ed.). Polity Press John Wiley & Sons.

Butler, A. (2019). The judges' decision is final: Judgement in music talent reality TV and school music education. *Journal of Popular Music Education, 3*(3), 399–415.

Butler, J. (1993). *Bodies that matter: On the discursive limits of 'sex'*. Routledge.

Butler, J. (1997). *The psychic life of power: Theories in subjection*. Stanford University Press.

Butler, J. (1990/2007). *Gender trouble: Feminism and the subversion of identity*. Routledge.

Chang-Kredl, S., Mamlok, D. and Venkatesh, V. (2023). Dark play and children's dyadic constructions of self and other. *American Journal of Play, 15*(2), 158–178.

Clark, A. (2010). *Transforming children's spaces: Children's and adults' participation in designing learning environments*. Routledge.

Collins, P. H. (2000). *Black feminist thought: Knowledge, consciousness, and the politics of empowerment*. Routledge.

Collins, S. (2008). *The hunger games*. Scholastic Press.

Conkling, S. W. (2019). Parenting and out-of-school music participation: An interrogation of concerted cultivation. *International Journal of Community Music, 12*(1), 129–143. https://doi.org/10.1386/ijcm.12.1.129_1

Craig, S. (1992). *Men, masculinity, and the media*. Sage.

Crenshaw, K. (1989). Demarginalizing the intersection of race and sex: A Black feminist critique of antidiscrimination doctrine, feminist theory and antiracist politics. *University of Chicago Legal Forum, 1*(8), 139–167. Retrieved 1 April 2018 from https://chicagounbound.uchicago.edu/cgi/viewcontent.cgi?referer=&httpsredir=1&article=1052&context=uclf

Crenshaw, K. (1991). Mapping the margins: Intersectionality, identity politics, and violence against women of color. *Stanford Law Review, 43*(6), 1241–1299. https://doi.org/10.2307/1229039

Cunningham, H. (2006). *The invention of childhood*. BBC Books.

Dahl, H. F. (1999). *Hallo-hallo! Kringkastingen i Norge 1920–1940* [Hello-hello! Broadcasting in Norway 1920–1940]. Cappelen.

de Jong, M. (2005). 'Rummets magt og magten over rummet' ['The power of space and the power over space']. In K. Larsen (ed.), *Arkitektur, krop og læring* [Architecture, the body and learning] (pp. 89–116). Hans Reitzels Forlag.

De Mink, F. M. and McPherson, G. E. (2016). 'Musical prodigies within the virtual stage of YouTube'. In G. E. McPherson (ed.), *Musical child prodigies: Interpretations from psychology, education, musicology, and ethnomusicology* (pp. 427–452). Oxford University Press.

Derrida, J. (1980). The law of genre. *Critical Inquiry, 7*(1), 55–81.

Derrida, J. (1997). *Of grammatology*. Johns Hopkins University Press.

Dugstadutvalget. (1989). *Musikkskolene. En dynamo i det lokale skole- og kulturmiljøet* [Music schools. A dynamo in the local school and cultural community]. The Ministry of Church Affairs and Education.

Dyndahl, P. (2015). Academisation as activism? Some paradoxes. *Finnish Journal of Music Education, 18*(2), 20–32.

Dyndahl, P. (2016). 'Everything except dance band music: Cultural omnivorousness, norms, and the formation of taboos'. In S. H. Klempe (ed), *Cultural psychology of musical experience* (Advances in Cultural Psychology: Constructing Human Development) (pp. 143–163). Information Age Publications.

Dyndahl, P. (2021). 'Musical gentrification: Strategy for social positioning in late modern culture'. In P. Dyndahl, S. Karlsen and R. Wright (eds), *Musical gentrification: Popular music, distinction and social mobility* (pp. 12–33). Routledge.

Dyndahl, P. (2021). 'Music education as qualification, socialisation and subjectification?' In R. Wright, G. Johansen, P. A. Kanellopoulos and P. Schmidt (eds), *The Routledge handbook to sociology of music education* (pp. 169–183). Routledge.

Dyndahl, P. (2024). 'Social class and cultural participation'. In J. L. Arostegui, C. Christophersen, K. Matsunobu and J. Nichols (eds), *SAGE handbook of school music education* (pp. 158–172). Sage.

Dyndahl, P. and Ellefsen, L. W. (2009). 'Music didactics as a multifaceted field of cultural didactic studies'. In F. V. Nielsen, S.-E. Holgersen and S. G. Nielsen (eds), *Nordic research in music education*. Yearbook 11 (pp. 9–32). NMH-publikasjoner.

Dyndahl, P., Karlsen, S., Nielsen, S. G. and Skårberg, O. (2017). The academisation of popular music in higher music education: The case of Norway. *Music Education Research, 19*(4), 438–454. https://doi.org/10.1080/14613808.2016.1204280

Dyndahl, P., Karlsen, S., Skårberg, O. and Nielsen, S. G. (2014). Cultural omnivorousness and musical gentrification: An outline of a sociological framework and its applications for music education research. *Action, Criticism, and Theory for Music Education, 13*(1), 40–69.

Dyndahl, P., Karlsen, S. and Wright, R. (eds) (2021). *Musical gentrification: Popular music, distinction and social mobility.* Routledge.

Dyndahl, P. and Nielsen, S. G. (2014). Shifting authenticities in Scandinavian music education. *Music Education Research, 16*(1), 105–118.

Dyndahl, P. and Vestad, I. L. (2017). Decades of recorded music for children: Norwegian children's phonograms from World War II to the present. *Nordic Journal of Art & Research, 6*(2). https://doi.org/10.7577/information.v6i2.2276

Early Education – The British Association for Early Childhood Education. (2021). *Friedrich Froebel.* Retrieved 24 March 2024 from https://early-education.org.uk/friedrich-froebel/

Eikemoutvalget. (1999). *Kulturskolen – kunststykket i kommunenes satsing for et rikere lokalmiljø* [The school of arts – 'kunststykket' in the municipals' commitment to a richer local community]. The Ministry of Church Affairs, Education and Research.

Elgaaen, G. (1960). Voi-voi [Song recorded by Nora Brockstedt]. Karusell.

Ellefsen, L. W. (2014). *Negotiating musicianship: The constitution of student subjectivities in and through discursive practices of musicianship in 'Musikklinja'* [Doctoral dissertation]. Norwegian Academy of Music.

Ellefsen, L. W. (2021). Sjangring som musikkdidaktisk praksis [Genring as a music educational practice]. *Nordic Research in Music Education, 2*(2). https://doi.org/10.23865/nrme.v2.2811

Ellefsen, L. W. (2022). Genre and genring in music education. *Action, Criticism, and Theory for Music Education, 21*(1), 56–79. https://doi.org/s10.22176/act21.1.56

Ellefsen, L. W. and Karlsen, S. (2019). Discourses of diversity in music education: The curriculum framework of the Norwegian Schools of Music and Performing Arts as a case. *Research Studies in Music Education, 42*(2). https://doi.org/10.1177/1321103X19843205

Ellefsen, L. W., Karlsen, S. and Nielsen, S. G. (2023). What happens in school music in Norway? Findings from a national survey of music teachers. *Music Education Research.* https://doi.org/10.1080/14613808.2023.2183494

Elliott, D. and Silverman, M. (2015). *Music matters: A philosophy of music education.* Oxford University Press.

English, F. (2011). *Student writing and genre: Reconfiguring academic knowledge.* Bloomsbury.

Fabbri, F. (1982). 'A theory of musical genres: Two applications'. In D. Horn and P. Tagg (eds), *Popular music perspectives* (pp. 52–81). Iaspm. Retrieved 19 January 2024 from https://www.tagg.org/others/ffabbri81a .html

Faber, S. T., Prieur, A., Rosenlund, L. and Skjøtt-Larsen, J. (2012). *Det skjulte klassesamfund* [The hidden class society]. Aarhus Universitetsforlag.

Faircloth, C. (2014). 'Intensive parenting and the expansion of parenting'. In E. Lee, J. Bristow, C. Faircloth and J. Macvarish (eds), *Parenting culture studies* (pp. 25–50). Palgrave Macmillan.

Faircloth, C. (2013). *Militant lactivism? Infant feeding and maternal accountability in the UK and France*. Berghahn Books.

Fargespill. (n.d.). *Fargespill* [Kaleidoscope]. Retrieved 11 December 2020 from https://fargespill.no/in-english/

Folkestad, G. (2006). Formal and informal learning situations or practices vs normal and informal ways of learning. *British Journal of Music Education*, 23(2), 135–145.

FolkOrg. (2024). Organisasjon for folkemusikk og folkedans [Organisation for folk music and folk dance]. Retrieved 17 May 2024 from https:// web.archive.org/web/20210126030646/https://folkorg.no/vinnarar -gjennom-tidene

Foucault, M. (1980). *Power/Knowledge: Selected interviews and other writings, 1972–79* (Colin Gordon, ed.). Pantheon.

Foucault, M. (1982). The subject and power. *Critical Inquiry*, 8(4), 777–795.

Foucault, M. (1997). 'Technologies of the self'. In P. Rabinow (ed.), *Ethics, subjectivity and truth* (pp. 223–251). Penguin Books.

Foucault, M. (2000a). 'The ethics of the concern for self as a practice of freedom'. In P. Rabinow (ed.), *Ethics: Subjectivity and truth* (pp. 281–301). Penguin Books.

Foucault, M. (2000b). 'Subjectivity and truth'. In P. Rabinow (ed.), *Ethics: Subjectivity and truth* (pp. 87–92). Penguin Books.

Foucault, M. (2007). *Security, territory, population: Lectures at the Collège de France, 1977–78*. (M. Senellart, ed.). Palgrave Macmillan.

Foucault, M. (1969/2010). *The archaeology of knowledge* (A. M. Sheridan Smith, Trans.). Pantheon.

Freeman, J. (2005). 'Permission to be gifted: How perceptions of giftedness can change lives'. In R. J. Sternberg and J. E. Davidson (eds), *Conceptions of giftedness* (pp. 80–97). Cambridge University Press.

Friedrich, D., Jaastad, B. and Popkewitz, T. S. (2010). Democratic education: An (im)possibility that yet remains to come. *Educational Philosophy and Theory*, 42(5–6), 571–587. https://doi.org/10.1111/j .1469-5812.2010.00686.x

Frith, S. (1996a). *Performing rites: On the value of popular music*. Harvard University Press.

Frith, S. (1996b). 'Music and identity'. In S. Hall and P. du Gay (eds), *Questions of cultural identity* (pp. 108–127). Sage.

Frith, S. (2000). 'The discourse of world music'. In G. Born and D. Hesmondhalgh (eds), *Western music and its Others* (pp. 305–322). University of California Press.

Frønes, I. (1998). *Den norske barndommen* [The Norwegian childhood]. Cappelen Akademisk.

Furedi, F. (2002). *Paranoid parenting: Why ignoring the experts may be best for your child*. Chicago Review Press.

Gadamer, H.-G. (1960/1989). *Truth and method*. Sheed and Ward Limited

Gagné, F. (1998). A proposal for subcategories within gifted or talented populations. *Gifted Child Quarterly*, 42(2), 87–95. http://doi.org/10 .1177/00169862980400203

Gagné, F. (2004). Transforming gifts into talents: The DMGT as a developmental theory. *High Ability Studies*, 15(2), 119–147. https://doi .org/10.1080/1359813042000314682

Gagné, F. and McPherson, G. E. (2016). 'Analyzing musical prodigiousness using Gagné's integrative model of talent development'. In G. E. McPherson (ed.), *Musical prodigies: Interpretations from psychology, musicology, and ethnomusicology* (pp. 3–114). Oxford University Press.

Geertz, C. (1980). 'Blurred genres: The refiguration of social thought'. *The American Scholar*, 49(2), pp. 165–179.

Gems, I. (2007). *Myten om det motsatta könet: Från förskolepedagogiken vid Tittmyran och Björntomten till det maskulina samhällets undergång* [The myth of the opposite sex: From pre-school pedagogy at Tittmyran and Björntomten to the decline of masculine society]. Idéimperiet KHL.

Georgii-Hemming, E. and Westvall, M. (2010). Music education – A personal matter? Examining the current discourses of music education in Sweden. *British Journal of Music Education*, 27(1), 21–33. https://doi .org/10.1017/S0265051709990179

Gethin, A., Martinez-Toledano, C. and Piketty, T. (2021). Brahmin left versus merchant right: Changing political cleavages in 21 Western democracies, 1948–2020. *Quarterly Journal of Economics*. https://doi .org/10.1093/qje/qjab036

Giæver, O. (Director). (2023). *Ellos eatnu – La elva leve* [Let the river live] [Film]. Mer Film, Bufo, Zentropa Sweden.

Goffman, E. (1969/1971). *Strategic interaction*. University of Pennsylvania Press.

Goffman, E. (1961/1972). *Encounters: Two studies in the sociology of interaction*. Penguin University Books.

Goldblatt, P., Castedo, A., Allen, J., Lionello, L., Bell, R., Marmot, M., von Heimburg, D. and Ness, O. (2023). *Rapid review of inequalities in health and wellbeing in Norway since 2014*. Institute of Health Equity. Retrieved 29 May 2024 from https://www.instituteofhealthequity.org /resources-reports/rapid-review-of-inequalities-in-health-and-wellbeing -in-norway-since-2014

Golding, W. (1954). *Lord of the flies*. Faber & Faber Ltd.

Goldson, B. (2004). '"Childhood": An introduction to historical and theoretical analyses'. In P. Scraton (ed.), *Childhood in crisis* (pp. 1–28). Routledge.

Gran, H. and Høien, G. (Directors). (1991–1999). *Sesam stasjon* [TV series]. NRK.

Gray, P. (2015). *Free to learn: Why unleashing the instinct to play will make our children happier, more self-reliant, and better students for life*. Basic Books.

Green, L. (2002). *How popular musicians learn: A way ahead for music education*. Ashgate.

Gulbrandsen, L. (2007). 'Barnehageplass – fra unntak til regel' ['Going to kindergarten – From exception to rule']. In M. Raabe (ed.), *Utdanning 2007 – muligheter, mål og mestring. Statistiske analyser 90* [Education 2007 – opportunities, goals and mastery. Statistical analyses 90] (pp. 50–68). Statistics Norway.

Hake, K. (2006). *Historien om Barne-TV: Barndomsbilder 1960–2005* [The history of children's television: Childhood memories 1960–2005]. Universitetsforlaget.

Hall, C. (2018). *Masculinity, class and music education: Boys performing middle-class masculinities through music*. Palgrave Macmillan. https:// doi.org/10.1057/978-1-137-50255-1

Hall, O. (2018). 'The Internet and cosmopolitanism'. In G. Delanty (ed.), *Routledge international handbook of cosmopolitan studies* (pp. 406–418). Routledge.

Hall, S. (1996). 'Introduction: Who needs "identity"?' In S. Hall and P. du Gay (eds), *Questions of cultural identity* (pp. 1–17). Sage.

Halvorsen, G. (Director). (2008–2011). *AF1* [TV series]. NRK. https://tv .nrk.no/serie/af1

Hansen, M. N. (2011). Finnes det en talentreserve? Betydningen av klassebakgrunn og karakterer for oppnådd utdanning [Is there a reserve of talent? The importance of class background and grades for the education achieved]. *Søkelys på arbeidslivet* [Spotlight on working life], *28*(3), 173–189.

Hansen, M. N. Andersen, P. L., Flemmen, M. and Ljunggren, J. (2014). 'Klasser og eliter' ['Classes and elites']. In O. Korsnes, M. N. Hansen and J. Hjellbrekke (eds), *Elite og klasse i et egalitært samfunn* [Elite and classes in an egalitarian society] (pp. 25–38). Universitetsforlaget.

Hansen, M. N., Flemmen, M. and Andersen, P. L. (2009). *The Oslo Register Data Class Scheme (ORDC)*. Final report from the classification project. Memorandum no 1:2009. Department of Sociology and Human Geography, University of Oslo.

Hansen, M. N. and Ljunggren, J. (2021). 'Arbeiderklassen i Norge – definisjon, sammensetning og endring' ['The working class in Norway – definition, composition and change']. In J. Ljunggren and M. N. Hansen (eds), *Arbeiderklassen* [The working class] (pp. 35–60). Cappelen Damm Akademisk.

Hansen, M. N. and Strømme, T. B. (2014). 'De klassiske profesjonene – fortsatt eliteprofesjoner?' ['The classic professions – still elite professions?']. In O. Korsnes, M. N. Hansen and J. Hjellbrekke (eds), *Elite og klasse i et egalitært samfunn* [Elite and classes in an egalitarian society] (pp. 39–53). Universitetsforlaget.

Hansen, M. N. and Uvaag, S. A. (2021). 'Arbeiderklassen og sosial mobilitet' ['The working class and social mobility']. In J. Ljunggren and M. N. Hansen (eds), *Arbeiderklassen* [The working class] (pp. 61–89). Cappelen Damm Akademisk.

Haraway, D. J. (1991). 'A cyborg manifesto: Science, technology, and socialist-feminism in the late twentieth century'. In D. J. Haraway (ed.), *Simians, cyborgs, and women* (pp. 149–181). Free Association Books.

Hawkins, S. (2016). *Queerness in pop music: Aesthetics, gender norms, and temporality*. Routledge.

Hays, S. (1996). *The cultural contradictions of motherhood*. Yale University Press.

Hebdige, D. (1979). *Subculture: The meaning of style*. Methuen.

Heimonen, M. (2003). Music education and law: Regulation as an instrument. *Philosophy of Music Education Review*, 11(2), 170–184.

Hendrick, H. (1997). *Children, childhood and English society 1880–1990*. Cambridge University Press.

Hermansen, T. H., Buljo, F.-R., Rotan, A., Tala, H., Schramm, R., Olsson, A. and Olsson, A. N. (2018). Spirit in the sky [Song recorded by KEiiNO]. Hugoworld AS.

Hesmondhalgh, D. (2008). Towards a critical understanding of music, emotion and self-identity. *Consumption, Markets and Culture*, 11(4), 329–343.

Hess, J. (2019). *Music education for social change: Constructing an activist music education*. Routledge.

Hilder, T. R. (2015). *Sámi musical performance and the politics of indigeneity in Northern Europe*. Rowman & Littlefield Publishers.

Hjellbrekke, J. and Korsnes, O. (2014). 'Intergenerasjonell mobilitet og sirkulasjon i norske elitar og profesjonar' ['Intergenerational mobility and circulation in Norwegian elites and professions']. In O. Korsnes, M. N. Hansen and J. Hjellbrekke (eds), *Elite og klasse i et egalitært samfunn* [Elite and class in an egalitarian society] (pp. 54–76). Universitetsforlaget.

Hofsli, E., Jakola, T. and Rishaug, H. (2013). *På vei til kulturskole for alle* [Towards a music and art school for all]. Retrieved 20 March 2022 from https://www.kulturskoleradet.no/_extension/media/114/orig/2013%20Jubileumsbok.pdf

Høien, G. (Director). (1971–1980). *Lekestue* [TV series]. NRK.

Høien, G., Gran, H., Dalchow, J. and Fosheim, L. (Producers). (1996). *Sesam Stasjon – Max Mekkers favoritter* [CD]. MilliGram.

Huizinga, J. (1944/1949) *Homo ludens: A study of the play-element in culture*. Routledge.

Hull, G. A., Stornaiuolo, A. and Sahni, U. (2010). Cultural citizenship and cosmopolitan practice: Global youth communicate online. *English Education*, 42(4), 331–367. Retrieved 2 August 2022 from http://www.jstor.org/stable/23018017

Ilari, B. (2018). Musical parenting and music education: Integrating research and practice. *Update: Applications of Research in Music Education*, 36(2), 45–52. https://doi.org/10.117/71/08.17157571/82735351273731717075173053

Ilari, B. and Young, S. (2016). 'MyPlace, MyMusic: Children's home musical experiences around the world'. In B. Ilari and S. Young (eds), *Children's home musical experiences around the world* (pp. 1–25). Indiana University Press.

Isenberg, J. P. and Jalongo, M. R. (1993). *Creative expression and play in the early childhood curriculum*. Macmillan

James, A. and Prout, A. (eds). (1990). *Constructing and reconstructing childhood: Contemporary issues in the sociological study of childhood*. Falmer Press.

Jensen, H. S. (2017). *From Superman to social realism*. John Benjamins.

Jeppsson, C. and Lindgren, M. (2018). Exploring equal opportunities: Children's experiences of the Swedish community school of music and arts. *Research Studies in Music Education*, 40(2), 191–210. https://doi.org/10.1177/1321103X1877315

Johansson, S., Werner, A., Åker, P. and Goldenzwaig, G. (2018). *Streaming music: Practices, media, cultures*. Routledge.

Johnsen, A. K., Touryguin, A., Eriksen, A. and Nilsen, E. (2008). Oro jáska beana [Song recorded by The BlackSheeps]. MBN.

Jonassen, T. (2015). – *Er frileken egentlig fri?* [– *Is free play really free?*]. Barnehage.no. Retrieved 31 July 2023 from https://www.barnehage.no/ forskning-kjonnsroller-likestilling/er-frileken-egentlig-fri/113665

Jordhus-Lier, A. (2018). *Institutionalising versatility, accommodating specialists: A discourse analysis of music teachers' professional identities within the Norwegian municipal school of music and arts* [Doctoral dissertation]. Norwegian Academy of Music.

Jordhus-Lier, A., Karlsen, S. and Nielsen, S. G. (2023). Meaningful approaches to content selection and ways of working: Norwegian instrumental music teachers' experiences. *Frontiers in Psychology, 14,* 1–10. https://doi.org/10.3389/fpsyg.2023.1105572

Jordhus-Lier, A. and Nielsen, S. G. (2025). Competing discourses of music as a discipline within Norwegian schools of music and arts: The teacher dimension. *Scandinavian Journal of Educational Research.* https://doi. org/10.1080/00313831.2025.2550261

Jordhus-Lier, A., Nielsen, S. G. and Karlsen, S. (2021). What is on offer within Norwegian extracurricular schools of music and performing arts? Findings from a national survey. *Music Education Research, 23*(1), 62–76. https://doi.org/10.1080/14613808.2020.1866518

Josefsen, E. and Skogerbø, E. (2021). 'Indigenous political communication in the Nordic countries'. In E. Skogerbø, Ø. Ihlen, N. Nörgaard Kristensen and L. Nord (eds), *Power, communication, and politics in the Nordic countries* (pp. 197–217). Nordicom.

Jørgensen, H. (2001). Sang og musikk i grunnskole og lærerutdanning 1945–2000 [Singing and music in primary school and teacher training 1945–2000]. *Studia musicologica Norvegica, 27*(1), 103–131.

Jugert, P., Kaiser, M. J., Ialuna, F. and Civitillo, S. (2021). Researching race-ethnicity in race-mute Europe. *Infant and Child Development, 31*(1), e2260. https://doi.org/10.1002/icd.2260

Källén, C. B. (2021). 'Binary oppositions and third spaces: Perspectives on the interplay between gender, genre practice, instrument and cultural capital in upper secondary schools in Sweden'. In S. V. Onsrud, H. Blix and I. L. Vestad (eds), *Gender Issues in Scandinavian Music Education* (pp. 74–94). Routledge.

Kallio, A. A. and Länsman, H. (2018). Sámi re-imaginings of equality in/through extracurricular arts education in Finland. *International Journal of Education & the Arts, 19*(7), 1–22. https://doi.org/10.18113 /P8ijea1907

Kallio, A. A. and Väkevä, L. (2017). 'Inclusive popular music education'. In F. Holt and A.-V. Kärjä (eds), *The Oxford handbook of popular music in the Nordic countries* (pp. 75–90). Oxford University Press. https://doi .org/10.1093/oxfordhb/9780190603908.013.0004

Kant, I. (1790/2007). *Critique of judgement.* (James Creed Meredith, Trans.). Oxford University Press.

Karlsen, S. (2014). Exploring democracy: Nordic music teachers' approaches to the development of immigrant students' musical agency. *International Journal of Music Education: Research*, *32*(4), 422–436.

Karlsen, S. (2017). 'Policy, access and multicultural (music) education'. In P. Schmidt and R. Colwell (eds), *Policy and the political life of music education* (pp. 211–230). Oxford University Press.

Karlsen, S. (2021). Assessing the state of sociological theory in music education: Uncovering the epistemic unconscious. *Philosophy of Music Education Review*, *29*(2), 136–154.

Karlsen, S. (2025, accepted for publication). 'Boundary work as feminist work: Deliberations on the growth and expansion of the Nordic field of music education research'. In M. Silverman and N. Niknafs (eds), *The Oxford handbook of feminism and music education*. Oxford University Press.

Karlsen, S., Jordhus-Lier, A. and Nielsen, S. G. (2024). Norwegian schools of music and arts: Local significance and strategies of inclusion. *International Journal of Music Education*, *42*(2), 271–284. https://doi .org/10.1177/02557614231157737

Karlsen, S. and Nielsen, S. G. (2021). The case of Norway: A microcosm of global issues in music teacher professional development. *Arts Education Policy Review*, *42*(2), 32–41. https://doi.org/10.1080/10632913.2020 .1746714

Karlsen, S. and Väkevä, L. (2012). *Future prospects for music education: Corroborating informal learning pedagogy*. Cambridge Scholars Publishing.

Keinonen, H., Jensen, P. M., Lemor, A. M. and Esser, A. (2018). Modes of engagement with musical talent shows: Studying audience engagement as a set of experiences. *Journal of Audience & Reception Studies*, *15*(2), 58–76.

Kjelsberg, S., Olsen, R. and Hætta, M. (1980). Sámiid ædnan [Song recorded by Sverre Kjelsberg and Mattis Hætta]. MAI.

Koops, L. H. (2020). *Parenting musically*. Oxford University Press.

Korsnes, O., Hansen, M. N. and Hjellbrekke, J. (2014). *Elite og klasse i et egalitært samfunn* [Elite and classes in an egalitarian society]. Universitetsforlaget.

Kragh-Müller, G. (2020). Hvor fri er børns fri leg i børnehaven? Om børns venskaber og leg i daginstitutioner [How free is children's free play in the kindergarten? About children's friendships and play in day care institutions]. *Psyke & Logos. Vitenskabeligt tidsskrift for psykologi*, *41*(1). https://doi.org/10.7146/pl.v41i1.121503

Kristeva, J. (1969/1986). 'Word, dialogue and novel'. In T. Moi (ed.), *The Kristeva reader* (pp. 34–61). Columbia University Press.

Kvaal, C. (2018). *Kryssende musikkopplevelser: En undersøkelse av samspill i en interkulturell musikkpraksis* [Crossing musical experiences: An investigation of interaction in an intercultural music practice] [Doctoral dissertation]. Inland Norway University of Applied Sciences.

Laclau, E. and Mouffe, C. (2001). *Hegemony and socialist strategy: Towards a radical democratic politics* (2nd ed.). Verso.

Lahire, B. (2003). From the habitus to an individual heritage of dispositions: Towards a sociology at the level of the individual. *Poetics, 31,* 329–355.

Lamont, M. (1992). *Money, morals, and manners: The culture of the French and the American upper-middle class.* University of Chicago Press.

Landskappleiken. (2024). Retrieved 17 May 2024 from https://landskappleiken.no

Lareau, A. (2011). *Unequal childhoods: Class, race, and family life.* University of California Press.

Lee, E., Macvarish, J. and Bristow, J. (2010). Editorial: Risk, health and parenting culture. *Health Risk and Society,* 12(4), 293–300.

Lee, T. T. (2021). Social class, intensive parenting norms and parental values for children. *Current Sociology,* 0(0). https://doi.org/10.1177/00113921211048531

Lijphart, A. (2012). *Patterns of democracy: Government forms and performance in thirty-six countries.* Yale University Press.

Ljunggren, L. and Hansen, M. N. (2021). *Arbeiderklassen* [The working class]. Cappelen Damm Akademisk.

Lund, R. E. (2010). 'I sangen møtes vi på felles grunn' – om sang og sangbøker i norsk skole ['In song we meet on common ground' – About song and songbooks in Norwegian schools]. *Acta Didactica Norge,* 4(1), 2–21.

Lunde, I. (2023). 'Digital landscapes of early childhood music learning and development: Music media and children's music culture of the past in the present'. In M. S. Barrett and G. F. Welch (eds), *The Oxford handbook of early childhood learning and development in music* (pp. 5–22). Oxford University Press.

Lyotard, J.-F. (1979/1984). *The postmodern condition.* Manchester University Press.

Malloch, S. and Trevarthen, C. (eds). (2010). *Communicative musicality: Exploring the basis of human companionship.* Oxford University Press.

Mantie, R. (2023). What should one expect from a sociology of music education? *Action, Criticism, and Theory for Music Education,* 22(1), 112–138.

Marsh, K. (2008). *The musical playground: Global tradition and change in children's songs and games.* Oxford University Press.

Marsh, K. and Young, S. (2006). 'Musical play'. In G. E. McPherson (ed.), *The child as musician: A handbook of musical development* (pp. 289–310). Oxford University Press.

Marx, K. (1867). *Das Kapital. Kritik der politischen Oekonomie* [Capital. Critique of political economy]. Verlag von Otto Meissner.

McCall, L. (2005). The complexity of intersectionality. *Signs, 30*(3), 1771–1800. https://doi.org/10.1086/426800

Meld. St. 18. (2020–2021). *Oppleve, skape, dele – Kunst og kultur for, med og av barn og unge* [Report to the Storting (white paper). Experience, create, share – Arts and culture for, with and by children and young people]. Ministry of Culture and Equality. Retrieved 21 March 2024 from https://www.regjeringen.no/no/dokumenter/meld.-st.-18-20202021/id2839455/

Merkelbach, F. (2022). *Cyborg talentification: YouTube as a hotspot for child pop stars, their fans, and critics* [Doctoral dissertation]. Inland Norway University of Applied Sciences. Retrieved 1 January 2023 from https://hdl.handle.net/11250/2977700

Mintz, S. (2012). 'The changing face of children's culture'. In P. S. Fass and M. Grossberg (eds), *Reinventing childhood after World War II* (pp. 38–50). University of Pennsylvania Press.

Midling, A. S. (2014, 7 December). A 'wow' ending of fog, jazz poetry and a tuba. *Gemini. Research News from NTNU and SINTEF.* Retrieved 8 December 2015 from https://geminiresearchnews.com/2014/12/a-wow-ending-of-fog-jazz-poetry-and-a-tuba-2/

Miller, C. (1984). Genre as social action. *Quarterly Journal of Speech, 70*(1), 151–167. Retrieved 2 March 2023 from https://www.researchgate.net/publication/238749675_Genre_as_Social_Action

Ministry of Culture. (2011). *Countryfestivalene får statsrådsbesøk* [The country festivals receive a ministerial visit]. Pressemelding nr. 59/11. Retrieved 30 June 2020 from https://www.regjeringen.no/no/aktuelt/countryfestivalene-far-statsradsbesok/id651449/

Ministry of Education and Research. (2020). *Curriculum for music MUS01–02.* Retrieved 29 March 2023 from https://data.udir.no/kl06/v201906/laereplaner-lk20/MUS01-02.pdf?lang=eng

Moore, A. (2002). Authenticity as authentication. *Popular Music, 21*(2), 209–223.

Møre og Romsdal Folkemusikklag. (2012). Kva er sjokoladekappleik? [What is sjokoladekappleik?]. Retrieved 20 May 2024 from http://www.folkemusikklag.no/kva-er-sjokoladekappleik.273496.nn.html

Mouffe, C. (2005). *On the political.* Routledge.

Mouffe, C. (2013). *Agonistics*. Verso Books.

Mouritsen, F. (2002). Child culture – play culture. In F. Mouritsen & J. Qvortrup (eds), *Childhood and children's culture* (pp. 14–42). University Press of Southern Denmark.

Mukherjee, U. and Barn, R. (2021). Concerted cultivation as a racial parenting strategy: race, ethnicity, and middle-class Indian parents in Britain. *British Journal of Sociology of Education*, 42(4), 521–536.

National Institute for Play. (2024). How we play: Many types of play. Retrieved 25 June 2024 from https://nifplay.org/what-is-play/types-of-play/

Nielsen, S. G. (2021). 'Musical gentrification and "genderfication" in higher music education'. In P. Dyndahl, S. Karlsen and R. Wright (eds), *Musical gentrification: Popular music, distinction and social mobility* (pp. 109–124). Routledge.

Nielsen, S. G., Jordhus-Lier, A. and Karlsen, S. (2023a). Selecting repertoire for music teaching: Findings from Norwegian schools of music and arts. *Research Studies in Music Education*, 45(1), 94–111. https://doi.org/10.1177/1321103X221099436

Nielsen, S. G., Jordhus-Lier, A. and Karlsen, S. (2023b). Classed approaches to musical parenting in the Norwegian schools of music and arts: Findings from an interview study with parents of music students. *Scandinavian Journal of Educational Research*. https://doi.org/10.1080/00313831.2023.2275803

Nokut. (n.d.). *General information about education in Norway*. Retrieved 11 May 2024 from https://www.nokut.no/en/norwegian-education/general-information-about-education-in-norway/

Nordin-Hultman, E. (2004). *Pedagogiske miljøer og barns subjektskaping* [Educational environments and children's subject construction]. Pedagogisk forum.

Norsk kulturskoleråd. (n.d.). *Vår visjon* [Our vision]. Retrieved 2 August 2024 from https://www.kulturskoleradet.no/om-oss/hvem-er-vi-hva-gjor-vi/var-visjon-kulturskole-for-alle

Norsk Rikskringkasting. (1996/2022). *Bylaws for NRK AS: Articles of Association for Norsk Rikskringkasting AS – NRK*. Retrieved 2 March 2023 from https://www.nrk.no/about/bylaws-for-nrk-as-1.4029867

Norwegian Education Act. (1998). Act relating to primary and secondary education and training (LOV-1998-07-17-61). Retrieved 1 December 2023 from https://www.regjeringen.no/contentassets/b3b9e92cce6742c39581b661a019e504/education-act-norway-with-amendments-entered-2014-2.pdf

Norwegian Council for the Schools of Music and Performing Arts. (2016). *Curriculum framework for schools of music and performing arts:*

Diversity and deeper understanding. Retrieved 2 February 2023 from https://kulturskoleradet.no/rammeplanseksjonen/planhjelp/plan-pa -flere-sprak

Norwegian Council for the Schools of Music and Performing Arts. (2021). «*Fordypning med mangfold*». *Norsk kulturskoleråds strategi for utvikling av kulturskolenes fordypningsprogram* ['In-depth learning with diversity'. Norwegian Council for the Schools of Music and Performing Arts' strategy for development of the school of music and arts' depth programme]. Retrieved 1 March 2023 from https://kulturskoleradet .no/nyheter/2021/september/strategi-utvikling-kulturskolenes -fordypningsprogram

Norwegian Directorate for Education and Training. (2020). *Curriculum for music*. Retrieved 2 May 2024 from https://www.udir.no/lk20/ MUS01-02

Norwegian Education Act. (2023). *Lov om grunnopplæringa og den vidaregåande opplæringa (opplæringslova)* [Act relating to primary and secondary education and training] (LOV-2023-06-09-30). Lovdata. Retrieved 21 August 2024 from https://lovdata.no/dokument/NL/lov /2023-06-09-30

NOU 2013:4. (2013). *Kulturutredningen 2014* [Norwegian public investigation on culture]. Ministry of Culture. Retrieved 2 March 2023 from https://www.regjeringen.no/no/dokumenter/nou-2013-4/ id715404/

Nysæther, E. T., Christophersen, C. and Sætre, J. H. (2021). Who are the music student teachers in Norwegian generalist teacher education? A cross-sectional survey. *Nordic Research in Music Education*, 2(2), 28–57. https://doi.org/10.23865/nrme.v2.2988

O'Connor, J. (2009). Beyond social constructionism: A structural analysis of the cultural significance of the child star. *Children & Society*, 23(3), 214–225. https://doi.org/10.1111/j.1099-0860.2008.00169.x

Olsson, B. (1993). *SÄMUS – en musikutbildning i kulturpolitikens tjänst* [SÄMUS – music education in the service of cultural policy] [Doctoral dissertation]. University of Gothenburg.

Onsrud, S. V. (2021). 'Thinking queer pedagogy in music education with Girl in Red'. In S. V. Onsrud, H. Blix and I. L. Vestad (eds), *Gender issues in Scandinavian music education* (pp. 135–155). Routledge.

Onsrud, S. V., Blix, H. and Vestad, I. L. (eds). (2021). *Gender issues in Scandinavian music education: From stereotypes to multiple possibilities*. Routledge.

Oslo kulturskole. (n.d.). *Instrumenter* [Instruments]. Retrieved 26 April 2024 from https://www.oslo.kommune.no/natur-kultur-og-fritid/kunst -og-kultur/oslo-kulturskole/undervisningstilbud/musikk/instrumenter/

Øyen, E. (1995). 'Velferdsstaten som kulturinstitusjon' ['The welfare state as a cultural institution']. In L. G. Lingås (ed.), *Myten om Velferdsstaten – 25 år etter. En antologi om norsk sosialpolitikk* [The myth of the welfare state – 25 years on. An anthology on Norwegian social policy] (pp. 28–36). Pax.

Papastergiadis, N. (2018). 'Aesthetic cosmopolitanism'. In G. Delanty (ed.), *Routledge international handbook of cosmopolitanism studies* (2nd ed., pp. 198–210). Taylor & Francis.

Parton, D. (1973). Jolene [Song]. *Jolene* [Album]. RCA Studio B.

Perkins, R. (2013). Learning cultures and the conservatoire: An ethnographically-informed case study. *Music Education Research*, 15(2), 196–213.

Peters, M. A. (2020): Wittgenstein/Foucault/anti-philosophy: Contingency, community, and the ethics of self-cultivation. *Educational Philosophy and Theory*, 54(10), 1495–1500. https://doi.org/10.1080/00131857.2020.1750039

Peterson, R. A. (1992). Understanding audience segmentation: From elite and mass to omnivore and univore. *Poetics*, 21(4), 243–258.

Peterson, R. A. and Kern, R. M. (1996). Changing highbrow taste: From snob to omnivore. *American Sociological Review*, 61(5), 900–907.

Peterson, R. A. and Simkus, A. (1992). 'How musical taste groups mark occupational status groups'. In M. Lamont and M. Fournier (eds), *Cultivating differences: Symbolic boundaries and the making of inequality* (pp. 152–168). University of Chicago Press.

Piketty, T. (2018). *Brahmin left vs merchant right: Rising inequality and the changing structure of political conflict (Evidence from France, Britain and the US, 1948–2017)*. World Inequality Database Working Paper Series No. 2018/7. Retrieved 18 July 2020 from http://piketty.pse.ens.fr/files/Piketty2018.pdf

Popkewitz, T. S. and Gustafson, R. (2002). Standards of music education and the easily administered child/citizen: The alchemy of pedagogy and social inclusion/exclusion. *Philosophy of Music Education Review*, 10(2), 80–91. https://doi.org/10.2979/PME.2002.10.2.80

Postman, N. (1982). *The disappearance of childhood*. Delacorte Press.

Prieur, A. and Savage, M. (2011). Updating cultural capital theory: A discussion based on studies in Denmark and in Britain. *Poetics*, 39, 566–580.

Prout, A. (2000). Children's participation: Control and self-realisation in British late modernity. *Children and Society*, 14(4), 304–315.

Prout, A. (2004). *The future of childhood*. Routledge.

Prout, A. and James, A. (1990). A new paradigm for the sociology of childhood? Provenance, promise and problems. In A. James and A.

Prout (eds), *Constructing and reconstructing childhood: Contemporary issues in the sociological study of childhood*. Falmer Press.

Rasmussen, K. (2001). Børnekulturbegrebet – set i lyset af aktuelle barndomstendenser og teoretiske problemstillinger [The concept of child culture – in light of current childhood trends and theoretical issues]. In B. Tufte, J. Kampmann and B. Juncker (eds). *Børnekultur. Hvilke børn? Og hvis kultur?* [Children's culture. Which children? And whose culture?] (s. 31–51). Akademisk Forlag.

Reay, D. (2017). *Miseducation: Inequality, education and the working classes*. Policy Press.

Regev, M. (2007). Cultural uniqueness and aesthetic cosmopolitanism. *European Journal of Social Theory*, *10*(1), 123–138. https://doi.org/10.1177/1368431006068765

Reed Jr, A. (2018). Antiracism: A neoliberal alternative to a left. *Dialectical Anthropology*, *42*, 105–115.

Rogers, C. S. and Sawyers, J. K. (1988). *Play in the lives of children*. National Association for the Education of Young Children.

Rollock, N. (2007). Legitimizing Black academic failure: Deconstructing staff discourses on academic success, appearance and behaviour. *International Studies in Sociology of Education*, *17*(3), 275–287. https://doi.org/10.1080/09620210701543924

Ruthsatz, J., Ruthsatz, K. and Stephens, K. R. (2014). Putting practice into perspective: Child prodigies as evidence of innate talent. *Intelligence*, *45*(1), 60–65. https://doi.org/10.1016/j.intell.2013.08.003

Ryzik, M. (2019, August 22). How 'Sesame Street' started a musical revolution. *New York Times*. Retrieved 2 June 2024 from https://www.nytimes.com/2019/08/22/arts/music/sesame-street-anniversary.html

Sakslind, R., Skarpenes, O. and Hestholm, R. (2018). *Middelklassekulturen i Norge: En komparativ sosiologisk studie* [Middle-class culture in Norway: A comparative sociological study]. Scandinavian Academic Press.

Salaby. (n.d.). *Salaby*. Retrieved 11 May 2024 from https://www.salaby.no/

Salvanes, K. G. (2017). Inntektsforskjeller og sosial mobilitet i Norge [Income differences and social mobility in Norway]. *Oppvekstrapporten 2017*. Bufdir. Retrieved 29 October 2023 from https://www2.bufdir.no/contentassets/e9df3a5c5087465eb09083d1be77ba10/inntektsforskjeller_og_sosial_mobilitet_i_norge_artikkel_3.pdf

Sannhets- og forsoningskommisjonen. (2023). Sannhet og forsoning : Grunnlag for et oppgjør med fornorskningspolitikk og urett mot samer, kvener/norskfinner og skogfinner [The Truth and Reconciliation Commission's report to investigate the Norwegianisation policy and injustice against the Sámi, Kvens/Norwegian Finns and Forest Finns].

Rapport til Stortinget fra Sannhets- og forsoningskommisjonen, avgitt til Stortingets presidentskap 01.06.2023. Dokument 19 (2022–2023). Retrieved 1 March 2024 from https://www.stortinget.no/globalassets /pdf/sannhets--og-forsoningskommisjonen/rapport-til-stortinget-fra -sannhets--og-forsoningskommisjonen.pdf

Savage, M. and Bennett, T. (2005). Editors' introduction: Cultural capital and social inequality. *British Journal of Sociology*, 56(1), 1–12.

Scruton, R. (2007). *The Palgrave Macmillan dictionary of political thought* (3rd ed.). Palgrave Macmillan.

Schechner, R. (1993). *The future of ritual: Writings on culture and performance*. Routledge.

Senter for talentutvikling Barratt Due. (2024, 11 May). *Tester 'toppidrettsgymnas' for musikere* [Testing 'toppidrettsgymnas' for musicians]. Retrieved 1 June 2024 from https://senterfortalentutvikling .no/tester-toppidrettsgymnas-for-musikere/

Shavinina, L. V. (1999). The psychological essence of the child prodigy phenomenon: Sensitive periods and cognitive experience. *Gifted Child Quarterly*, 43(1), 25–38.

Sjöberg, J. (2013). *I marknadens öga: barn och visuell konsumtion* [In the eye of the market: children and visual consumption] [Doctoral dissertation]. University of Linköping.

Skard, Å. G. (1953, January 14). Merknader til barne- og ungdoms- programma i tida 31. aug. 1952–10. jan. 1953 [Notes regarding programs for child *barn och visuell konsumtion* ren and youth from 31 August 1952–10 January 1953]. Unpublished document for NRK.

Skard, Å. G. (1954, January 3). Om barnetimen for dei minste [On the 'Children's Hour for the Youngest']. Unpublished letter to NRK.

Skeggs, B. (2004). *Class, self, culture*. Routledge.

Ski-Berg, V. (2023). *Pressures to change: Institutional politics in higher music education* [Doctoral dissertation]. The Norwegian Academy of Music.

Skjelstad, E. and Ellefsen, L. W. (2024). Challenging stereotypes? Norwegian music teachers' repertoires on gender roles and gender-expansiveness. *Journal of Research in Music Education*, 71(4), 398–417. https://doi.org /10.1177/00224294231175859

Skogvang, S. F. (2024). Fosen-saken [The Fosen conflict]. In *Store norske leksikon*. Retrieved 31 May 2024 from https://snl.no/Fosen-saken

Small, C. (1998). *Musicking: The meanings of performing and listening*. Wesleyan University Press.

Solomon, T. (2016). The play of colors: Staging multiculturalism in Norway. *Danish Musicology Online Special Edition*, 187–201.

Sørensen, A. (2016). Participation. *Nordisk Kulturpolitisk Tidsskrift*, *19*(1), 4–18. Retrieved 3 August 2023 from https://www.idunn.no

Spivak, G. C. (1988). 'Can the subaltern speak?' In C. Nelson and L. Grossberg (eds), *Marxism and the interpretation of culture*. University of Illinois Press.

Stabell, E. M. (2018). *Being talented – becoming a musician: A qualitative study of learning cultures in three junior conservatoires* [Doctoral dissertation]. Norwegian Academy of Music.

Stabell, E. M. (2023). 'Talent og talentutvikling – et gammelt felt i nye klær?' ['Talent and talent development – an old field in new clothing?']. In Ø. Varkøy, E. M. Stabell and B. Utne-Reitan (eds), *Høyere musikkutdanning: Historiske perspektiver* (pp. 301–325). Cappelen Damm Forskning/NOASP (Nordic Open Access Scholarly Publishing).

Stabell, E. M. and Jordhus-Lier, A. (2017). 'Fordypningsprogram i kulturskolen – i spennet mellom bredde og spesialisering' ['In-depth programme in the schools of music and arts – in the span between breadth and specialisation']. In E. Angelo, A. Rønningen and R. J. Rønning (eds), *Forskning og utvikling i kulturskolefeltet: IRIS – den doble regnbuen* [Research and development in the field of municipal schools of music and arts: IRIS – the double rainbow]. Cappelen Damm Akademisk/NOASP (Nordic Open Access Scholarly Publishing).

Statistics Norway. (2024). *Barnehager* [Kindergartens]. Retrieved 3 August 2024 from www.utdanningsforbundet.no/globalassets/var-politikk/publikasjoner/faktaark/faktaark_06.2024_2.pdf

Stearns, P. N. (2009). Analyzing the role of culture in shaping American childhood: A twentieth-century case. *European Journal of Developmental Psychology*, *6*(1), 34–52.

Steinmetz, K. (2020, 7 February). She coined the term 'intersectionality' over 30 years ago. Here's what it means to her today. *Time*. Retrieved 31 May 2024 from https://time.com/5786710/kimberle-crenshaw-intersectionality/

St. meld. nr. 8. (1973–1974). *Om organisering av kulturtilbud* [About the organisation of cultural services]. Ministry of Culture and Education. Retrieved 3 March 2024 from https://www.stortinget.no/no/Saker-og-publikasjoner/Stortingsforhandlinger/Lesevisning/?p=1973-74&paid=3&wid=b&psid=DIVL41&s=True

St. meld. nr. 39. (2002–2003). *'Ei blot til Lyst'. Om kunst og kultur i og i tilknytning til grunnskolen* [Report to the Storting (white paper). On arts and culture in and in relation to the compulsory school]. Ministry of Education and Research.

Sutton-Smith, B. (1997). *The ambiguity of play*. Harvard University Press.

Sutton-Smith, B. (2008). Play theory: A personal journey and new thoughts. *American Journal of Play*, *1*(1), 80–123.

Syvertsen, T., Enli, G. S., Mjøs, O. S. and Moe, H. (2014). *The media welfare state: Nordic media in the digital era*. University of Michigan.

Tagg, P. (1997). The Göteborg connection: Lessons in the history and politics of popular music education and research. *Popular Music*, *17*(2), 219–242.

Thornton, S. (1995). *Club cultures: Music, media, and subcultural capital*. Blackwell.

Thorsen, D. E. (2021). 'Introduction: Social democracy in the 21st century'. In N. Brandal, Ø. Bratberg and D. E. Thorsen (eds), *Social democracy in the 21st century* (Vol. 35, pp. 1–14). Emerald Publishing Limited. https://doi.org/10.1108/S0195-631020210000035001

Tosi, J. and Warmke, B. (2020). *Grandstanding: The use and abuse of moral talk*. Oxford University Press. https://doi.org/10.1093/oso /9780190900151.002.0003

Tønnessen, E. S. (2000). *Barns møte med TV: Tekst og tolkning i en ny medietid* [Children meeting television: Text and interpretation in new times of media]. Universitetsforlaget.

Tønnessen, E. S. (2015). 'Alf Prøysen som radiokunstner for barn' ['Alf Prøysen as a radio artist for children']. In H. K. Rustad and A. Skaret (eds), *Alf Prøysen, kunsten og mediene* [Alf Prøysen, the art and the media] (pp. 91–114). Novus.

Trulsson, Y. H. (2015). 'Striving for "class remobility": Using Bourdieu to investigate music as a commodity of exchange within minority groups'. In P. Burnard, Y. Hofvander-Trulsson and J. Söderman (eds), *Bourdieu and the sociology of music education* (pp. 29–41). Ashgate.

Union of Education Norway. (2024). *Nøkkeltall for grunnskolen t.o.m. skoleåret 2023/24* [Key numbers for compulsory school 2023/24]. Union of Education Norway, Department for Society and Analysis. Retrieved 30 August 2024 from https://www.utdanningsforbundet.no /globalassets/var-politikk/publikasjoner/faktaark/faktaark-02.2024.pdf

United Nations. (1966). *International covenant on civil and political rights*. UN General Assembly Resolution 2200A.

Utdanningsdirektoratet. (2020). Læreplan i musikk (MUS01-02) [The national curriculum for the music subject]. Fastsatt som forskrift. Læreplanverket for Kunnskapsløftet 2020. Retrieved 6 June 2024 from https://www.udir.no/lk20/mus01-02?lang=nob

van den Berg, M. (2011, July 7–9). *City children and genderfied neighbourhoods: The new generation as urban regeneration strategy* [Conference presentation]. RC21 Conference 2011, University of Amsterdam. Retrieved 18 October 2019 from http://www.rc21.org/

conferences/amsterdam2011/edocs2/Session%2022/RT22-1-Van-den -Berg.pdf

van Leeuwen, T. (1999). *Speech, music, sound*. Macmillian Press.

Varkøy, Ø. (2015). '*Bildung*. Between cultural heritage and the unknown, instrumentalism and existence'. In M. Fleming, L. Bresler and J. O'Toole (eds), *The Routledge international handbook of the arts and education* (pp. 19–29). Routledge.

Vestad, I. L. (2010). To play a soundtrack: How children use recorded music in their everyday lives. *Music Education Research*, 12(3), 243–255. https://doi.org/10.1080/14613808.2010.504811

Vestad, I. L. (2013). *Barns bruk av fonogrammer: Om konstituering av musikalsk mening i barnekulturelt perspektiv* [Children's uses of recorded music: On the constitution of musical meaning from the perspective of children's culture] [Doctoral dissertation]. University of Oslo.

Vestad, I. L. (2014a). Children's subject positions in discourses of music in everyday life: Rethinking conceptions of the child in and for music education. *Action, Criticism & Theory for Music Education*, 13(1) 248–278.

Vestad, I. L. (2014b). 'Now you see it, now you don't': On the challenge of inclusion in the perspective of children's everyday musical play. *Nordisk musikkpedagogisk forskning: Årbok*, 15, 85–103.

Vestad, I. L. (2016). 'Passing on musical knowledge and ideas about music through television: The Norwegian children's programmes *Lekestue* and *Sesam stasjon*'. In O. Kramer and I. Malmberg (eds), *Open ears – Open minds: Listening and understanding music* (pp. 135–150). Hellbling.

Vestad, I. L. (2018). 'Children's music and nostalgia. Digging in the past with an eye to the future'. In L. Wesseling (eds), *Reinventing childhood nostalgia: Books, toys, and contemporary media culture* (pp. 255–273). Routledge.

Vestad, I. L. (2022). 'The sound of Norwegian children's television: Narrating the nation, childhood and the welfare state'. In D. Olson and A. Schober (eds), *Children, youth, and international television* (pp. 171–194). Routledge.

Vestad, I. L. and Dyndahl, P. (2017). 'This one Grandma knew, too, exactly this one!': Processes of canonization in children's music. *Nordic Journal of Art and Research*, 6(2), 1–19. https://doi.org/10.7577/information .v6i2.2279

Vestad, I. L. and Dyndahl, P. (2021). 'Musical gentrification, parenting and children's media music'. In P. Dyndahl, S. Karlsen and R. Wright (eds). *Musical gentrification: Popular music, distinction and social mobility* (pp. 66–79). Routledge.

Vestby, S. (2017). *Folkelige og distingverte fellesskap: Gentrifisering av countrykultur i Norge – en festivalstudie* [Popular and distinguished communities: Gentrification of country music culture in Norway – A festival study] [Doctoral dissertation]. Inland Norway University of Applied Sciences. Retrieved 3 August 2019 from http://hdl.handle.net /11250/2437613

Vestby, S. (2021). 'Musical gentrification and the (un)democratisation of culture'. In P. Dyndahl, S. Karlsen and R. Wright (eds), *Musical gentrification: Popular music, distinction and social mobility* (pp. 50–65). Routledge.

Vilbli.no. (n.d.). *Studiekompetanse med musikk (studiekompetanse)*. Retrieved 11 May 2024 from https://www.vilbli.no/nb/no/yrke/v .md3001/studiekompetanse-med-musikk?utdanningsprogram=v.md

Vincent, C. (2017). 'The children have only got one education and you have to make sure it's a good one': Parenting and parent-school relations in a neoliberal age. *Gender and Education*, *29*(5), 541–557.

Vincent, C. and Martin, J. (2002). Class, culture and agency: Researching parental voice. *Discourse: Studies in the Cultural Politics of Education*, *23*(1), 108–127. https://doi.org/10.1080/01596300220123079

Vincent, C., Rollock, N., Ball, S. and Gillborn, D. (2012). Raising middle-class Black children: Parenting priorities, action and strategies. *Sociology*, *47*(3), 427–442.

von Neumann, J. and Morgenstern, O. (1944/2004). *Theory of games and economic behavior*. 60th Anniversary Commemorative Edition. Princeton University Press.

Vulliamy, G. (1984). A sociological view of music education: An essay in the sociology of knowledge. *Canadian University Music Review*, *5*, 17–37.

Wahlberg, I. H. (2020). *Att göra plats för traditioner. Antagonism och kunskapsproduktion inom folk- och världsmusikutbildning* [Making room for traditions: Antagonism and knowledge production within folk and world music education] [Doctoral dissertation]. University of Gothenburg.

Walkerdine, V. (1998). 'Popular culture and the eroticization of little girls'. In H. Jenkins (ed.), *The children's culture reader* (pp. 254–264). New York University Press.

Warwick, J. and Adrian, A. (2016). 'Introduction'. In J. Warwick and A. Adrian (eds), *Voicing girlhood in popular music: Performance, authority, authenticity*. Routledge.

Weber, M. (1922/2013). *Economy and society* (eds G. Roth and C. Wittich). University of California Press.

Weisberg, D. S., Hirsh-Pasek, K. and Golinkoff, R. M. (2013). Guided play: Where curricular goals meet a playful pedagogy. *Mind, Brain, and Education*, 7(2), 104–112.

Wells, J. J. (2014). Keep calm and remain human: How we have always been cyborgs and theories on the technological present of anthropology. *Reviews in Anthropology*, 43(1), 5–34. https://doi.org/10.1080 /00938157.2014.872460

Whale, M. J. (2022). Review of the book *Class, control and classical music*, by Anna Bull. *Philosophy of Music Education Review*, 30(1), 100–106. Retrieved 6 August 2024 from https://www.muse.jhu.edu/ article/851852

Wittgenstein, L. (1953/1986). *Philosophical investigations*. Second Edition. Translated by G. E. M. Anscombe. Basil Blackwell Ltd.

Young, S. (2009a). Towards constructions of musical childhoods: Diversity and digital technologies. *Early Child Development and Care*, 179(6), 695–705. https://doi.org/10.1080/03004430902944908

Young, S. (2009b). *Music 3–5*. Routledge.

Zuckerman, E. (2015). *Digital cosmopolitans: Why we think the Internet connects us, why it doesn't and how to rewire it*. Norton.

Index